Material Powers

This edited collection is a major contribution to the current development of a 'material turn' in the social sciences and humanities. It explores new understandings of how power is made up and exercised by examining the role of material infrastructures in the organisation of state power and the role of material cultural practices in the organisation of colonial forms of governance.

A diverse range of historical examples is drawn on in illustrating these concerns – from the role of territorial engineering projects in seventeenth-century France through the development of bureaucratic information systems in nineteenth-century Britain to the relations between the state and road-building in contemporary Peru, for example. Similarly, the colonial contexts examined are varied, ranging from the role of photographic practices in the constitution of colonial power in India and the measurement of the bodies of the colonised in French colonial practices to the part played by the relations between museums and expeditions in the organisation of Australian forms of colonial rule. These specific concerns are connected to major critical re-examinations of the limits of the earlier formulations of cultural materialism and the logic of the 'cultural turn'.

The collection brings together a group of key international scholars whose work has played a leading role in debates in and across the fields of history, visual culture studies, anthropology, geography, cultural studies, museum studies and literary studies.

Tony Bennett is Research Professor of Social and Cultural Theory in the Centre for Cultural Research at the University of Western Sydney. He is also a Professorial Fellow in the School of Culture and Communication at the University of Melbourne and Visiting Research Professor at the Open University in the UK. Recent publications include *Culture: A Reformer's Science* (Sage, 1998), *Pasts Beyond Memory: Evolution, Museums, Colonialism* (Routledge, 2004) and *Culture, Class, Distinction*, with Mike Savage, Elizabeth Silva, Alan Warde, Modesto Gayo-Cal and David Wright (Routledge, 2008).

Patrick Joyce is Professor of History Emeritus at the University of Manchester, and currently Visiting Professor of Sociology at the London School of Economics and Fernand Braudel Fellow in History at the European University Institute, Florence. He has published widely on the history of work, class and popular politics, in recent times developing an interest in historical aspects of governmentality. His publications include *Visions of the People* (Cambridge University Press, 1991), *The Oxford Reader on Class* (Oxford University Press, 1995), *The Social in Question* (Routledge, 2001) and *The Rule of Freedom* (Verso, 2003).

Culture, economy and the social

A new series from CRESC – the ESRC centre for research on socio-cultural change

The *Culture, Economy and the Social* series is committed to innovative contemporary, comparative and historical work on the relations between social, cultural and economic change. It publishes empirically-based research that is theoretically informed, that critically examines the ways in which social, cultural and economic change is framed and made visible, and that is attentive to perspectives that tend to be ignored or side-lined by grand theorising or epochal accounts of social change. The series addresses the diverse manifestations of contemporary capitalism, and considers the various ways in which the 'social', 'the cultural' and 'the economic' are apprehended as tangible sites of value and practice. It is explicitly comparative, publishing books that work across disciplinary perspectives, cross-culturally, or across different historical periods.

The series is actively engaged in the analysis of the different theoretical traditions that have contributed to the development of the 'cultural turn' with a view to clarifying where these approaches converge and where they diverge on a particular issue. It is equally concerned to explore the new critical agendas emerging from current critiques of the cultural turn: those associated with the descriptive turn for example. Our commitment to interdisciplinarity thus aims at enriching theoretical and methodological discussion, building awareness of the common ground that has emerged in the past decade, and thinking through what is at stake in those approaches that resist integration to a common analytical model.

Series titles include:

The Media and Social Theory (2008)
Edited by David Hesmondhalgh and Jason Toynbee

Culture, Class, Distinction (2009)
Tony Bennett, Mike Savage, Elizabeth Bortolaia Silva, Alan Warde, Modesto Gayo-Cal and David Wright

Material Powers (2010)
Edited by Tony Bennett and Patrick Joyce

The Social after Gabriel Tarde: Debates and Assessments (forthcoming)
Edited by Matei Candea

Cultural Analysis and Bourdieu's Legacy (forthcoming)
Edited by Elizabeth Silva and Alan Warde

Milk, Modernity and the Making of the Human (forthcoming)
Richie Nimmo

Creative Labour – Media Work in Three Cultural Industries (forthcoming)
David Hesmondhalgh and Sarah Baker

Rio de Janeiro: Urban Life through the Eyes of the City (forthcoming)
Beatriz Jaguaribe

E·S·R·C ECONOMIC & SOCIAL RESEARCH COUNCIL

CRESC Centre for Research on Socio-Cultural Change

Material Powers

Cultural studies, history and the material turn

Edited by
Tony Bennett
and Patrick Joyce

Routledge
Taylor & Francis Group
LONDON AND NEW YORK

First published 2010
by Routledge
2 Park Square, Milton Park, Abingdon, Oxon, OX14 4RN

Simultaneously published in the USA and Canada
by Routledge
270 Madison Avenue, New York, NY 10016

Routledge is an imprint of the Taylor & Francis Group, an informa business

Typeset in Times New Roman by Glyph International Ltd.
Printed and bound in Great Britain by CPI Antony Rowe, Chippenham, Wiltshire

British Library Cataloguing in Publication Data
A catalogue record for this book is available from the British Library

Library of Congress Cataloging in Publication Data
A catalog record for this book has been requested

ISBN: 978-0-415-48303-2 (hbk)
ISBN: 978-0-415-60314-0 (pbk)
ISBN: 978-0-203-88387-X (ebk)

Contents

Figures

Contributors

Tony Bennett is Research Professor in Social and Cultural Theory in the Centre of Cultural Research at the University of Western Sydney. He is also Visiting Professor at the Open University and a Professorial Fellow in the School of Culture and Communication at the University of Melbourne. Recent publications include *Culture: A Reformer's Science; Pasts Beyond Memory: Evolution, Museums, Colonialism; New Keywords: A Revised Vocabulary of Culture and Society* (edited with Larry Grossberg and Meaghan Morris); and *Culture, Class, Distinction* (with Mike Savage, Elizabeth Silva, Alan Warde, Modesto Gayo-Cal and David Wright).

Bill Brown is George M. Pullman Professor of English and the History of Culture at the University of Chicago and co-editor of *Critical Inquiry*. He is the author of *The Material Unconscious* (1996) and *A Sense of Things: The Object Matter of American Literature* (2003). He is also the editor of *Things* (2004).

Nélia Dias is Associate Professor in the Department of Anthropology at the University of Lisbon (Portugal). She is the author of *Le Musée d'Ethnographie du Trocadéro. Anthropologie et Muséologie en France* (Paris, CNRS, 1991) and *La Mesure des Sens. Les Anthropologues et le corps humain au 19e siècle* (Paris, Aubier, 2004) and of several articles on the history of French anthropology and on ethnographic museums from the nineteenth century to the present. She is currently working on the relationships between quantification and the classification of categories of people in nineteenth-century physical anthropology and medical discourses.

John Frow is Professor of English Language and Literature at the University of Melbourne. He is the author of *Marxism and Literary History* (1986); *Australian Cultural Studies: A Reader* (ed. with Meaghan Morris, 1993); *Cultural Studies and Cultural Value* (1995); *Time and Commodity Culture* (1997); *Accounting for Tastes: Australian Everyday Cultures* (with Tony Bennett and Michael Emmison, 1999), and *Genre* (2006).

Penny Harvey is Professor of Social Anthropology at the University of Manchester. Her regional specialisation is in South America and Europe, and she has conducted fieldwork in Peru, Spain and the UK. Her research interests focus on the modern state, and in how ethnographic work can inflect standard accounts of political economy by extending standard approaches to power, value and knowledge. She is the author of *Hybrids of Modernity: Anthropology, the Nation State and the Universal Exhibition* (Routledge, 1996), editor of *Sex and Violence: Issues of Representation and Experience* (with Gow, Routledge, 1994); of *Anthropology and Science: Epistemologies in Practice* (with Edwards and Wade, Berg, 2007) and of *Technologized Images, Technologized Bodies* (Berghahn, 2010).

Patrick Joyce is Professor of History Emeritus at the University of Manchester, and currently Visiting Professor of Sociology at the London School of Economics and Fernand Braudel Fellow in History at the European University Institute, Florence. He has held visiting fellowships and professorships at, among others, the University of California, New York University, and the Max Planck Institute, Göttingen. He has published widely on the history of work, class and popular politics, in recent times developing an interest in historical aspects of governmentality, particularly in relation to materiality, an interest which has resulted in a recent book on the city, and current work on the state. His publications include *Visions of the People* (Cambridge 1991), *The Oxford Reader on Class* (Oxford 1995), *The Social in Question* (London 2001), *The Rule of Freedom* (London 2003). He also works in the area of social theory and historiography, and has contributed to debates on history and postmodernism. His current work in progress on the state *The Soul of Leviathan* represents a rethinking of the British state since the early nineteenth century in terms of the nature of governance and material power.

Hannah Knox is a research associate at CRESC. Her work is broadly concerned with the anthropological study of technologies of modernisation and progress. Her ethnographic research has spanned the UK and Peru, to look at the ways in which complex social, technical and expert knowledges intersect in projects of planned social change. In the UK, she conducted an ethnography of the development of a regional new media industry and investigated the cultural expectations implicit in contemporary attempts to engineer the economic prosperity promised by new technologies. She has also worked on an interdisciplinary project which looked at how the principles and practices of multinational business organisation are shaped and mediated by technology-driven 'information systems'. Most recently she has been working with Penny Harvey, conducting an ethnography of road building in Peru.

Chandra Mukerji is Professor of Communication and Science Studies at the University of California, San Diego. She is author of *Territorial Ambitions and the Gardens of Versailles* (Cambridge 1997); *From Graven Images: Patterns of Modern Materialism* (Columbia 1983) and *A Fragile Power: Science and the State* (Princeton 1989). Her newest book, *Impossible Engineering*: *Technology and Territoriality on the Canal du Midi*, was published by Princeton University Press (2009).

Chris Otter is Assistant Professor of Modern European History at the Ohio State University. He is the author of *The Victorian Eye: A Political History of Light and Vision in Britain, 1800–1910* (University of Chicago Press, 2008). He is currently working on the history of food in modern Britain and the environmental history of Europe.

Christopher Pinney is Professor of Anthropology and Visual Culture at University College London and Visiting Crowe Chair in Art History at Northwestern University. He has held visiting positions at the University of Chicago, Australian National University, University of Cape Town and Jawarharlal Nehru University in New Delhi. His most recent book is *'Photos of the Gods': The Printed Image and Political Struggle in India* (2004). *The Coming of Photography in India*, based on the 2006 Panizzi Lectures is forthcoming.

Acknowledgements

The initial impetus for this book came from a workshop on the subject of New Cultural Materialisms that was organised by CRESC – the Economic and Social Research Council (ESRC) for Research on Socio-cultural Change – that was held at the Open University in 2006. We are, then, first and foremost indebted to the ESRC for funding CRESC. Its support for the development of an interdisciplinary research environment in CRESC that made a workshop of this kind possible has been invaluable. We are also grateful to our colleagues in the research theme – Culture, Government, Citizenship: The Formation and Transformations of Liberal Government – from which the workshop derived, and particularly those members of the theme who attended the workshop and contributed to its discussions. Special thanks to Francis Dodsworth and Liz Mcfall in this regard. Our thanks also to Donald Pressiozi for his advice and contributions regarding the relations between the material and the immaterial.

We are also indebted to the anonymous reviewers of our original publishing proposal who convinced us of the need to adopt a tighter and more closely focused organisation for the book than we had originally envisaged. And a very special thanks to Karen Ho, the secretary of CRESC at the Open University, for her help in both organising the New Cultural Materialisms workshop with her customary good cheer and efficiency, and for her assistance in finalising the manuscript for this book. Finally, many thanks to Michelle Kelly from the Centre for Cultural Research at the University of Western Sydney for her eagle-eyed help in collating the proof corrections from ourselves and our contributors.

Material powers

Introduction

Patrick Joyce and Tony Bennett

We have called our book *Material Powers* because we want to bring power and materiality closer together than has hitherto been the case. In attempting this, however, does not our title entail giving a hostage to fortune? This in the sense that the logic of its meaning seems to contradict the logic of our aspirations, one of which is to extend thinking beyond the familiar division between what is and is not 'material'. For in invoking its opposite, heavenly powers, does not the term material powers describe a cosmos which is divided into two completely different substances, lofty spirit and base matter? Does this not simply reproduce the contention, apparent from the Enlightenment onwards, that the material is somehow earthly or basic in its earthliness, and because of this more real, and indeed more powerful, and certainly something generically different from that which is above the earth, namely, what is not material, which is to say ideas, values and so on?

The social historian William Sewell has in fact pointed out the irony whereby certain exponents of 'materialism' – in the 1990s of which he writes, Marxists – have unconsciously and unquestioningly reproduced Christian and aristocratic discourse in assigning the material to the earthly, and ideas to the empyream (Sewell, 1987). Nineteenth-century materialism, and many subsequent versions (extending into the present) simply inverted the Christian division by now finding reality in the laws and hence order of the earthly and illusion in the heavens. Well, we would wish the rhetorical aspect of our title to take precedence over the strictly logical, for by its use we point to the limitations of those still fairly numerous cousins of the nineteenth-century materialists who, inverting the old pattern still, assign power to anything but the material. The material indeed has 'powers', but at this stage it is necessary to address both terms, power and the material, if we are to move forward. What do we mean by these terms?

Power

Our contributors share a view of power that is at variance with most mainstream accounts. In these power is akin to a quantity, a property, essentially to a thing. Some have more, some less, some none at all. And this power originates in particular places, for example in classes, institutions and states. Now, this view of power is not 'wrong', but there are grave limitations to what it can actually tell us about how power works. The view of power adopted here involves conceiving of it as omnipresent, and as constantly ebbing and flowing, collecting and dispersing, in changing combinations and arrangements. Rather than a thing or property, it is more like a condition of action that is made manifest in the practices through which it is performed and exercised. This view of power of course is deeply indebted to the work of Michel Foucault (Faubion, 2005).

According to this perspective, if power is dispersed in such a manner it cannot have a single source, or set of sources, from which it springs, as if these sources were the places where power is made. These sources have traditionally numbered classes, institutions, persons, the human subject itself, and especially important in the present regard, the state.

Let us consider the state. When it is written about it still tends to be in the familiar terms of its constitutional and administrative manifestations, its social and economic role (welfare, educational and economic policy and practice, for instance), or in terms of ideas or experiences of the state. The state is in such understandings decidedly an 'it'. Much the same view of the state is evident as regards the chief conceptual schools of understanding the state. This is so whether these be the liberal and pluralist ones which envisage the state as the autonomous and neutral regulator of society and of its rights and obligations, or Marxist and 'elite' notions of the state as the projection or instrument of interests and classes. While there are, of course, significant differences between these approaches in other respects, they share a tendency to ontologise the state.

This view of the state does not easily bear the critical scrutiny of the positions developed in this book. Patrick Joyce, for example, speaks of the state not as a reified entity, but as something like a site of passage of and between different powers, thinking of power here in the Foucauldian vein. The accretion or clustering of these systems of power, or more simply powers, at the level of 'the state' since the sixteenth century forms a process that, in academic discourse, has come to be called the governmentalisation of the state, something which the state may sometimes drive but of which it is very often neither the author nor the master.[1] From a parallel viewpoint the state might be thought of in terms of relationships, in particular as a constantly shifting relationship between what we are used to calling 'state' and 'society'. In one of Foucault's more famous formulations, the state is thus 'nothing else but the mobile effect of a regime of multiple governmentalities' (Foucault, 2008: 77). It is in this vein that Timothy Mitchell, for example, talks of the 'state effect', the particular configuration of state and society being seen as the outcome of the transaction of powers which are themselves diversely located in the social (Mitchell, 2002).

Taking the example of bureaucracy, considered directly by Joyce and Mukerji in this book, it has proved productive to think about the state as a site where bureaucratic power congregates or clusters, rather than a site from which this form of power originates or at which it terminates. Bureaucratic forms of organisation, and the powers they call upon and elaborate, emerge in many places, for example in business, the military, and within religious institutions. These then 'migrate' to and from the state. Clustering there, they are redeployed and multiplied, but they may also lodge themselves so firmly as to outlive the state, or to function in ways that are parasitic upon it and inimical to it, as for example in some contemporary African states.[2] So, it might be better to talk not of state power per se but of bureaucratic power, emphasising the adjectival over the nominative. This view has in fact now begun to be dominant in the social sciences, a recent reader in the anthropology of the state drawing precisely on some of the figures considered here, for instance Timothy Mitchell, Michel Foucault, Nikolas Rose and James Ferguson.[3]

Similar tendencies are evident in the literature on colonialism. In the wake of Ann Laura Stoler and Frederick Cooper's (1997) challenge to one-way constructions of the flow of power from metropolis to colony, work across a range of disciplines has focused on the operations of plural flows of power arising from the networks of relations between both metropolitan and colonial sites. Miles Ogborn, in summarising this literature, argues that colonialism is 'constituted through its arrangements of spaces, places, landscapes, and networks of connection', involving the interplay of powers between a multiplicity of such sites as 'trading posts, mercantile offices, imperial and colonial cities, and plantation and slave gardens' (Ogborn, 2007: 4). Nélia Dias, in this book, would agree given the close attention she pays to the relations between trading stations and railways in the exercise of colonial power in colonial French West Africa. So would Tony Bennett and Christopher Pinney in extending the range of the colonial sites in which distinctive forms of power are made up and exercised to include the relations between the ethnographer's field site and the museum, and the photographer's studio.

It is apparent, then, that a critical interrogation of the concept of power enables us to think of the mechanisms of power in new ways. However, our particular concern here is to deepen this understanding of power by relating it to materiality, just as in turn the richness of the latter concept is augmented by linking it to power. One major area of scholarship in which the links between materiality and power have been greatly strengthened in recent times is that which we previously referred to as 'governmentality'. This can be defined as the study of the various rationales and technologies that are involved in the governance of human conduct generally and, especially but not exclusively, those concerned with the governance of the state. Work in this particular conceptual frame has been strongly marked by an interest in how rationales and technologies invariably take material forms. However, this still leaves us the question of what 'material' means in our title, *Material Powers.*

The material

When we speak of material powers are we saying that objects and things themselves *have* powers? Surely this cannot be the case, for would we not then inhabit a deterministic world? Yet, equally, if we are to speak of material powers, this entails recognising distinctive forms of agency and effectivity on the part of material forces. How are we to designate the material as something which exercises, but does not *have* powers, without courting the difficulties of determinist positions? To unravel these comments we turn to recent notions of 'the social', another term, like 'the material', needing discussion.[4] Recent ideas about the social bear directly on our theme of the material. After the major 'turn' of the cultural, there has, in the USA as well as in Britain, been a series of what might be called secondary 'turns' – 'empirical', 'affective', 'descriptive' and so on – which all to one degree or another have built upon and further developed a critique of familiar and inherited conceptual dualisms: those between the material and the ideal, the material and the cultural and so on. In the process they have moved 'beyond documentary positivism, simplistic notions of causality, and quasi-philosophical social theories of change'.[5] One of the most productive if not contentious developments in this agenda of inquiry into the nature of the social involves the trans-national initiatives crystallising around the work of Bruno Latour,[6] although his work is only one of the influences involved in this 'science studies' agenda.[7] His work marks this book in several respects.

The crucial intellectual move in this view is one that turns away from notions of a coherent social totality, and towards the erasure of familiar conceptual distinctions between the natural and the social, the human and the non-human, and the material and the cultural, divisions that are all in the first place predicated on the immaterial/material divide. The social, in this intellectual departure, is seen to be performed by material things just as much as by humans, so that labelling one thing a person and one a machine, one thing material and one thing not, is not given in the order of things but is itself a product of the ordering of people and things that make up the social in the first place. The general idea here is therefore that the social does not lie outside the actors and networks in which it is located (say in 'society' or 'nature'), as John Frow explains in his chapter. 'Society' is therefore seen to be radically contingent, not necessary, this view being marked by a keen apprehension of the difficulty and complexity of achieving order. The social and society are seen in terms of the 'path building' and 'order making' activities of the networks and the actants involved – the latter being the term Latour has coined to describe the non-human as well as the human elements of networks. The job of analysis, and the moral of this metaphysical story, is that one follows the actants and the networks themselves and in particular those that become 'strategic' because of the number of connections they make possible in a highly contingent world.

This is a useful point at which to make good our opening promise of explaining what me mean by materiality and, as its plural extension, 'materialities'. There are difficulties here, though, since the meanings of these terms are neither settled nor undisputed. Daniel Miller's work, while important and always insightful, rests on different premises from those we have outlined so far. While embracing the language of 'materialities', he insists that any concern with the agency of material things has to be part of a larger account of culture and looks to Hegel's account of the dialectic between subject and object for this purpose. For it suggests, he argues,

> that there can be no fundamental separation between humanity and materiality – that everything that we are and do arises out of the reflection upon ourselves given by the mirror image of the process by which we create and form and are created by this same process.
>
> (Miller, 2005: 8)

In such formulations, material things become effective in shaping social relations and conduct only through the mediating agency of human consciousness.

We do not, of course, doubt that this is often so. It is a claim, though, that stands in marked contrast to the traditions of work arising from science studies and actor-network theory which argue for the independent agency of material things and processes. This is not, however, an agency that is autonomous in relation to human practices and the relations between human agents. Nor is it a matter of attributing intentionality to the components of the material world. It is, rather, a matter of taking account of the distinctive kinds of effectivity that material objects and processes exert as a consequence of the positions they occupy within specifically configured networks of relations that always include human and non-human actors. The issues to be considered here concern less the ways in which objects become effective by being integrated into the subjective world of human consciousness, and more the difference they make in their own right as a consequence of their specific material properties considered relationally: the immense differences, for example, particularly for the management of waste, between glass and plastic bottled water (Hawkins, 2009). There are differences, too, between the Latourian tradition and the stress on the agency of things that comes from recent work in the anthropology of art, particularly Alfred Gell's *Art and Agency* (Gell, 1998).[8] However, as Miller usefully notes, while both Latour and Gell attribute 'agency to guns and landmines as against those who fire or plant them,' the key difference between them is that 'Gell is looking through objects to the embedded human agency that we infer they contain' (Miller, 2008: 279). The same is true of the account of distributed personhood proposed by Marilyn Strathern (1999); this remains human-centred even as it distributes agency across a network of human and non-human agents.

There is, however, a second aspect of our approach to materialities that needs to be highlighted here. This concerns its post-representational logic. The key influence here is that of Gilles Deleuze and Félix Guattari, particularly their contention that social life is to be understood in terms of the operation of assemblages made up of 'semiotic flows, material flows, and social flows simultaneously' but without there being any clear ontological distinction between these capable of establishing 'a tripartite division between a field of reality (the world) and a field of representation (the book) and a field of subjectivity (the author)' (Deleuze and Guattari, 1987: 22–23). This locates the analysis of the relations between semiotic, material and social flows in an entirely different conceptual space from that of dualistic or tripartite schemas which set up divisions between different levels (between that of culture, for example, and the social or the economy) and then seeks some general formula for deciphering the relations between them (the economic base determines the ideological superstructure; or the role of culture, in the logic of the cultural turn, is to construct the social). As Paul Patton notes, although Deleuze and Guattari speak of social relations and social formations, their account of assemblages affords no place for a conception of 'the social' as such. Instead, attention is paid to the way in which the components of assemblages work to secure the ordering, and disordering, of social/economic/political life as an intersecting set of 'flat multiplicities' (Patton, 2006) whose interactions are, in Deleuze and Guattari's famous imagery, those of a 'thousand plateaus'.

The legacy of Deleuze and Guattari is evident in Latour's employment of spatial metaphors, talking for instance about a 'flat' social, instead of received understandings of a surface/depth one.[9] It is the latter that suffuse common sense and much of academic usage, when we talk for instance of the 'social context' or the social setting or social ground of something, and above all when we speak about notions of 'social construction'. 'Social context' is meaningless when the distinction between text and context is dissolved, as it is here, and 'social construction' is equally meaningless because it presupposes already a distinction between what is and what is not the social. Similarly, still prevalent if often unacknowledged notions of the social either as akin to a structure or an organism are called into question: the force of this questioning should be recognised, for this is a root and branch departure from mainstream conceptions of the social and society.[10] For, in this 'flat' social, forms of addressing the social that are part of disciplinary common sense, such as foreground and background, figure and context, actor and system, and therefore micro and macro, are all dissolved. Historical outcomes and events are not therefore the reflection of something else which lies hidden beneath the surface of things.[11] It is the 'surface' itself that constitutes the effective level at which material and semiotic relations are entangled with one another.

As well as a 'flat' social replacing 'society', the process of social ordering itself replaces the traditional model of social order. In place of the idea of a single social order the emphasis is placed on criss-crossing and often conflicting practices of social ordering, and on the constitution of such practices as, in John Law's terms, 'materially heterogenous' (Law, 1994: 2) involving talk, bodies, texts, machines, architectures, etc. The problem of social order is replaced by a concern with 'the plural processes of socio-technical ordering' (Law, 1994: 2). Therefore, questions of agency come to the fore, and to some extent displace questions of identity and of meaning. The latter have been the calling cards of cultural history and cultural studies, but from these new perspectives on the social the central question is how agency is mobilised and performed by a vast array of human and non-human actors. As Christopher Otter observes 'Action is not simply something humans do: in a collective, action is distributed between multiple agents'.[12] Although agency has of course been emphasised in cultural and social history and cultural studies, it has tended to be from an anthropocentric and humanist perspective, dwelling on individual and collective actions, or else agency has been conceived in highly structural or organic ways as manifestations of what is in one sense or another hidden below the surface.

There are other traditions that would need to be taken into account in a fuller rendering of the relations between a concern with materialities and the development of post-representational agendas across the humanities and social sciences. The work of Michel Callon, for example, has been influential in shaping the development of new 'cultural economy' approaches to the ordering of markets. This has been particularly true of his translation of Deleuze and Guattari's concept of *agencement* into an account of the hybrid constitution – a mix of human and non-human, textual and material, social and technical elements – of the market devices which organise and equip economic actors with the capacities for certain kinds of action (Callon, 2005, 2007; Callon, Millo and Muniesa, 2007). Recent accounts of the ordering practices peculiar to the organisation of insurance markets (Mcfall, 2009) or grocery retailing (Cochoy, 2008) are indebted to this aspect of Callon's work. Posthumanist perspectives have similarly informed the development of new approaches to race which stress the role of material forces and their affordances in organising the terrain of racialising practices (Anderson and Perrin, 2009).

From these multiple perspectives, then, all with their own separate agendas and influences at work, it becomes apparent that one might appropriately talk about a 'material turn' in history and the social sciences, and that this might be the most important of all the recent intellectual turns that have been taken. Certainly, its force can already be felt in relation to the intersections between the concerns of historical and cultural analysis which inform this collection in seeking to push these on beyond the logic of the cultural turn. For it is clear, in retrospect, that the cultural turn occupied the same 'problem space' as the economic or social deterministic schools of thought it was defined against in sharing the assumption that culture, the economy and the social can be clearly differentiated from one another in a fashion that then makes it intelligible to ask questions concerning the relative power of the flows between them. When John Law remarks that what is social is never just social but is also 'simultaneously technical, architectural, textual, and natural' he goes on to argue that 'the division between such categories is itself a relational achievement rather than something given in the order of things' (Law, 1991: 166). It is in these terms, we suggest, that questions concerning the relations between culture, economy and the social now need to be posed: not as a matter of enfolding culture within the economy or the social, or, on the contrary, of attributing to it the power to construct these, but as historically contingent divisions between different sectors of activity each of which is composed of the same heterogeneous 'mangle of practices' and is situated on the same plane.[13]

The virtue of Foucauldian conceptions of the social is that of avoiding any false ontologisation of the social as a universal while simultaneously recognising the complex set of interacting forces that have gone into making up the social as a historically specific 'transactional reality' mediating the relations between government and population.[14] It is here, we should add, that we part company with Latour's project of a sociology of associations. For while we have no objection to his substitution of collectives for the sociological object of 'society', his methods are ultimately too formalist to offer a properly historical understanding of the social as a product of, and relay for, practices of government.

Material powers

The contributions to this book take up a number of the questions, difficulties and possibilities in these positions. This is so first of all in terms of questions about agency, questions that are of primary importance for social scientists and historians seeking to build new accounts of the processes and mechanisms of social change. Again, the state proves to be a productive arena. As a number of our contributors indicate, the state is not founded fully formed but is a process of continual 'improvisation'. In Mukerji's account of the 'unintended state', for example, political control in seventeenth-century France was made possible through the means of territorial engineering, which in turn gave rise to the development of 'administrative stewardship'. What was in fact a very early incidence of the emergence of modern form of administration involved multiple 'entanglements' of things and persons, of human and non-human agency. Other contributions echo this: Christopher Pinney for instance, in considering photography in nineteenth-century colonial India, writes not of photography but of 'corpography' in order to denote this way of understanding connections between the body and the technical. He also writes of what he calls 'image acts', instead of 'photography' and the 'logics of technosocial practice' instead of 'technology'. Tony Bennett is similarly concerned with the role played by photography as one amongst other inscription devices through which the 'other worlds' produced by anthropological fieldwork are made mobile, translated from field to museum and back again via the route of their association with colonial forms of administration.[15]

In fact, evident across the book are what can be called logics of practice, although the word 'logic' does not quite do justice to the vagaries of how these eventuate. In relation to the state what is apparent in the case of seventeenth-century France is a particular logic of state practice, and Patrick Joyce's contribution on the materiality of files and filing systems in governing the British Empire in nineteenth-century London and India similarly emphasises such a logic. In France key servants of the King in the engineering dimension of land stewardship entered the collective world of engineers, masons, draughtsman and other workers, and collectively developed new forms of expertise and new understandings of this expertise and its possibilities which were at variance with its ostensible purpose, namely the augmentation of the royal will. A new kind of state therefore emerged in an unintended fashion out of the logic of practice evident in land stewardship, a logic that was proto-technocratic. Similarly, in considering administrative paperwork Joyce emphasises how a particular logic of bureaucratic practice – in which human agency and the material agencies involved in writing were combined – brought into being a new kind of state, born in large part out of a new concern with system and systematicity. Rather than territorial, this was now extra- or trans-territorial, in the case of the British Empire. What Joyce also shows is the unpredictability of outcomes, a particular logic of practice leading to results which were anything but functional for the new bureaucratic institution of the India Office. Harvey and Knox in analogous fashion show the various convergences and divergences of different logics of practice at work in Peruvian state formation, as interpreted through the means of road building, the logics of engineers and the different logics of workers.

In recent work Miles Ogborn, in looking at the writing and accountancy practices of the early, commercial East India Company has shown how these practices can be understood as performing historically specific logics of capitalism (Ogborn, 2007). However, the important point to emphasise here is that in employing the term logic of practice one is not imputing an innate, somehow immanent, force and direction to either capitalism or the state, a 'state logic' for instance.[16] Instead, the history of both, and of other 'historical forces' (such as technology itself) that have been reified in similar fashion needs to be taken apart and if necessary rewritten in terms of detailed reconstructions of what can be said to have formed such 'logics' (Joyce, 2010). In such reconstructions the agency of things needs to be carefully considered. So far, we have emphasised the ways in which human and non-human agency are linked, or not linked, and the logic of our own position is that 'agency' is apparent only when agents, or better perhaps the less anthropocentric technical term 'actants', exist in a network, which is to say that agency is always relational. However, we are concerned with the interaction of material agency with material agency as well is with human agency. This ground of non-human, 'material' agency presents many problems of understanding.

In beginning this task of understanding, the field of infrastructure has proved to be particularly rewarding, whether the framework of understanding be the state, the city or the technological itself. It is not surprising, then, that a number of contributions are explicitly concerned with the analysis of infrastructures, for instance Dias on communication systems in colonial West Africa, Harvey and Knox on road building projects in Peru, Mukerji on the relations between canals and absolutism, and Joyce on the role of filing systems in the development of colonial bureaucracies. Nélia Dias, whose work on railway infrastructures parallels Manu Goswami's (2004) concerns with the effects of such infrastructures in organising the material geographies of colonial administrations, adds to this a concern with the material management of colonised bodies, showing how the languages and techniques for the development of colonial infrastructures and for managing colonial labour intersected. From a similar perspective too, Bill Brown's account of literature's power to produce distinctive 'materiality effects' has an infrastructural component in its concern with the role of plate glass in changing the relation among human subjects, and between those subjects and inanimate objects. Brown, however, adds to this a concern with the ways in which literary texts are active mediators of such relations, thus encompassing a concern with the functioning of literary technologies as active components in the make-up of the social worlds they inhabit.

Christopher Otter addresses similar questions directly in arguing for an account of material power that not only embraces, critically, recent social theory such as actor-network theory but also human subject-centred phenomenological work and the long-established tradition of what he calls 'new historical materialism', something in fact going back to the great historian Fernand Braudel and the *Annales* School of historical writing. All, and more, are indeed necessary to unpick the workings of material powers, especially when the agency that is apparent in material things and processes not only seems to but actually has a power of its own.

We think then of the 'muteness' of power, and how the operation of infrastructure, for instance the growing system and quality of systematicity that Joyce finds in paperwork procedures, is revealing. Such systems involve the 'engineering in' of different capacities and possibilities for agency to things and material processes. There are many instances of this in the literature, particularly notable ones being the work of Ken Alder on the role of machine tools and technical information in transposing social relations in late eighteenth-century France into material forms, or in this regard the rather similar work of Richard Biernacki on how the material forms of factories and of payment systems embedded different notions of human labour, in the process transmitting these over very long periods of historical time. Of course, if certain capacities or affordances are 'built-in' to the material world this is very far from dictating outcomes, for these affordances are continually disrupted and transformed through the action of the innumerable other agencies of things and people. Nonetheless, infrastructure is a good location for understanding how material powers can to varying extents operate outside human consciousness and language: indeed, their power lies in this very muteness, this capacity to be left to operate by themselves. This operation is of course shaped by human agency and intention, but the very purpose of this very often lies in the creation of durability and connectability (or 'connectivity') in objects and processes. The work of Otter on the creation of durability in the infrastructural components of cities, for instance, and its links to a liberal, political history of vision shows how the attempt worked but failed to work fully (Otter, 2008a). And, as Joyce shows, the extent to which the mute power of things seems to have worked can be gauged by the very great extent to which bureaucracy and the state both have become naturalised.

However, the naturalisation of the state in turn depended upon the inculcation, or partial inculcation, of a particular ontology, and as the contribution of Harvey and Knox shows, in a context outside the 'Western' one, different ontologies were at play among different social groups. These might converge and coexist but also diverge, and as these authors show, these different ontologies were always materialised and materialising. Knowledge was not an intellectual exercise and is best approached, via these materialising activities they point to, not as a question of epistemology but of ontology. This shifts the ground of power and especially of political accounts to a recognition that there are always multiple ontologies at play in the world, and that these are inseparable from the ways in which these are materialised and materialising. However, recognising this, it has rightly been remarked that contemporary social theory of a Latourian kind deals with an attenuated and still dualistic notion of ontology, in the shape only of the distinction between the human and the non-human. Whatever the degree to which this attenuation is tactical, it certainly points to the difficulties of employing inherited epistemological and ontological terms and vocabularies in order to describe realities whose complex, multiply stranded constitution, is simply not rendered sensible or understandable by them.

We must, however, forego any further exploration of these matters here in order to review the organisation of this collection and the ways in which the papers it brings together address the issues reviewed earlier.

The collection

There are three sections to the book. The first is concerned with historicising the categories of matter and materialism, and with clarifying the significance of the newer vocabularies of materialities alongside these older terms. This task is undertaken by novel means: through the lens of the city, and via analysis of the relations between literary technologies, things and social life, as well as by the route of the history of thought. The second section concerns the state, where the interest in relations between materialities and power is combined directly with questions about the nature of the state itself. And in the last section on colonial materialities, the colonial encounter represents a particularly fertile area (being politically particularly fraught and particularly demanding) for exploring the forms of knowledge involved in the prosecution of material powers.

Our point of entry into the history of the categories of matter and materialism in the first section is a selective one via a particular tradition of thought, Marxism, that has been central to modern understandings of materialism. By concentrating on Marxism we explore some of the key developments in the history of materialism and how to move beyond these to resist the dualistic ways of thinking that have been so characteristic of modern understandings. By also exploring the history of matter, the chapters in this section push the exploration of this theme beyond philosophical doctrines alone to give some account of how matter has traditionally been understood within Western culture, an account which begins with a consideration of the city, and then moves to the relationship between materiality and literature.

In his opening discussion of the relations between the categories of matter, materialism and materialities, John Frow argues that the privileged place that the concept of materialism occupies in the Marxist tradition has its origins in Marx's philosophical interest in Enlightenment materialism, an interest which later merges with the discovery, first by Engels and then by Marx, of political economy, and with this 'inversion' of Hegelian idealism. Together these three strands form a new theoretical object: the concept of the complex unity of the forces and relations of production understood as a determinant structure. Frow suggests that the ontological weight lent to this object by its description as 'material' has produced major theoretical difficulties for the Marxist and post-Marxist traditions and argues that these have obstructed the development of adequate analytical understandings of the place of materiality in social and cultural processes. The chapter therefore concludes with a discussion of the new logic of 'materialities' and its departures from both materialisms and the cultural turn.

Chris Otter's ensuing discussion of the relations between theory, materiality and the city takes up the baton from Frow in reviewing the ways in which the city – probably, he suggests, the largest and most complex material artifact with which historians, sociologists and cultural theorists routinely deal – has been analysed across a range of intellectual traditions. His starting point is with the way in which urban life has been dematerialised in three influential bodies of work developed in sociology, where he focuses on the influence of Georges Simmel's accounts of city life, in geography, where he takes issue with David Harvey's work on the relations between capital accumulation and urban life, and in the tradition of urban cultural history running from Carl Schorske to Judith Walkowitz's account of the role of cultural texts in mediating urban identities. While respecting their accomplishments, and recognising that none of these traditions ignores the role of material things, he argues that this is nonetheless largely taken for granted – black-boxed, he says, as largely a backdrop to the real social action which takes place elsewhere in the encounters between human subjects. He then looks to the work of urban historians who, drawing eclectically on multiple intellectual traditions – architectural theory, environmental history, Foucauldian theory, science studies, urban geography – have turned their attention to the nitty-gritty aspects of the social life of things in order to foreground their roles as discrete actors or mediators, rather than intermediaries for any deeper level of reality (capital, discourse, psyche). These concerns are exemplified by examinations of the role of urban infrastructures associated with the delivery of water and meat to city populations. In the sketches he offers of these, Otter postulates an urban materiality that is multiple, heterogeneous, dispersed and totally immanent or self-sustaining, as opposed to one that is singular, monistic, focused and merely the surface effect of a truer real existing beyond or behind the material.

Re-theorising urban materiality, Otter argues, involves re-theorising ontology itself. Bill Brown's purpose is to argue that what he calls 'literary mediations' – that is, the ways in which literary texts and technologies mediate the relations between human actors and objects – have to be factored into any such re-thinking of the ontological organisation of cities. He broaches his topic, initially, by a careful reading of C.L.R. James's account of his first experience of the 'object culture' of London in 1932. This serves as a means for reviewing the currency of objects across a range of contemporary disciplines, particularly material culture studies and ethnography, and for a more focused assessment of the accomplishments and the limitations of the 'cultural materialism' that Raymond Williams advocated as a corrective to the determinist implications of traditional Marxist forms of materialism. Tracing the connections between these concerns and those of new historicist criticism Brown notes that, while allowing for a greater fluidity of reciprocal determination between culture and the economy, their materialist credo remained curiously 'dematerialised' in its lack of any effective engagement with the role of objects in social and cultural life. These commentaries on earlier critical traditions serve to locate Brown's own distinctive concerns with the often intense engagement with different object worlds that characterises literary narratives, particularly those which take the modern city as their setting. To illustrate these concerns, he turns his attention to an American text, Theodore Dreiser's *Sister Carrie*, that has long served to illustrate both commodity fetishism and class relations. Brown's focus, by contrast, is on the work of a particular material in that novel – the work of plate glass, and the history of glass manufacture to which it gave rise – as a way of suggesting how that material comes to structure events in the novel (and, indeed, to figure a certain kind of consciousness). By considering the attraction of objects within literary representation, Brown highlights the role that the mediated materiality of literary representations plays in the processes through which subjects are constituted as agents in the midst of, and are affected by, the inanimate object world.

How can we approach understandings of power, especially political power, using new approaches to the concept of materiality and new understandings of the material world? This is the question that guides our concerns in the second section of the book. In talking about material powers the chapters engage with the manifold ways in which, in concert with the human, material things and processes assemble or format the state. In the first chapter in this section, Chandra Mukerji argues that the 'territorialisation' of the seventeenth-century French state operated in such a way as to eventuate in new state forms that were not the conscious product of political agents themselves so much as the unintended results of an investment in territorial infrastructures. In the second contribution, Patrick Joyce is concerned with the role of material processes and artefacts in shaping the persona and the institutions of bureaucracy itself with particular regard to the India Office in London. In the third chapter, Harvey and Knox's study of roads and road construction in Peru shows that the state is as much a product of the civil engineer, and the technical expert more generally, as of the politician.

Chandra Mukerji's starting point, to develop each of these points in more detail, is that no one intended to build a territorial state in seventeenth-century France. It was rather, she argues, an accident on the road to empire that had its roots in the material transformation of French land that resulted from a series of engineering projects. Louis XIV and his Minister of the Treasury, Jean-Baptiste Colbert, had dreams of France as a New Rome: an empire to rival that of the Hapsburgs. But to realise this goal, Colbert needed more money for the treasury, and tried to assert new powers over French lands to get it. Arguing that they had exercised poor stewardship, Colbert began to take land away from local nobles and use it for state projects. The resulting infrastructural improvements restructured the conditions of possibility for the lives of peasants, merchants and aristocrats alike, while also manifesting a form of government that did not depend upon the sacred status of the king, but instead the worldly effectiveness of the administration. The engineers who redesigned French territory for political purposes began to see their skills as sources rather than as expressions of the king's powers. The king took action against all of them for acting independently of his will, rejecting state territoriality as a political strategy. But what these engineers had built had already changed France, and the notion of stewardship they realised on the land remained a powerful model of government as France continued to become a territorial state in spite of the will of sovereign power.

Patrick Joyce in his chapter moves on naturally from this interest in a logic of practice which as has been seen as proto-technocratic. By the late nineteenth century, as compared with the seventeenth century, the technocratic state had more fully emerged, though in forms somewhat removed from those usually imagined, where technical expertise is understood as mastered by more or less elaborate forms of technical training. While this did exist, and in Britain from the middle of the nineteenth century included a civil service that was made increasingly 'technical', the technostate revealed by the management of information in the British empire, as evident in the India Office, was a matter of very unelaborated knowledge and practice, for techniques were learned on the job 'informally', often by the low-grade officers exerting their own initiative. This was a low-tech rather than a high-tech technocrat, and contrary to many present-centred accounts of empire and the state, the material technologies that so often mattered were also low-tech. It was pens, ink, paper that mattered, if not exclusively then much more than is usually understood. Material powers are so often based on a bedrock of quotidian technologies.

Human agency therefore mattered, and intention mattered also, but this agency gained its powers only to the extent that it was able to stabilise and capture material agencies. However, this was invariably only temporary, partial and qualified, each new rationale of paperwork organisation, for example, leading to numerous unforeseen and often contradictory consequences. Such consequences were the result of material agencies themselves, which operated autonomously so that their own powers, the powers of ink, pens and paper, have to be taken into the very centre of accounts of what empire was. This question is approached in this chapter in terms of the stabilisation of empire, the achievement of a 'centre' that would harness and curb the centripetal tendencies of empire (and similarly the analogous tendencies within the nation state itself). The human and non-human agencies so mobilised in paperwork management achieved increasingly sophisticated levels of systematicity at the time, and it is precisely in this achievement of system and the creation of 'connectivity' that state power was rooted. Filing and other management systems show how the agency of material entities operated according to logics of their own, often independent of human intention and indeed awareness.

Such systems also operated more directly on human sensibilities in that they also 'performed' the legitimacy of the institution of bureaucracy and the personae of the bureaucrats, and hence the legitimacy of the state. All states are rooted in writing, and the performance of the state in the routines of writing can be understood in the sense that such routines operated as embodied practice, in pre-discursive and pre-cognitive ways, which produced 'effects' that were fundamental to state formation, and as a consequence of their character fundamental to the naturalisation of the state as well. This was one way through which dispersed and fragmented governmental reasons and techniques came to be perceived as a unitary, purposeful state, when in practice it was most often anything but. 'Performance' operated in a rather different sense also, one involved with the repeated public performance of efficiency and political accountability as symbolising the rightness of imperial governance.

In the next chapter, Penny Harvey and Hannah Knox take a comparative look at road building in contemporary Peru and at the Inka construction at Macchu Picchu. These examples allow them to work through some of the key contributions of anthropological thinking in relation to the study of material culture: the holistic study of technological processes as embodied and embedded in complex social and cultural understandings; the social and cultural dynamics of abstraction, and the compromises made between the abstract and the material in the re-materialisation of analytic models. By contrasting modern laboratory practices with ancient Andean construction techniques, they explore distinctions between analytical and analogical thinking in relation to knowledge about the material world and the ways in which such knowledges are intrinsic to the shaping of particular state forms. However, their study also shows how, despite an explicit resistance to the intrinsic sociality of matter, modern engineering practice continually undermines its own assertion of the discontinuities between 'nature' and 'politics'. By focusing on experimental practice as negotiation and not simply control, the chapter reveals the continuities between the modern engineers and Inka builders (and by extension the state forms they are enabling) as each looks for ways to reveal the properties inherent in the matter they seek to transform. Modern engineers are thus shown to be instrumental in assembling the 'modern' state, and in ensuring its deferred modernity. Equally important, though, are the limits to this which arise from the operation of other material powers deriving from the quite different relations to the land and what it holds associated with traditional Inka and local cosmologies. By showing how these were brought into play in association with a fatal accident during the roadbuilding project, Harvey and Knox foreground the instability of the purifications – between nature and culture, the material and the immaterial – associated with modernist state-building projects. Albeit reluctantly, they argue, the engineers are obliged to put to one side the forms of engagement with the earth's materiality derived from laboratory soil sampling in a struggle – never entirely successful – to fend off the 'ghosts' that Indigenous practices implanted in the same soil.

Our concerns in the final section shift to 'colonial materialities', that is, to a consideration of the role of 'material powers' in the organisation and exercise of power in the specific contexts of colonial forms of rule. It is also effects a change of emphasis away from a primary concern with the organisation of technical infrastructures (although Dias is concerned with these questions) toward the role played by specific cultural knowledges and practices in organising particular techniques of governing. These matters are addressed in three different colonial contexts: British rule in India, late nineteenth-century colonial practices in the French colonies, and the 'internal colonialism' of the early twentieth-century Australian state. The practices considered range across railway building, photography, anthropometry and ethnographic collections of various kinds: of objects, film and sound recordings.

In his account of camerawork as technical practice, Christopher Pinney asks how we can avoid seeing photography, on the one hand, as simply a screen onto which the social and/or the state is projected, or on the other, as a determining 'technology'. His analysis assumes that the potentiality of photography, and the objects which it proved capable of picturing, were both initially *unknown*. The camera and its objects evolved within a shared space (a 'corpography'), an experimental, networked zone of technical *practice*. This is explored through experiments with the use of the camera as a prosthetic extension in colonial jurisprudence, the attempt to integrate the photography of convicts with the network of telegraphy in the 1870s, and photographic portraiture's 'prophetic' individuating role in mid-nineteenth century Lucknow and Bhopal. In his consideration of these practices, Pinney constantly stresses the need to *historicise* the relation of photography to colonial power by considering the changing relations between apparatus and *habitus*. As photographers became less dependent on the kinds of official support (finance, transport, labour-agents, staging bungalows, etc) which had been so vital to the canonical photographers of the nineteenth century, they became far more mobile and their *habitus* changed with significant consequences for the conduct of photography as a technical practice. In concluding his discussion, Pinney argues that a historicised and materialised approach to photography starkly reveals the inadequacy of post-Foucauldian accounts of photography as entirely inscribed within discourses of knowledge and power.

Nélia Dias's concerns centre on the relations between French colonial administration and anthropological concerns with the body in general and with the senses in particular in the late-nineteenth and early-twentieth centuries. How were anthropological concerns with the sensory capacities of the colonised and the development of railroads connected? Dias interprets both as parts of a process of intervention into both natural and human 'milieus' so that the economic capacity of colonial society might be improved. The construction of massive colonial infrastructures (through railroads and the telegraph) informed and was informed by the analysis of the senses, and both shared the same conceptual, social and material relations. Dias thus examines how the terms in which anthropologists codified and defined the meanings for a variety of bodily measures, including sensory acuity and susceptibility to pain, echoed and were derived from those developed for the management of infrastructures. The standardisation of measurement that this permitted along with the uniformity of observational and experimental practices allowed anthropological knowledge to travel from the metropolis to the colonies. Far from being mere objects of such knowledge, however, the colonised reworked anthropological representations of their bodies into new forms of somatic resistance to the work regimes imposed by colonial administrations. By pointing out the contingent nature of colonial administration, its strategies of adaptation to local differences and the ways in which its policies were constantly contested, Dias's account allows for considerable agency on the part of the colonised population.

In the final chapter, Tony Bennett takes his title from Bruno Latour's remarks, in *Pandora's Hope* (Latour, 1999) on the role played by the relationships between expeditions and museums in 'making and mobilising worlds', that is, the processes through which non-humans are loaded into discourse, and thereby made mobile in the sense of being made available for varied forms of social enrolment. Latour sees museums as having played a critical role in such processes by serving as the centres at which objects collected in expeditions are assembled and made available for mobilisation in new contexts. Bennett draws on this perspective and the more general formulations of assemblage theory to examine how a particular version of Aboriginal culture was produced and mobilised in the relations between Baldwin Spencer's anthropological fieldwork in Central Australia, his work as Director of the National Museum of Victoria, his influence on the development of the administration of Aboriginal affairs, and the development of the assimilationist strategies that characterised the early decades of state formation in post-Federation Australia. In developing this account, Bennett draws on the principles of Foucault's historical method to locate Spencer's racial production of the Aborigine as a new 'transactional reality' across which the relations between coloniser and colonised took place, and considers the part that his museum and photographic practices played in developing new socio-material arrangements for the management of Aborigines in the increasingly nationalised space of Australia.

Notes

1 For some of these historical applications see Alan Hunt (1999); Matthew G. Hanna (2000); Oleg Kharkhordin (1999); Gyan Prakash (1999); Nicholas Dirks (2001); Tony Bennett (2004). See also Thomas Osborne, Andrew Bary and Nikolas Rose (1996); Nikolas Rose (1999a, 1999b, 2007); Mitchell Dean (1999); Colin Gordon, Peter Miller and Graham Burchill (1991); Mike Gane and Terry Johnson (1993).
2 James Ferguson (1994).
3 Aradhana Sharma and Akhil Gupta (2006).
4 Patrick Joyce (2010).
5 See especially the anniversary issue of the British *Sociological Review*, vol. 56, No. 4, November 2008, 'Introduction: Inscribing the history of British sociology ', editorial introduction by Tom Osborne, Mike Savage and Nikolas Rose. The issue represents what might be called the 'descriptive term', in which there is a shift from emphasising causality to description itself. See also Patricia Ticineto Clough (2007); Nigel Thrift (2008); Manual De Landa (2006) and De Landa (1997).
6 Bruno Latour (2006). Also Latour (1993, 1999, 2001, 2002).
7 This line of thinking runs from Foucault and Deleuze through to actor-network theory, and postconstructivist science studies, including Latour, Michel Callon and John Law. In his account of modernity, John Law draws on the work of his colleague Bruno Latour who locates the arbitrary division of the world historically in terms of modernity itself. In turn, in his *We Have Never Been Modern*, Latour is heavily indebted to a classical work in the history of science and technology, namely, Steven Shapin and Simon Shaffer (1985). See John Law (1994).
8 Gell's work has had a considerable influence on the recent increased significance assigned to the agency of objects within anthropology where, however, the influence of actor-network theory and related approaches is also evident. For a representative range of

studies reflecting these concerns, see Edwards, Gosden and Phillips (2006), Myers (2001), Pinney and Thomas (2001) and Henare (2005).

9 Bruno Latour, 'How to keep the social flat', (2006)

10 For a more extended discussion of these questions, see Callon and Law (1997).

11 Some of the key debates here have been between Latour's call for a sociology of associations, modelled on the work of Gabriel Tarde, to Bourdieu's conception of sociology as a science whose objectifying procedures bring to light the operation of hidden structures which order the activities of social agents in ways that such agents are not conscious of. Latour explicitly targets aspects of Bourdieu's work for criticism along these lines (Latour, 2004, 2005). Bourdieu's response to these criticisms (Bourdieu, 2004) is an unfortunate one in that it all too evidently misunderstands the claims of the tradition of science studies from which Latour writes. For a better and more balanced account of the relations between Bourdieu's and Latour's understandings of sociology, see Schinkel (2007).

12 Christopher Otter, ' From the social to the collective', unpublished seminar paper (2008b). See also Otter (2004, 2005, 2008a).

13 The reference to 'mangle of practices' here is to Pickering (1995), though see Pickering (2009) for a statement of his divergences from Latourian principles of analysis. Bennett (2007) develops more fully the point we argue for here concerning the historical ordering of the relations between culture and the social.

14 See Foucault (2008) for the significance he accords to the analysis of historically specific and mutable 'transactional realities' in place of universals.

15 See Bennett (2009) for a parallel analysis of the relations between field, museum and colonial administration exemplified by the development of the Musée de l'Homme.

16 In this respect, if not all others, we concur with Luc Boltanski and Eve Chiapello's (2005) contention that the logics of capitalism have been historically plural and diverse.

Bibliography

Anderson, Kay and Colin Perrin (2009) 'Thinking *with* the head: race, craniometry, humanism,' *Journal of Cultural Economy*, 2 (1–2), 83–98.

Bennett, Tony (2004) *The Birth of the Museum*, London: Routledge.

—— (2006) *Pasts Beyond Memory: Evolution, Museums, Colonialism*, London: Routledge.

—— (2007) 'Making culture, changing society: the perspective of culture studies', *Cultural Studies*, vol. 21, nos 4–5, 610–629.

—— (2009) 'Museum, field, colony: colonial governmentality and the circulation of reference', *Journal of Cultural Economy*, 2 (1–2), 91–116.

Bourdieu, Pierre (2004) *Science of Science and Reflexivity*, University of Chicago Press.

Boltanski, Luc and Eve Chiapello (2005) *The New Spirit of Capitalism*, London: Verso.

Callon, Michel (2005) 'Why virtualism paves the way to political impotence: a reply to Daniel Miller's critique of *The Laws of the Markets*', *Economic Sociology: European Electronic Newsletter*, vol. 6, no. 2 (February), 3–20.

—— (2007) 'What does it mean to say that economics is performative?' in D. Mackenzie, F. Muniesa and L. Sui (eds) *Do Economists make Markets?* Princeton University Press, 311–357.

Callon, Michel and John Law (1997) 'After the individual in society: lessons on collectivity from science, technology and society', *Canadian Journal of Sociology*, 22 (2), 165–181.

Callon, Michel, Yuval Millo and Fabian Muniesa (eds) (2007) *Market Devices*, Oxford: Blackwell Publishing/The Sociological Review.

Cochoy, Frank (2008) 'Hans and Gretel at the grocery store: *Progressive Grocer* and the little American consumers (1929–59)', *Journal of Cultural Economy*, 1 (2), 145–164.

Dean, Mitchell (1999) *Governmentality*, London: Sage.
DeLanda, Manual (1997) *A Thousand Years of NonLinear History*, New York and London: Zone Books.
—— (2006) A *New Philosophy of Society: Assemblage Theory and Social Complexity*, New York and London: Continuum.
Deleuze, Gilles and Félix Guattari (1987) *A Thousand Plateaus: Capitalism and Schizophrenia* (trans. B. Massumi), London: The Athlone Press.
Dirks, Nicholas (2001) *Castes of Mind: Colonialism and the Making of Modern India*, Princeton University Press.
Edwards, Elizabeth, Chris Gosden and Ruth B. Phillips (eds) (2006) *Sensible Objects: Colonialism, Museums and Material Culture*, Oxford and New York: Berg.
Ferguson, James (1994) *The Anti Politics Machine: 'Development', Depoliticisation, and Bureaucratic Power in Lesotho*, University of Minnesota Press.
Faubion, James D. (ed.) *Power: The Essential Works of Michel Foucault 1954–1984*, London: Allen Lane, The Penguin Press.
—— (2008) *The Birth of Biopolitics: Lectures at the Collège de France, 1978–1979*, London: Palgrave Macmillan.
Gane, Mike and Terry Johnson (eds) (1993) *Foucault's New Domains*, London: Routledge.
Gell, Alfred (1998) *Art and Agency: An Anthropological Theory*, Oxford: Clarendon Press.
Gordon, Colin, Peter Miller and Graham Burchill (eds) (1991) *The Foucault Effect: Studies in Governmentality*, Brighton: Harvester Wheatsheaf.
Goswami, Manu (2004) *Producing India: From Colonial Economy to National Space*, Chicago and London: University of Chicago Press.
Hanna, Matthew G. (2000) *Governmentality and the Mastery of Territory in Nineteenth Century America*, Cambridge University Press.
Hawkins, Gay (2009) 'The politics of bottled water: assembling bottled water as brand, waste and oil', *Journal of Cultural Economy*, 2 (1–2), 183–196.
Henare, Amiria (2005) *Museums, Anthropology and Imperial Exchange*, Cambridge University Press.
Hunt, Alan (1999) *Governing Morals: A Social History of Moral Regulation* Cambridge University Press.
Joyce, Patrick (2003) *The Rule of Freedom: Liberalism and the Modern City*, London: Verso.
—— (forthcoming, 2010) 'What is the social in social history?', *Past and Present*, Oxford University Press.
Kharkhordin, Oleg (1999) *The Collective and the Individual in Russia: A Study of Practices*, California University Press.
Latour, Bruno (1993) *We Have Never Been Modern*, Brighton: Harvester Press.
—— (1999) *Pandora's Hope: Essays on the Reality of Science Studies*, Cambridge, Mass.: Harvard University Press.
—— (2001) 'When things strike back: a possible contribution of "science studies" to the social sciences', *British Journal of Sociology*, 51 (1).
—— (2002) 'Gabriel Tarde and the end of the social', in Patrick Joyce (ed.) *The Social in Question: New Bearings in History and the Social Sciences*, London and New York: Routledge.
—— (2004) 'Why has critique run out of steam? From matters of fact to matters of concern' in Bill Brown (ed.) *Things*, Chicago and London: University of Chicago Press.
—— (2006) *Reassembling the Social: An Introduction to Actor-Network-Theory*, Oxford: Oxford University Press.

Law, John (1991) 'Power, discretion and strategy' in John Law (ed.) *A Sociology of Monsters: Essays on Power, Technology and Domination*, Sociological Review Monograph 38, Oxford: Routledge, 165–191.

—— (1994) *Organising Modernity*, Oxford: Blackwell.

—— (2004) *After Method: Mess in Social Science Research*, London and New York: Routledge.

Mcfall, Liz (2009) 'The agencement of industrial branch life assurance', *Journal of Cultural Economy*, 2 (1–2), 49–66.

Miller, Daniel (2005) 'Materiality: an introduction' in Daniel Miller (ed.) *Materiality*, Durham and London: Duke University Press.

—— (2008) 'Material culture' in Tony Bennett and John Frow (eds) *The SAGE Handbook of Cultural Analysis*, London: SAGE.

Mitchell, Timothy (2002) *The Rule of Experts: Egypt, Techno-Politics, Modernity*, University of California Press.

Myers, Fred (eds) (2001) *The Empire of Things: Regimes of Value and Material Culture*, Santa Fe and Oxford: School of American Research Press/James Currey.

Ogborn, Miles (2007) *Indian Ink: Script and Print in the Making of the English East India Company*, University of Chicago Press.

Osborne, Thomas, Andrew Barry and Nikolas Rose (eds) (1996) *Foucault and Political Reason: Liberalism, Neoliberalism and Rationalities of Government* London: UCL Press.

Osborn, Thomas, Mike Savage and Nikolas Rose (2008) 'Introduction: Inscribing the history of British sociology', *Sociological Review*, vol. 56, No. 4, November.

Otter, Christopher (2004) 'Cleaning and clarifying: technology and perception in 19th-century London', *Journal of British Studies*, 43 (1, January).

—— (2005) 'Making liberalism durable: vision and civility in the late Victorian city', in *Social History*, 27 (1).

—— (2008a) *The Victorian Eye: A Political History of Light and Vision in Britain, 1800–1910*, University of Chicago Press.

—— (2008b) 'From the social to the collective', unpublished seminar paper.

Patton, Paul (2006) 'Order, exteriority and flat multiplicities in the social' in Fuglsang, Mark and Bent Meier Sørensen (eds) *Deleuze and the Social* (2006) Edinburgh University Press.

Pickering, Andrew (1995) *The Mangle of Practice: Time, Agency, and Science*, Chicago: University of Chicago Press.

—— (2009) 'The politics of theory: producing another world with some thoughts on Latour', *Journal of Cultural Economy*, 2 (1–2), 197–212.

Pinney, Christopher and Nicholas Thomas (eds) (2001) *Beyond Aesthetics: Art and the Technologies of Enchantment*, Oxford and New York: Berg.

Prakash, Gyan (1999) *Another Reason: Science and the Imagination of Modern India*, Princeton University Press.

Rose, Nikolas (1999a) *Powers of Freedom: Reframing Political Thought*, Cambridge University Press.

—— (1999b) *Governing the Soul: The Shaping of the Private Self*, second edition, London: Free Association Books.

—— (2007) *The Politics of Life Itself: Biomedicine, Power and Subjectivity in the Twenty-First Century*, Princeton University Press.

Schinkel, Willem (2007) 'Sociological discourse of the relational: the cases of Bourdieu & Latour', *The Sociological Review*, 55 (4), 707–729.

Sewell, William Jnr. (1987) 'A post-materialist rhetoric for labour-history', *International Labor and Working Class History*, 31, 1–13.

Sharma, Aradhana and Akhil Gupta (eds) (2006) *The Anthropology of the State: A Reader* Oxford: Blackwell.

Stoler, Ann Laura and Frederick Cooper (1997) 'Between metropole and colony: rethinking a research agenda' in Laura Ann Cooper and Frederick Stoler (eds) *Tensions of Empire: Colonial Cultures in a Bourgeois World*, Berkeley, Los Angeles, London: University of California Press.

Strathern, Marilyn (1999) *Property, Substance and Effect: Anthropological Essays on Persons and Things*, London and New Brunswick, NJ: The Athlone Press.

Thrift, Nigel (2008) *Non-Representational Theory: Space, Politics, and Text*, London and New York: Routledge.

Ticineto Clough, Patricia (ed.) (2007) *The Affective Turn: Theorizing the Social*, Durham and London: Duke University Press.

Part 1

A history of the categories

1 Matter and materialism

A brief pre-history of the present

John Frow

I

For the last half century or thereabouts the linked concepts of the material, materiality and materialism have worked in the social and human sciences as a very particular kind of fetish. Distantly deriving from the tradition of dialectical materialism, their use promises serious commitment to a methodology that situates cultural or political, legal or experiential matters in relation to social power, social institutions, economic forces, or some bundle thereof. Yet the word 'material' here is not self-explanatory, since 'it does not have a great deal to do with the type of force, causality, efficacy, and obstinacy non-human actants possess in the world. "Matter" … is a highly politicised interpretation of causality' (Latour, 2005: 76).

Let me begin my exploration of the antecedents and the aporias of these concepts with a representative, if unusually complex and nuanced, example of their usage. In the 1980 collection *Problems in Materialism and Culture*, describing the development of the philosophical position he calls 'cultural materialism', Raymond Williams writes of the emphasis he had come to place 'on the production (rather than only the reproduction) of meanings and values by specific social formations, on the centrality of language and communication as formative social forces, and on the complex interaction both of institutions and forms and of social relationships and formal conventions'. Cultural materialism, he continues, is

> a theory of culture as a (social and material) productive process and of specific practices, of 'arts', as social uses of material means of production (from language as material "practical consciousness" to the specific technologies of writing and forms of writing, through to mechanical and electronic communication systems).
>
> (Williams, 1980: 243)

In these passages, as in many others in Williams's oeuvre, we witness a process of translation by which an older Marxist language of base and superstructure is recast to assimilate the 'superstructures' ('meanings and values', culture, language and communication) to the forces of production, and in the same movement the aestheticising language of literary and cultural criticism (formal conventions, culture, the 'arts') is displaced into the language of practice, of materiality, and of technology.

These are familiar enough moves in the trajectory of Western Marxism away from the crippling metaphors of reduction, derivation and determination with which Marxist orthodoxy accounted for the domain of culture. They govern Williams's repeated assertion of the 'materiality' of cultural production (cf. Milner, 1993: 62–63) or, to take a more finely-grained example, his insistence on treating writing as a system not of signs but of notations (Williams, 1977: 169). 'Notations' puts the emphasis on a process rather than its result, and displaces attention from meanings to the physical particularity of the mark on the page.

Yet that particularity cannot be the whole point, for the difference between writing and those objects (paintings, for example) whose semiotic force lies in their difference from every other such object[1] is that the notations making up writing are necessarily repeatable; unless our interest is in type-faces or calligraphy, we attend not to the variations between notations but to the element of commonality that we call meaning. It is true, of course, that meaning is inflected by what we think of as the materiality of the signifier: by intonation and cadence as they are carried by the voice, by font and layout, by script; yet these signifiers are also, for the most part, repeatable; it is not their materiality of itself that matters but their repeated organisation of phonic and graphic matter.

The invocation of materiality thus seems to me either wrong or trivial: trivial because no one doubts that meanings and practices are always and necessarily materially embedded; wrong because it is not the materiality of meanings and practices that gives them their social force but rather the particular social and cultural frameworks that govern how they are deployed. What puzzles me, and what I want to explore here, is how readily the concept of the material has come to act as a shorthand for something quite different (Bhaskar, for example, casually notes that in Marx's 'practical materialism' the concept of matter 'is to be understood in the sense of "social practice" ': a non-sequitur for anybody not in the know) (Bhaskar, 1983: 327); and I'll ask whether it is worth hanging on to this shorthand that shores up a truth claim rather than doing serious intellectual work.

II

Philosophical materialism in the West is carried in two major waves: that of classical antiquity, and that of the European Enlightenment.[2] The former develops around an ontological question about the basic stuff of the universe and how it is organised, and its most interesting answer is the thesis that the fundamental matter of being is atoms moving in random motion through the void. The *Great Diakosmos*, a lost work written by one or both of Leucippus and Democritus in the Athens of the late fifth century BCE, argues that moments of organisation of matter come about as a result of the collision of atoms, resulting in vortices which push the heavier atoms to the centre and thus form bodies. In the later work of Epicurus and of Lucretius, it is the slight deviation of atoms from uniform motion that produces collisions, vortices and thus moments of random order in a context of universal entropy. In this tradition consciousness, too, is understood in terms of the impact of atoms upon the human senses, and thus as a purely physical process.

The materialism of the European Enlightenment is intimately connected with the experimental method of the new physics and its refusal of non-material explanations of physical processes. The methodological starting point for such writers as Gassendi and Hobbes is an assumption that there is no part of the universe that is not a material body, and that no part of the universe contains no body; change and variation take place through the motion and contact of bodies, and sensation is an interchange between two material entities. The central philosophical questions here tend to be not so much about the primordial stuff of the universe as about the laws of motion and interaction of bodies, and the relations between matter and consciousness: that is to say, the relation of secondary representations of matter to matter (is thought also material, or is it different in kind from matter? Or, as Marx succinctly put it, 'can matter think'? [*Ob die Materie nicht denken könne*?] [Marx, 1975: 128]). In the later phases of the Enlightenment – in the work of La Mettrie, d'Holbach and Helvétius – these questions shift on the one hand into questions of causality and determinism organised by the figure of the machine, and on the other into the systematic critique of religion.

At the core of both of these traditions is an assumption that matter is in some sense fundamental and independent of human representations of it. What might be meant by the term 'matter' itself is, of course, a more complex question. From the enquiries of the Ionian metaphysicians of 600 BC onwards, the key question has been about the nature of that substance that underlies the multiplicity of its instantiations: what Robert Boyle in 1666 called 'one universal matter, common to all bodies, an extended, divisible, and impenetrable substance' (quoted in Toulmin and Goodfield, 1962: 180). Matter in this sense is an abstraction from the materials of the world. Atomism answers the primary question about the basic stuff (the world is made up of particles and the forces that hold them together or apart – forces that Empedokles called 'Love and Strife'); but it gives much less satisfactory answers to the question of how this stuff becomes differentiated into the actual variety of specific forms. Various continuist theories posit a principle or a medium of organisation of matter: the Stoics' *pneuma*, Newton's aether, or the force fields of contemporary physics all seek to move beyond the notion of a merely random agglomeration of particles. If relatively stable answers seemed to emerge within the framework of the Newtonian cosmos, however, they have been greatly complicated with the emergence of quantum mechanics, where the components of that cosmos – mass and energy, particles and forces – have come increasingly to be seen as moments of each other rather than analytically distinct entities.

III

My concern here, however, is not directly with these questions, but rather with the formation of the versions of materialism associated with Marx, since I take it that it is these materialisms and the models of causal interaction associated with them that feed most strongly into contemporary uses of the concept of materiality in the social and human sciences. Marx always explicitly associated himself with the materialist tradition; his doctoral dissertation explored the differences between the atomic materialisms of Democritus and Epicurus, and his decisive break with Hegel was mediated by Feuerbach's materialist inversion of Hegel's idealist ontology. In Marx's earliest works the force of materialism is primarily to underpin the critique of religion, which he sees as being central to any process of revolutionary change; with the 'Theses on Feuerbach', however, the simple opposition of an anthropological materialism to an ultimately theological idealism is complicated by an assertion of the constitutive role of human praxis in the shaping of the world and our knowledge of it.

What is striking about the 'Theses' is the way they explicitly marry materialist and idealist positions in seeking to move beyond what for Marx is the passive way in which Feuerbach conceives of the external world as an objective given. Avineri, contrasting Marx's position with Engels's later mechanical materialism, summarises its originality as well as its continuing indebtedness to Hegel as follows:

> Marx's postulate about the ultimate possibility of human self-emancipation must be related to his philosophical premise about the initial creation of the world by man. Philosophically such a view is a secular version of the Hegelian notion that actuality [*Wirklichkeit*] is not an external, objective datum, but is shaped by human agency. For Hegel this shaping is performed by consciousness; Marx extricates the activist element of Hegel's doctrine from its metaphysical setting and combines it with a materialist epistemology.
>
> (Avineri, 1968: 65)

This move, which was combined as early as the *1844 Manuscripts*, but more systematically in *The German Ideology*, with a grounding of human practice in the system of production of material life (that is, in work performed in an organised and socially systemic manner upon raw materials), initiates a more complex model of materialism than that of Helvétius and d'Holbach or of Feuerbach.

This is the first sentence of the crucial first thesis:

> The chief defect of all previous materialism (that of Feuerbach included) is that things [*Gegenstand*], reality, sensuousness are conceived only in the form of the *object or of contemplation* [*Anschauung*], but not as *sensuous human activity* [*menschliche sinnliche Tätigkeit*], *practice*, not subjectively.
>
> (Marx, 1976a: 3)

'Contemplation' here is used in the sense of 'registration of the external world in the form of sensory data'; rather than positing a more active engagement with the world, for Feuerbach 'man the species-being, provided with merely natural qualities, confronts the dead objectivity of nature passively and intuitively rather than actively and practically, in a subjectivity which remains empty' (Schmidt, 1971: 27). The more active relation to the object world that Marx proposes is associated with the idealist tradition, which however 'does not know real, sensuous activity as such' (Marx, 1976a: 3).

Praxis works in the 'Theses on Feuerbach' not just as an anthropological concept or an asocial individualism but also as the beginnings of a conception of the human 'subject' as a network of social relations. This is obscured by a certain naïve empiricism in Marx's assertion that to the abstraction of idealist conceptions of the subject (as consciousness or spirit) he will oppose the concrete reality of 'living human individuals' (Marx, 1976b: 31) (itself, of course, another abstraction in which the 'concrete' is understood as a quasi-immediacy rather than as a concept mediated by its conditions of possibility). Yet the force of the concept of praxis, understood in Marx's early writings above all as the work of transformation of nature, lies in the way it combines with the critique of political economy to generate a theory of the subject and object of work that fuses the two terms as moments of the social relations of production. Displacing an anthropology of the subject and a metaphysics of the (material) object,[3] Marx's critique develops an account of the class-based organisation of the system of production and appropriation of value which allows for no simple separation of these two poles.

This is, in its mature form, an account of the relationality of the social, not of its materiality. As Richard Osborne puts it:

> The question of how a network of relations in flux can be encompassed within a view that calls itself 'materialism' is frustratingly left unaddressed by Marx in these fragments. He simply stresses the sensible character of human practices. But these are social only because they relate to each other, rather than because of their sensuous materiality … We are not told how social relations themselves might be explained 'materially'.
>
> (Osborne, 2005: 30)

In particular, the turn that Marx's work takes in the 'Theses' decisively distances it from the problematic of an ontology of matter. There can be no nature 'in itself' and apart from or prior to human mediation, since 'on the one hand, it includes the forms of human society; on the other, it only appears in thought and in reality in virtue of these forms' (Schmidt, 1971: 29). The writings of Marx thus have little to do with the traditional preoccupations of philosophical materialism: the metaphysical postulate 'that there is only one "substance" in the world, matter, and everything else (thought, for example) is a modification or an attribute of it' (Osborne, 2005: 27). Yet this is how they have been read within what is perhaps the dominant, tradition of Marxist thought.

One form taken by this reading is the apparently 'weak' doctrine 'that something exists independently of thought (and mind)' (Rubin, 1977: 63). Materialism, on this account, is not a 'strong' reduction of cognition to matter, but merely asserts the ontological distinction of the object from human interaction with it. Yet even this apparently innocuous thesis fits poorly with Marx's understanding of the constitutive role of praxis, and Rubin – who is at least scrupulous about whether his claims correspond to the text of Marx – concedes that his argument holds true only for fully natural objects, not for the social world. Rubin cites a passage from *The German Ideology* which apparently asserts the independence of 'external nature'. As the culmination of a long argument that Feuerbach 'does not see that the sensuous world around him is not a thing given direct from all eternity, remaining ever the same, but a product of industry and of the state of society', Marx adds the qualification that 'Of course in all this the priority of external nature remains unassailed, and all this has no application to the original men produced by *generatio equivoca*' (1976b: 39–40); but Marx's immediate qualification is then that

> nature, the nature that preceded human history, is not by any means the nature in which Feuerbach lives, it is nature which today no longer exists anywhere (except perhaps on a few Australian coral islands of recent origin) and which, therefore, does not exist for Feuerbach.
>
> (Marx, 1976b: 40)

Nature is now, for all intents and purposes, socialised, or at least Marx's whole interest is in the social world and its constant transformations of the natural: not matter in itself but matter transformed into the stuff of social interaction, and 'known' to the extent that it is the object of human praxis. For Rubin to object – as the core of his counter-claim – that 'there are distant parts of the universe which … can never by mediated by man' (1977: 82) is at once trivial, contestable (since those 'distant parts of the universe' are known and can be posited only within a human framework), and, most importantly, irrelevant to whatever it is that is 'materialist' about Marx's work.

Sebastiano Timpanaro takes this 'theological fiction of "Matter"' (Colletti, 1972: 70–71) somewhat further in arguing for a materialism that posits the priority 'of the physical level over the biological level, and of the biological level over the socio-economic and cultural level' (Timpanaro, 1975: 35). In this view the emphasis must fall not so much on human *action* as on 'that which is passivity and external conditioning in the human condition' (Timpanaro, 1975: 36). By this criterion,

> Marxism, especially in its first phase (up to and including *The German Ideology*) is not materialism proper. Physical and biological nature is certainly not denied by Marx, but it constitutes more a prehistoric antecedent to human history than a reality which still limits and conditions man.
>
> (Timpanaro, 1975: 40–41)

Even the later Marx and Engels, while they apparently felt the need for it, never managed actually to construct 'a materialism which was not purely socio-economic but also "natural"' (Timpanaro, 1975: 41).

IV

Behind both Rubin and Timpanaro stands, of course, the supreme theologian of matter, the Lenin of *Materialism and Empirio-Criticism*, for whom 'materialism, in full agreement with natural science, takes matter as primary and regards consciousness, thought and sensation as secondary' (Lenin, 1927: 38), with the corollary that 'the object exists independently of the subject and is reflected more or less adequately in the subject's mind' (Lenin, 1927: 100), or, in another formulation, is 'copied, photographed and reflected by our sensations, while existing independently of them' (Lenin, 1927: 128). On the one hand, then, is an ontology of matter and on the other an account of knowledge as a merely derivative registration of the object, and of praxis as a confirmation rather than a transformation of the known world ('the practice of humanity, by verifying our ideas, corroborates what in those ideas corresponds to absolute truth', Lenin, 1927: 103). These arguments posit nature as an abstract generality. Their critique is well put by Schmidt:

> Men are not concerned in their production with matter 'as such', but always with its concrete, quantitatively and qualitatively determined forms of existence. Its general form, i.e. its independence of consciousness, exists only in particular shapes. There is no fundamental matter, no fundamental ground of being. Material reality can no more provide an ontological principle in the 'being for the other' it owes to its relativity to men, than it can in its 'being-in-itself' … Not the abstract nature of matter, but the concrete nature of social practice is the true subject and basis of materialist theory.
>
> (Schmidt, 1971: 34, 40)

A more productive way of understanding what is innovative about Marx's 'materialism' must surely take its starting point, then, not in philosophical materialism's preoccupation with the ontological and epistemological status of matter, but rather in that 'practical materialism' which is concerned at one level with the transformative work of humankind upon a natural world constantly shaped and re-shaped to its ends, and at another with the particular historical configuration of the forces and relations of production: the use of capital, tools and plant, and raw materials within a particular 'mode of production of material life' which structures the creation and appropriation of value by means of specific relations between owners and producers. The shorthand term in Marxist thought for this complex of 'forces' and 'relations' is 'the economic base', and for Marx this sphere embraces 'both the production of *things* and the production (objectification) of *ideas*; production and intersubjective communication; material production and the production of social relations' (Colletti, 1972: 65). This is to say, as Colletti argues, that the economic is not '*one isolated factor*, separated from the other "moments" and thereby emptied of any effective *socio-historical* content, representing ... an antecedent sphere prior to any human mediation' (Colletti, 1972: 65). Production and social relations cannot be separated because

> In production, men not only act on nature but also on one another. They produce only by cooperation in a certain way and by mutually exchanging their activities. In order to produce, they enter into definite relations with one another and only within these relations does their action on nature, does production, take place.
>
> (Marx, *Wage Labour and Capital*, quoted in Colletti, 1972: 66)

What emerges from this model of the interaction and mutual constitution of moments of the social is a conception of a causality which has no outside, no *external* object to be acted upon. Although the simple form in which Marx sometimes casts his account of the social – the model of base and superstructure, in which an economic instance is causally prior to the institutions of law, religion, state and culture – supposes such an exteriority, it is clear that the relations of production enter into, and are formative of, every moment of the process (by which in turn they are shaped). There is no 'materiality' with causal force vis-à-vis social relations, indeed no ground on which such a materiality could be posited; the material is a moment of production, not the outside of the social.

Yet much of the later history of Marxist thought has to do with an 'interpretation of the "economic base" as a "purely material" or "*technical*-economic" domain, not including social relations and hence inter-subjective communication' (Colletti, 1972: 65n.). In the case of G.A. Cohen's influential analytic account of Marx's theory of history, for example, the materiality of production is grounded in a distinction between 'material' forces of production and 'social' relations of production, which is also a distinction between content and form: 'People and productive forces comprise [society's] material content, a content endowed by production relations with social form. On entering production relations, persons and productive forces receive the imprint of the form these relations constitute' (Cohen, 1978: 89). First there is matter, and then it enters the social. 'Persons' are included as part of the social 'content' in so far as they are physical bodies, but this corporeality is distinct from their social being. What is wrong with this before-and-after account is its reduction of the forces of production to their materiality (that of tools, plant and bodies). But it is strictly impossible to imagine technologies apart from their uses and the systems of use that govern them; technologies are complexes of scientific and practical knowledge, systems of use, legal ownership, financial calculation, and materiality, and no moment of this complex precedes any other.

It is difficult not to conclude that the work done by the concept of the material in the Marxist tradition – whether in the most complex formulations of Marx or in the crudest reductionisms of Soviet orthodoxy – is rhetorical rather than conceptual. Bérubé comments that 'in law as in history as in physics ... it is worth noting the association of the "material" with the "basic" and the "elemental" ' (Bérubé, 2005: 210). It is the authority of this association, with its metaphorical grounding in the dualism of mind and body, that lends itself to a description of economic activity that powerfully implies its primacy over other levels of the social. The concept of the material pushes the distinctiveness of Marxist analysis towards the materiality of the commodity rather than the inscription within it of the process and the relations of production which determine its value *and which are not, strictly speaking, material*. Indeed, the great paradox of Marx's analysis of capitalist production is his discovery of the sheer *im*materiality of the commodity form: 'Not an atom of matter', he writes in Volume I of *Capital*, 'enters into the objectivity of commodities as values ... their objectivity as values is purely social' (Marx, 1976c: 14).

Underlying this critique of the commodity form is something like a nostalgia for a world (past or to come) in which complex systems of value would give way to the simplicity, immediacy and sensuous materiality of use values. Yet the whole weight of what is original and perhaps still compelling in Marx's work has to do not with this nostalgia but with the analysis of historically particular systems of abstract value forms: with immaterial structures and the constraints they impose upon human action. The invocation of materialism serves only, and I think invalidly, to posit either the forces of production or the complex of forces and relations of production as a prediscursive or presymbolic real. The assumption is problematic, however, to the extent that both the forces and the relations of production involve, indeed are in part constituted by, knowledge and communicative relationships (between people, and between people and things). To posit the greater reality of the 'material' assumes that the division *between* the real and the symbolic is established *prior to* the symbolic. However, that distinction is not ontologically given but is a social and historical result. The discursive is a socially constructed reality which constructs the categories of the real and the symbolic *and this distinction between them*. It assigns structure to the real at the same time as it is a product and a moment of real structures. It is thus unproductive to accept at face value the distinction of ontological levels of the social that this couple imposes. The dichotomy of material and immaterial, real and symbolic, forces of production and knowledge, separates and hierarchises elements that are better understood as being inextricably fused.

The Marxist model of the determinant effectivity of the complex of forces and relations of production is not in any meaningful sense a materialism. Rather, we could think of it as something like a 'socialism', meaning not, in the first place, a political doctrine but a general model of the causal force of the socio-economic moments of the social whole. (In its reductive form, this schema is that of an economism.) What the model necessarily supposes is the possibility at any moment of apprehending or at least predicating the totality of the social and of the play of forces within it. It posits general laws of structure and constraint, and a homogeneous but hierarchised space within which these laws operate. This is to say that the closed sphere of the social is informed by a general principle (that of the self-present organisation of a mode of production, for example) which informs all aspects of a social order equally, and which renders time a principle of rupture between social orders rather than an inherent dimension of any order. If Nature is in one sense absorbed into the social by virtue of its constant human mediation, it continues to work nevertheless as a principle of contrast which sustains the distinctiveness of the social world.

V

Such a model of closure and of an internal hierarchy of constitutive moments offers at once too much and therefore too little to a theory of materiality; it leaves no space for the specificity of material things, since that specificity is absorbed into the all-encompassing principle that unifies the social totality. It is at this point, I think, that the limitations of the Marxist model most clearly emerge: not because it is a materialism, but precisely because it subsumes the material within an order that must always precede it. I conclude this chapter by thinking briefly about how the material might be conceptualised in its specificity, its modesty, and without reduction to meaning, structure, or law.

The chapters in this volume seem to me by and large to be grappling with an alternative way of thinking about the materiality of the 'material' that owes much to late twentieth-century attempts to rethink the importance of material culture, on the one hand, and of technology on the other, while attempting to avoid the assumption that artefacts and technologies are most authentically *matter* before they are the structures and uses that inform and organise matter. The crucial move here is perhaps the one that, in refusing a model of social totality ('the social'), seeks to bypass the dualistic division of the world into elements that are permanently and essentially on one or the other side of a causal trajectory. Rather than thinking in terms of an opposition of inanimate material entities to bodies endowed with consciousness and intention, or of more to less real components of the social, such a model would recognise the heterogeneity both of things and of persons in the world – categories complexly ordered along intersecting scales running from the material to the immaterial, the simple to the complex, the functional to the nonfunctional, the living to the inert, the relatively immediate to the highly mediated – *and* the fluidity of the relations between these categories.

The relevant genealogy here runs from Foucault and Deleuze through to actor-network theory, with important contributions from material culture theory and elsewhere. The importance of Foucault lies in his formulation of a model of ontologically indifferent and open-ended structures to replace his earlier, bounded models of the *episteme* and (to a lesser extent) the discursive formation. Thus the *dispositif* is defined as 'a thoroughly heterogeneous ensemble consisting of discourses, institutions, architectural forms, regulatory decisions, laws, administrative measures, scientific statements, philosophical, moral and philanthropic propositions. … The apparatus [*dispositif*] itself is the system of relations that can be established between these elements' (Foucault, 1980: 194). But 'system of relations' here means not an internally coherent structure but something more like a 'system of dispersion' (Foucault, 1972: 38): a contingent tying-together of unlike elements for temporary structural purposes. If it is this contingent process, rather than its apparently stable end-product, that becomes the focus of analysis, then any account of structure shifts from an attention to determinants, whose effectivity is known and calculable in advance, to the play of elements and forces that operate under variable conditions to produce temporary and always unstable crystallisations of form.

This is a matter of metaphors: how do we move from figures evocative of a closed totality to figures of heterogeneous becoming? A series of concepts – *dispositif*, *agencement*, assemblage, network, chain, performativity, hybridisation … – propose ways of thinking a relationality without ontological divisions, in which 'material' and 'immaterial' elements interact on the same plane to form structures and in this process are at once constrained and formed by those interactions. The replacement by actor-network theory of the dichotomy of 'persons' and 'things' with the undifferentiated term 'actants', taken from Greimasian semiotics, performs a refusal of ontological division at the level of structures in favour of a *multiplicity* of differences in kind. The payoff of such an indifferentiation at the macro level is an account of interaction that can attend to the specific forms of difference at the micro level, where the affordances of material things translate human intentions and shape human uses; human persons shape themselves in constant, active or passive interaction with a world of humanised things; and persons, too, operate in part *as* things in a world formed of things, texts, codes, regulations, spatial environments, institutions, frames of understanding and action, bodies, reflexive knowledges, and the accumulated weight of the interaction over time of all of these materials of the world.

The 'material', in this framework, designates not substance in its opposition to ideality, not matter conceived of as existing in some pure pre-social state, abstracted from its uses, but rather 'a continuously enacted relational effect', something 'endlessly generated and at least potentially reshaped' (Law, 2004: 161). And it is perhaps in this sense, a deliberately neutral use of the concept of the 'material' that strips it of its connotations of substantiality, that we might imagine a quite different kind of materialism.

Notes

1 Cf. Kubler's (1962: 24–25) distinction between self-signification and adherent signification.

2 Within Western Christianity there is a third, very powerful theological and folk tradition of materialism, stretching from the early patristic period to the fourteenth century, which has to do with the resurrection of the body at the last trumpet by means of a reassembling of all and only those material components of which it was composed in life, thus guaranteeing a continuity between the living self and the reborn self which 'in [its] flesh shall … see God' (see Bynum, 1995, passim). I have not discussed this tradition here because its materialism is, in a sense, always disavowed; but it does serve as a bridge between the materialisms of antiquity and modernity, and its influence on modern Western conceptions of the person is fundamental.

3 Cf. Pinney: 'Any discussion of materiality that starts and ends with the object is doomed to fail. In configuring materiality as objectness, it accidentally champions one half (objects) of a binary whose other half (subjects) it wishes to attack. Hence it intensifies the work of purification' (2005: 257).

Bibliography

Avineri, Shlomo (1968) The *Social and Political Thought of Karl Marx*, Cambridge: Cambridge University Press.

Bennett, Tony, Lawrence Grossberg and Meaghan Morris (ed.) (2005) *New Keywords*, Oxford: Blackwell.

Bérubé, Michael (2005) 'Materialism', in Bennett, Grossberg and Morris (2005), 209–211.

Bhaskar, Roy (1983) 'Materialism', in Bottomore (1983), 324–329.

Bottomore, Tom (ed.) (1983) *A Dictionary of Marxist Thought*, Cambridge, Mass.: Harvard University Press.

Bynum, Caroline Walker (1995) *The Resurrection of the Body in Western Christianity, 200–1336*, New York: Columbia University Press.

Cohen, G.A. (1978) *Karl Marx's Theory of History: A Defence*, Oxford: Oxford University Press.

Colletti, Lucio (1972) *From Rousseau to Lenin: Studies in Ideology and Society* (trans. John Merrington and Judith White), New York: Monthly Review Press.

Foucault, Michel (1972) *The Archaeology of Knowledge* (trans. A.M. Sheridan Smith), London: Tavistock.

—— (1980) *Power/Knowledge: Selected Interviews and Other Writings*, 1972–1977 (ed. Colin Gordon), New York: Pantheon.

Kubler, George (1962) *The Shape of Time: Remarks on the History of Things*, New Haven: Yale University Press.

Latour, Bruno (2005) *Reassembling the Social: An Introduction to Actor-Network-Theory*, Oxford: Oxford University Press.

Law, John (2004) *After Method: Mess in Social Science Research*, London: Routledge.

Lenin, Vladimir (1927) *Materialism and Empirio-Criticism*, New York: International Publishers.

Marx, Karl (1975) *The Holy Family. Collected Works*, vol. 4, London: Lawrence and Wishart.

—— (1976a) 'Theses on Feuerbach' [1845], *Collected Works*, vol. 5, London: Lawrence and Wishart.

—— (1976b) *The German Ideology. Collected Works*, vol. 5, London: Lawrence and Wishart.

—— (1976c) *Capital: A Critique of Political Economy*, vol. 1 (trans. Ben Fowkes), Harmondsworth: Penguin.

Miller, Daniel (ed.) (2005) *Materiality*, Durham, NC: Duke University Press.

Milner, Andrew (1993) *Cultural Materialism*, Melbourne: Melbourne University Press.

Osborne, Peter (2005) *How to Read Marx*, London: Granta.

Pinney, Christopher (2005) 'Things happen: or, from which moment does that object come', in Miller (2005), 256–272.

Rubin, David-Hillel (1977) *Marxism and Materialism: A Study in Marxist Theory of Knowledge*, Sussex: The Harvester Press.

Schmidt, Alfred (1971 [1962]) *The Concept of Nature in Marx* (trans. Ben Fowkes), London: NLB.

Timpanaro, Sebastiano (1975 [1970]) *On Materialism* (trans. Lawrence Garner), London: Verso.

Toulmin, Stephen and June Goodfield (1962) *The Architecture of Matter*, London: Hutchinson.

Williams, Raymond (1977) *Marxism and Literature*, Oxford: Oxford University Press.

—— (1980) *Problems in Materialism and Culture*, London: Verso.

2 Locating matter

The place of materiality in urban history

Chris Otter

Of all the fields of historical study, urban history perhaps has the most reassuringly tangible, material focus. However the urban is understood, its physicality – in the form of buildings, streets, and pipes – is seldom in doubt. Yet cities have always been much more than dense collections of technologies and networks. They are sites of the symbolic, the poetic and the imaginary. The same urban modernity that produced electricity networks and municipal sewage systems produced *The Interpretation of Dreams* and *Ulysses*. Cities have also been the physical locus where abstract entities like social structure and capital have been most manifest. In cities, the material and the immaterial appear simultaneously opposed and intertwined.

Throughout much of the twentieth century, a range of scholars tended to privilege the immaterial dimensions of the city over the material ones. Urban sociologists, for example, often followed Robert Park's dictum that the city was 'a state of mind' (cited in Donald, 1999: 8), and addressed social formations rather than physical ones. Even Marxist approaches to the city tended to study abstract forces of capital rather than the physical texture of urban space. The cultural turn merely amplified this trend towards immateriality. The material world featured in such analyses, to be sure, but it was relegated to a limited series of roles which left materiality as such largely unexamined. At present, this trend is beginning to be reversed. New and reworked theoretical tools, drawn from phenomenology, science studies, poststructuralism, post-Marxist materialism and environmental studies, have allowed scholars to approach urban materiality in ways which transcend the rather exhausted dichotomies of social–technical and cultural–natural.

These dichotomies can be transcended by exploring the history of particular substances: their changing form, modes of circulation, range of distribution and type of political control. In this chapter, I will address two particular substances consumed in vast quantities by cities throughout history: water and meat. The history of water and meat is at once material, political and environmental. Today's purified water consumed in the west is a historically unique substance, far different to that consumed in ancient times or in large parts of nonwestern megacities or 'shadow cities'. The material history of water is thus a history of the production of very primal forms of inequality. Similarly, the historically unprecedented levels of meat consumed in western cities have major environmental ramifications, from deforestation and methane emissions to the fossil fuels and refrigerants needed to perpetuate cold chains. In these kinds of analyses, the material world – at a very basic, molecular level – is reincorporated into the social, economic, cultural and political worlds. It is relocated, as a dynamic, differentiated and interactive force, within processes from which it has sometimes been analytically expunged.

This chapter will begin by addressing this process by which materiality was demoted or purged from urban studies, before using the examples of water and meat to demonstrate how reincorporation can be achieved. It uses multiple literatures, from urban history, geography, sociology and anthropology to emergent interdisciplinary fields like critical urban studies and industrial ecology (Brenner, 2004: 24; Bourg and Erkman, 2003). My discussion covers the past 300 years, but primarily addresses the nineteenth century. Geographically, I concentrate on Western Europe and North America, but gesture to global issues. Because of this breadth, my claims are very general, and there will doubtless be many exceptions to these generalities.

Three varieties of dematerialization: sociological, Marxist, cultural

Richard Sennett once noted that only after the industrial revolution were cities seen as manifesting 'a special, unique form of social life' and hence amenable to specific forms of sociological analysis (Sennett, 1969: 3). This formulation includes a constitutive tension between a more material process (the industrial revolution) and a less obviously material one (social life). This bifurcation underpinned the foundational works of urban sociology. In 1916, Park observed that 'the city possesses a moral as well as a physical organization, and these two mutually interact in characteristic ways to mold and modify one another' (1916: 92).

Early urban sociologists invariably privileged this moral organization over the physical one. In 'The metropolis and mental life' (1903), Georg Simmel famously explored how urbanization created historically particular forms of individual psychic life, like loneliness and the blasé attitude. While such states were never wholly divorced from their material milieux, Simmel's primary causal explanation was social: new structures of human relationship or 'social forces' generated psychic conditions (1903: 47). Park furthered this causal framework, analyzing the impact of modern social patterns (the division of labour, the separation of work and home, the collapse of primary social relationships and traditional kinship systems) on urban social groups (1916: 102, 110, 129). This sociologization of urban topography reached its abstract, schematic apogee in Robert Burgess's concentric zonal model of the city, which was disentangled from any environmental context.

Urban sociologists never denied the existence or importance of more material forces. Park made much of transportation and communication technologies, while Simmel argued that 'economic life' would disintegrate if all urban clocks simultaneously went wrong (Simmel, 1903: 50). When technology appeared, then, it was often as a rather crude determinant. More commonly, analytic attention gravitated from a technological substrate towards a primary field of social relations (Konvitz, Rose and Tarr, 1990: 286). Finally, the social dimension of existence was both ontologically distinct from, and superior to, the technological substrate. The city, Park revealingly concluded, was not 'merely a physical mechanism' (1916: 91). Indeed, cities threatened to become simply places where 'larger' and more 'abstract' processes, like differentiation, rationalization and individuation, occurred in concentrated form (Katznelson, 1992: 18; Mitchell, 2002: 28). Material things remained rather obscure, generally functioning as either an uninteresting backdrop for social relations, or, periodically, a brute determinant of social transformation.

This particular ontology undoubtedly influenced later scholarship in urban history. Cities were often studied as loci of class formation and segregation. The pioneering works of Dyos (1961) and Stedman Jones (1971), for example, fused social concerns with an economic analysis of markets in speculative building and casual labour respectively. Such work was, however, as influenced by Marxism and economic history as by other sociological traditions. Let us turn to Marxist approaches here. Marxism might intuitively suggest more materially satisfying approaches to the city, but it has often generated parallel problems to sociological models. Marxist work has often privileged abstract forces (usually capital) over physical structure. Cities again lose much of their specificity, becoming epiphenomena of deeper, larger processes.

Friedrich Engels's *The Condition of the Working Classes in England* (first published in German in 1845) focused explicitly on capitalism's impact on urban space and social formation. Capitalist cities, Engels concluded, were spatially divided into residential and industrial zones, the former being split again into middle- and working-class zones, within which class consciousness germinated. Engels's insights, unfortunately, were developed neither by Marx nor subsequent generations of Marxist scholars. This situation changed, however, with the work of Lefebvre, Castells and Harvey, for whom the urban was the critical site for, and medium of, the production and reproduction of capital and capitalist social relations. Harvey's modern city is a capitalist city, 'an agglomeration of productive forces built by labour within a temporal process of circulation of capital' (Harvey, 1985a: 250). His primary analytic focus was the complex but empirically traceable causal relationship between capitalist overaccumulation and urban form (Harvey, 1985b). When capitalists overproduce, undersell or experience surplus labour, Harvey argued, they tend to invest in the built environment, or the 'secondary circuit of capital,' which functions as a profitable outlet for capital and labour (1985b: 4–7). The city's physical structure, then, is a tangible vector through which capitalism prolongs its existence, by becoming 'welded fast to the surface of the earth' (Marx, 1973: 740). A classic example of this process is postwar suburbanization (Harvey, 1985b: 28). Such 'spatial fixes,' however, produce an obdurate landscape which future waves of capitalist activity necessarily destroy: such is the 'creative destruction' of capitalism (Harvey, 2001: 284–311; Harvey, 1990: 106).

Harvey's thesis is a powerful one, with which I have much sympathy. The material form of the city, however, appears little more than the outcome of the abstract force of capital, mediated through the rational minds of capitalist actors:

> The study of urbanization is a study of that process [the capital process] as it unfolds through the production of physical and social landscapes and the production of consciousness. *The study of urbanization is not the study of a legal, political entity or of a physical artifact.* It is concerned with processes of capital circulation; the shifting flows of labor power, commodities, and money capital; the spatial organization of production and the transformation of space relations; movements of information and geopolitical conflicts between territorially-based class alliances; and so on.
>
> (Harvey 1985b, xvi–xvii, emphasis added)

This ultimate reduction of the material to the congealed result of capitalist logic became standard fare in economically inflected urban theory and history (Dear and Scott, 1981). Cities, again, are ultimately material epiphenomena of bigger, more abstract forces, something which is traceable to Marx (Katznelson, 1992: 33). Harvey's work tells us much about the logic of capital, but rather less about the material texture of particular cities.

Such abstraction parallels a broader process through which academic economists have divorced pure economic forces, expressed in laws and equations, from the messy, local world of material practice (Mitchell, 2002: 85, 94). It also forms part of an evolutionary narrative which traces economic progress from face-to-face barter to today's dematerialized forms of value like derivatives (Maurer, 2005: 140). This abstraction, deterritorialization and dematerialization undergirds numerous contemporary arguments about the 'virtual' or 'weightless' economy and corporate power operating without spatial constraints. Such processes are captured in expressions like Castells' (2000) 'space of flows'. Such methodological trends have not entirely divested the economic of its material components, but they have, again, analytically privileged the abstract over the concrete (Brenner, 2004: 55).

Urban experience and form, then, have often been explained by referring to immaterial social or economic 'forces' existing outside or above a physical city which is a backdrop for social relations or a residue of, and obstacle to, the force of capital. The material city, then, often appears to be located *outside* the dynamic, abstract forces that are the true object of scholarly focus. These forces did, of course, operate within, or actually produced, physical space itself. With the 'cultural turn', however, purely physical entities (or at least human comprehension of, and interaction with, them) effectively evaporated (Bonnell and Hunt, 1999). The cultural turn powerfully affected urban studies. Cities were now studied in terms of symbols, languages and imagination, producing a more radical form of dematerialization.

Urban cultural history has a rather longer history. Carl Schorske's *Fin-de-Siècle Vienna* (1981 [1961]) demonstrated how physical form could express political values without being a straightforward consequence of capital. Vienna's Reichsrat building, for example, could have been built in numerous ways: its classical style embodied the historicist, liberal ethos of the rising bourgeoisie (Schorske 1981: 33, 36, 39–42). This focus on the expressive character of buildings appeared to direct analysis from an ideational to a physical plane, but more often did the reverse. In the 1990s, the cultural turn greatly expanded this focus on meaning to include seemingly all urban space, which became a script to be read or signs to be decoded (Donald, 1992). Analysis of material forms themselves practically disappeared. Texts were no longer analyzed to reveal extratextual entities, whether immaterial or material (social and economic forces, individual intentions, physical artifacts). Rather, discursive patterns themselves became the object of analysis. In *City of Dreadful Delight* (1992), Judy Walkowitz brilliantly demonstrated how narrative forms, from melodrama to psychopathology, mediated all social experience. Rather than study the Ripper murders 'in themselves', she analyzed the ways that discourse structured the responses of the police and the public, which were themselves textualized as newspaper reports, testimonies of witnesses, and so on (Walkowitz, 1992: 191–228).

Walkowitz's London is a place of fluid and multiple identities, all of which are strongly mediated, or even produced, by texts. These identities were analytically liberated from extrinsic and Procrustean explanatory structures of class and capital. Urban historians could now view culture as an autonomous variable with causal power. While Harvey had viewed suburbanization as the consequence of capitalist overaccumulation, Robert Fishman regarded it as the materialization of preformed bourgeois cultural values, such as veneration of the nuclear family, desire for nature, and segregation of the masculine world of work from the feminine domestic sphere (Fishman, 1987: 62). A primary concept here is the 'imagination' or 'imaginary', which refers to the shared but culturally specific ways in which social groups conceive of themselves and others (Donald, 1999). In Walkowitz's London, the East End was rarely physically experienced by the wealthy, but its imagined attributes structured their perception of both themselves and their city.

Geographers, too, experienced a cultural turn, which manifested itself in many rich and remarkable analyses of the iconography of landscape and the historically protean nature of urban meaning and representation (Cosgrove and Daniels, 1988; Stilgoe, 1988). The textual paradigm generated exploration of the 'discourses, symbols, metaphors and fantasies' producing urban meaning, however evanescent (Donald, 1999: 422). Carried to its logical extreme, the immaterial, psychological and imaginary, located in the heads of urban actors, might become the truest reality of the city (Donald, 2000: 46–54). Even Marxist geographers underwent this cultural and psychological turn. In *Paris, Capital of Modernity* (2003), Harvey considers myths, gender and the geographical imagination. Whether this marks a genuine methodological break with his earlier work, is, however, questionable. Haussmann's Paris was ultimately shaped by the first great international capitalist crisis of overaccumulation. A built environment incompatible with capitalism was replaced by one eminently suited to the purpose. Paris's physical structures remain mediated epiphenomena of capital, and materiality sinks beneath the level of analysis.

Complicating materiality: technological determinism, the force of things, and material agency

Material things, to repeat, were never entirely ignored in such analyses, but they remained undifferentiated and black-boxed. Little serious attention was devoted to physical qualities, molecules, forces and textures. In urban sociology, material space was primarily a backdrop for social action: 'physical space and time … are not the fundamental determinants of cultural "motion" as they are of physical motion' (Redfield and Singer, 1954: 231). The city remained 'a state of mind.' For Marxist urban geography, the 'materiality of space relations' is ultimately an effect of capital (Harvey, 2003: 102). Although some notable works of cultural history, like Lynda Nead's *Victorian Babylon* (2000) and Simon Gunn's *The Public Culture of the Victorian Middle Class* (2000) have incisively discussed material systems and spaces, these remain exceptional. The cultural turn threatened a wholesale, reductive dematerialization of the city. In 2000, Chris Philo expressed concerns about geography's 'current preoccupation with immaterial cultural processes', and 'intersubjective meaning systems'. 'Less-than-tangible' entities, like 'texts, signs, symbols, psyches, desires, fears, and imaginings' had taken precedence over 'the more "thingy", bump-into-able, stubbornly there-in-the-world kinds of "matter" (the material) with which earlier geographers tended to be more familiar' (2000: 33).

These three approaches to the city, then, have turned away from the material towards more immaterial systems and determinants: social, economic and cultural. With urban sociology, the material is a *background* or *arena* within which social forces act and social structures are formed. With capital, the material is an *outcome*, but also a *medium* through which capitalist social relations are reproduced and an *obstacle* to later capitalist development. With culture, the material is a *text* to be decoded or a *symbolic* bearer of meaning. Obviously, material things and systems *do* often function as background, arena, outcome, medium, obstacle, text or symbol. However, every one of these functions leaves materiality itself – the forms, states and qualities of matter – analytically underexplored.

The material often played another role in twentieth-century urban literature: as *technological determinant*. Technological determinism can be defined most basically as the idea that changes in the technological substrate inevitably cause changes in the social superstructure (Winner, 1977). At its most reductive, technological transformation, and concomitant social transformation, can appear entirely unavoidable. Technological determinism often appears in urban literature. As noted earlier, urban sociologists, while ultimately valorizing the social, occasionally attributed great causal weight to technological systems. 'Transportation,' argued Wirth, 'has made the city accessible to rural people. The radio and, more lately, television promise to produce a virtual revolution' (Wirth, 1956: 165). Suburbia, for technological determinists, was produced neither by capital nor the bourgeois imagination, but by trams, railways and automobiles.[1] While urban historians and geographers have been more attuned to the built environment than other scholars, they have still usually divided the urban sphere into technological and social realms, with the former now determining or overdetermining the latter. Thomas Misa concludes that urban historians 'frequently affirm that technological change determines social change' (1988: 315).

To escape technological determinism, scholars have regularly argued that technology is socially constructed. The Social Construction of Technology (SCOT) approach argues that technological forms and choices are always shaped by human groups, usually powerful ones (Feenberg, 1999: 79). Apparent technological autonomy is actually overdetermined by the social. In *Inventing Accuracy* (1990), Donald MacKenzie argues that highly accurate nuclear weapons only made sense as part of a military strategy of 'counterforce,' which involved destroying enemy weapons before they were launched. If one simply wanted weapons as a deterrent, to be launched if one's enemy launched their weapons, such accuracy was unnecessary. Thus 'accuracy,' as materialized in particular missile designs, was a social construction produced by a very particular strategy and its military, political, industrial and academic promoters. Nuclear missile guidance is 'a historical product and social creation' (MacKenzie, 1990: 2). Nuclear weapons, which have often exemplified technological determinism, actually possess no innate technological logic. A more urban example of SCOT is Peter Norton's *Fighting Traffic* (2008). In the early twentieth century, Norton shows, American urban streets ceased to be places for pedestrians and became places for cars. This was not, again, due to any intrinsic 'technological logic'. Instead, it was a result of one social group, 'motordom', creating a vision of the automotive street, associating this with freedom, and making this vision hegemonic. 'Before the city could be physically reconstructed for the sake of motorists,' Norton notes, 'its streets had to be socially reconstructed as places where motorists unquestionably belonged' (2008: 1).

Different social groups, then, have different ideas about material technologies. These ideas, particularly when institutionalized, shape pathways of material development which seem autonomous. Such pseudo-autonomy is often called 'momentum'. In *Networks of Power* (1983), Thomas Hughes criticized the idea that electricity networks had inevitable social effects by charting their very different material trajectories in Berlin, Chicago and London. These trajectories were, ultimately, formed by powerful social groups and sustained by institutions mobilizing capital, expertise and dominant representations. Putatively pure material force is actually mediated or translated social force: 'technological systems, even after prolonged growth, do not become autonomous; they acquire momentum. They have a mass of technical and organisational components; they possess direction, or goals; and they display a rate of growth suggesting velocity' (Hughes, 1987: 76).

Such approaches eschew technological determinism but not necessarily materiality. MacKenzie addresses very specific materials like the beryllium used in stable platforms for minutemen rockets, and the enriched uranium necessary for nuclear warheads (MacKenzie, 1990: 209, 280). However, MacKenzie's work is perhaps rather exceptional. Norton, despite splendid vignettes on parking meters and traffic lights, concentrates heavily on the social domain. Cars and street surfaces rarely feature in his story. SCOT ontology splits the world into social and technological-material domains, with the former carrying most causal weight. As MacKenzie argues, 'a technology is not just social up to the point of invention and self-sustaining thereafter. Its conditions of possibility are always social' (1990: 4).

Despite the genuine brilliance of some SCOT works, they fail to enrich the understanding of materiality. Materiality is more nuanced than in the work of, say, Harvey, but its effects remain effects of deeper, social forces. It might appear, then, that materiality is doomed to be treated either as pure effect (as in urban sociology), mediated effect (as in SCOT), or pure cause (as in technological determinism). The key question, then, is this: *can materiality be apprehended as more than an effect but less than a determinant? In other words, can we restore force, qualities and immanence to material things without reducing them to clumsy, brute determinants*?? This question, in various forms, has animated recent work on materiality in numerous disciplines: history, sociology, anthropology, science studies, literature and geography (Joyce, 2003; Miller, 2005; Pickering, 1995; Brown, 2004). This work promises to move analysis of materiality beyond the impasses of cultural theory, SCOT and technological determinism. I will briefly outline three relevant clusters of concepts here, which I will call 'thing theory', 'material agency', and 'new historical materialism'.

The basic premise of 'thing theory' is phenomenological and Heideggerian: things are more than objects (Heidegger, 1962 [1927]: 95–102; Brown, 2004). While objects exist only for subjects, things have a broader, thicker, less anthropocentric existence. Every thing emits a peculiar combination of different forces (physical, sensory, emotive) which cannot be reduced to something as unified or monodirectional as determinism (Dant, 2005: 62–65; Tisseron, 1999). Things are heterogeneous. Some of these forces – fetishistic or totemic, for example – have an affective, intangible nature entirely in 'excess' of a tamed, revealed scientific object (Brown, 2004: 5). Things are not simply screens onto which humans project ideas. Indeed, some forces, or some aspects of forces, are, to use an unfashionable word, innate, even if this innateness lies phenomenologically dormant until the point where it is encountered by a human being. According to Peter-Paul Verbeek, 'what a thing does, the way in which a thing is present as a thing, cannot be reduced to something non-thingly and must be conceived from the thing itself' (2005: 89). The world of physical things, then, always contains a certain amount of mystery.

'Material agency' is particularly associated with the work of Bruno Latour and actor-network theory (ANT). Even if devoid of consciousness or intentionality, ANT argues, matter generates effects. It makes things happen; it has agency. Again, this implies commitment to a form of revived innateness. Like thing theory, ANT approaches suggest that sealed, autarkic innateness or potential is, by itself, insignificant. Only when linked to, and concatenated with, other material innatenesses does significant agency occur. Force or power is, from the start, neither possessed nor centred. It is always in motion, circulating, rippling, meandering. This 'active and distributed materialism' resists attempts at ontological bifurcation and undermines efforts to relate a material realm to a social one (Latour, 2005: 129). The rather rigid ontology of sociology, Marxism, cultural theory and SCOT begins to blur. Latour concludes that 'there exists no relation whatsoever between "the material" and "the social world", because it is this very division which is a complete artifact' (Latour, 2005: 75–76).

'New historical materialism' refers to an eclectic range of non-, post- and (less commonly) neo-Marxist materialisms, including Braudel's sweeping historical materialism, environmental history, Wallerstein's world-systems theory and the poststructuralism of Deleuze and Guattari. Everyday life, Braudel argued, was 'rich zone, like a layer covering the earth, I have called for want of a better expression *material life* or *material civilization*' (Braudel, 1981: 23). Braudel argued that western cities played a vital role in the generation of capitalism, by developing command over increasingly diverse, durable and differentiated material flows – wood, coal, metals, grain. This focus on material flow is central to many works of environmental history (Cronon, 1991; Klingle, 2007). Deleuze and Guattari, like Latour, refused *a priori* division of the world into material and immaterial dimensions. They argued that self-organization extends beyond the organic world, a hypothesis reflected in concepts like 'nonorganic life', 'machinic phylum', and ' the body without organs' (Deleuze and Guattari, 1987). The work of Braudel and Deleuze and Guattari has been imaginatively fused by Manuel de Landa (1997), who explores the evolving physical organization of large-scale entities like cities as part of an exploration of 'geological history'. In cities, material life is more concentrated, structured, differentiated and purified. At certain historical junctures, specific materials have played a pivotal role in constituting particular forms of western urban system: wood and stone in the medieval period, iron and coal in the early industrial period, and steel and glass in high modernity.

These three clusters of theory, thing theory, material agency, and new historical materialism, are not straightforwardly compatible. In particular, the phenomenological tradition is hard to satisfactorily combine with Latour's or Deleuze's antihumanism. Grand theoretical synthesis, however, is not my concern here. More importantly, for these theories, materiality is not simply background, outcome, medium, obstacle, text, symbol or determinant. Materiality's analytical location shifts, its agency becomes multiple, connected and interactive. It ceases to be an external environment within which social, economic and cultural forces circulate. Substances produce multiple and unpredictable effects. In order to explicate these points, I will now turn to two substances consumed in vast quantities by modern cities: water and meat.

Water: infrastructure, power, ecology

Infrastructure has been a particular object of focus for recent theorists of materiality, who have prised it open, revealing complicated, interactive material systems and concomitant political, economic, environmental and even strategic questions (McFarlane and Rutherford, 2008: 364). Sewers, roads, airports and railways can no longer be regarded simply as the backdrop for social relations, the effect of capital or cultural constructions. Neither, however, are they straightforward determinants of social behaviour, as Stephen Graham and Simon Marvin observe in *Splintering Urbanism* (2001). Infrastructures are multiple, interlaced, and synergistic. They 'dramatically, but highly unevenly, "warp" and refashion the spaces and times of all aspects of interaction – social, economic, cultural, physical, ecological' (11). Their intrinsic material multiplicity undermines simplistic notions of causality. They must, rather, 'be considered as sociotechnical *assemblies* or 'machine complexes' rather than as individual, causal agents with identifiable 'impacts' on cities and urban life' (31). Such complexes operate across significant distances, embedding very particular types of agency and material relations of power.

Of all such systems, hydraulic infrastructure has perhaps received the most academic attention (Smith, 1975; Goubert, 1989; Hamlin, 1998; Gandy, 2002; Blackbourn, 2006). All urban settlements need water, for drinking, cooking, cleaning, washing, fire-fighting and ceremonial purposes. Water is essential for the agriculture upon which all cities depend. Since the late nineteenth century, hydroelectric power has provided substantial quantities of urban energy. Western water culture, in which nearly everything (bodies, cars, lawns) is regularly doused with large quantities of water, is an enormous historical artifact, involving physical systems, cultural codes, laws and capital flows. Here, I will sketch some salient aspects of the system's recent physical history, before examining the phenomenological, political and ecological dimensions of western water culture.

In 1800, European cities drew water from numerous sources: rivers, wells, cisterns and occasional longer-distance conduits. Waste accumulated in dunghills and cesspools, and was periodically removed to the countryside by horse and cart. During the nineteenth century, western cities, at varying rates, developed new infrastructures to supply water and remove waste. Water was distributed through mains made of numerous substances (iron, cement, lead, wood). Large reservoirs were built at significant distances from urban settlements to capture, store and distribute rainwater to cities via longer networks of mains and aqueducts. Some reservoirs were modifications of existing lakes, while others were completely new. Demand soon exceeded supply: Rennes built one reservoir in 1882, a second in 1889, and a third in 1919 (Goubert, 1989: 202). Reservoir construction expanded globally after 1900, meaning that an increasing percentage of global water is now consumed in urban settlements. Today, an area approximately the size of France is impounded in reservoirs.

Water was simultaneously introduced as a means of waste disposal. The accumulation of dung in heaps, pools and middens was replaced, again at various rates, first by nonhydraulic closets, and then the water closet itself. Most English towns with a population of over 50,000 had water closets by 1911 (Daunton, 1983: 258). Such closets were increasingly connected to drainage networks rather than individual cesspools. London's drains were separate from the runoff water system. This 'separate system' was used in American cities, while Paris, along with other major European cities, developed a combined system (Goubert, 1989: 61). In late nineteenth-century Amsterdam, canals, *fosses mobiles* (portable barrels) and the Liernur pneumatic system were all used to remove human waste. In the early twentieth century, a British-style system was introduced (Buiter, 2008: 149–150). This process was generally urban: in 1967, only around 17 per cent of French agricultural workers had domestic bathrooms (Goubert, 1989: 87). Such sewerage networks developed at such variegated rates, and were too materially idiosyncratic, for their development to be attributed totally, or even largely, to capitalist overaccumulation.

Water, of course, is not chemically homogeneous: it varies from place to place. During the modern period, however, numerous large-scale processes have been introduced to manipulate its qualities and produce water that is both homogenized and chemically enhanced. Filters, to remove various impurities, first appeared in hospital and domestic cisterns and on a larger scale in clarification and treatment plants. Paris had a plant from 1806 (Goubert, 1989: 53). Early filters were made of gravel or charcoal; by the later nineteenth century, following Fuller's American experiments, aluminium sulphate (alum), was commonly used (Smith, 1975: 130–131). Meanwhile, the hardness of water was, slowly, being modified. Hard water's high mineral content, which makes it good to drink, means that it scales the inside of pipes, boilers and kettles. It also fails to produce a good lather with soap. These material reactions meant that soft water was generally deemed better for an evolving urban hydraulic infrastructure and its attendant practices. The hydrometer, invented in 1856, allowed water's hardness to be calculated, and areas with exceptionally hard water identified (Goubert, 1989: 44). The addition of lime and soda softened water: an 1888 Southampton softening plant remained the world's largest for some time (Smith, 1975: 132). By the later nineteenth century, chemical standards of water purity were developed, although these standards were flexible and contested (Hassall, 1876: 15–90). In the early twentieth century, water was both chlorinated (to neutralize certain bacteria) and fluorinated (to protect teeth). Modern water, then, is a historically unique substance, of regulated hardness, purged of organic and mineral 'impurities', and augmented with highly specific chemicals. It is subjected to a regime of calculation and technological manipulation that is quite unlike anything previously seen on earth.

Both ANT and thing theory sharpen analysis of these vast 'material agents'. The cumulative agency of reservoirs, mains, bathrooms and sewage plants makes possible a supply of chemically standardized, objectified, 'secularized' water which secures the private hygiene, cleanliness and health that is a foundational dimension of 'modern' western material life and subjectivity (Goubert, 1989: 27). The 'modern subject' is less a product of discourse than of technological imbrication, a result of a body 'hooking up' to chains of material agents (Latour, 1999: 23). This materialising of subjectification is a great insight of ANT. However, as Goubert suggests, water's sacred, purifying qualities persist. For rites like baptism, water remains a thing. In an age of aqueous homogenisation, spa towns thrived on the mysterious promise of the idiosyncratic (if chemically calculated) effects of minerals suspended in their untreated water (Blackbourn, 2006: 169). The subjective experience of water (invigorating showers, priestly sprinklings, relaxing baths) is seldom a cold molecular encounter between a living body and a liquid. It is neither mechanistic nor straightforwardly immaterial. This is the great insight of phenomenological approaches to materiality.

Material networks clearly shape subjectivity in ways that are irreducible to straightforward technological determinism. Human subjects acquire at least some of their powers from the networks with which they interact. Here, however, we approach the limits of new theories of materiality. ANT and thing theory cannot explain the asymmetrical access to such material forms of empowerment and experience (Rowlands, 2005: 75). Material agency and effects, then, must be situated within a politico-economic narrative. Let us do this for water. Since the mid-nineteenth century, there have been three phases of European water provision: liberal, social and neoliberal. Liberal systems of water provision aimed to secure individual health and cleanliness, and collective economic agency. Social ones tried equalize access to, and quality of, water, with states and municipalities, not private interests, overseeing provision. Neoliberal infrastructure returned to the individual, the private and the economic, at a global and national scale. These 'broad phases' are not absolutely distinct. There was no straightforward, absolute rupture dividing one regime from another, and different management systems often co-existed. Timescales of transformation varied from nation to nation, and more dramatically from global region to global region.

The liberal model thrived in the early and mid-nineteenth century. This liberality had three dimensions. First, private companies often supplied water (Gandy, 2002: 27–28). Second, as Joyce shows (2003: 73), linking houses to sanitary networks facilitated cleanliness, privacy, and individuation, which were vital dimensions of 'liberal subjectivity.' Third, the ensuing 'sanitary city' would eliminate the fevers produced by rotting organic matter, and thus ensure a healthy, productive labour force without intervening in economic affairs (Joyce, 2003: 67; Hamlin, 1998). Individual and economic concerns were paramount, meaning that the 'sanitary city' of fresh water and bathtubs first appeared among more individuated classes and thus translated social into material inequality and asymmetry (Platt, 2005: 70–74, 164–171). This process was even more pronounced in colonial cities.

The social model emerged out of a critique of a system which subjugated collective provision to individual and private interests. In Halle, for example, an 1864–1867 commission concluded that allowing private companies to supply water to German cities 'damage[d] … public interests' (cited in James, 1901: 82). With the exception of France, private companies largely ceased to supply water to European cities: by the early twentieth century all Swedish and Finnish, and most German water systems, were municipal (Juuti, Katko and Hukka, 2007: 239, 242; Goubert, 1989, 176). This was not, again, a product of capitalist overaccumulation, but primarily a consequence of a socialized vision of infrastructural provision which placed collective right to water over individual and private interests.

Later nineteenth-century International Conferences on Hygiene recommended that every individual receive 1,000 litres of water daily. Even if rarely achieved in practice, the premise was established that a certain volume of water should be provided to everyone. This social model reached its pinnacle after 1945, when European states constructed multiple large-scale infrastructures, like motorway systems (Brenner, 2004: 123–124).

Following the financial crises of the 1970s and the rise of neoliberalism, however, this social provision of infrastructure has been supplanted by multiple forms of privatization. Water privatisation has been a global phenomenon, occurring in, for example, Britain, Bolivia, Poland, South Africa and Indonesia (Bakker, 2003: 329). Large World Bank loans are awarded to municipalities, usually on the condition that the contract is awarded to a private corporation, which then provides filtered, chlorinated, fluorinated, objectified water to those who can pay (Barlow, 2007: 39). In the global south, however, the poor use isolated standpipes, polluted wells, rivers or expensive bottled water from peripatetic vendors. In Mahira in Nairobi, a single toilet with ten units and two bathrooms serves 1,500 inhabitants in 332 households (Hukka and Seppälä, 2007: 583). Waterborne diseases (cholera, typhoid, diarrhea) thrive in such circumstances. The global poor have a radically different material life to the global rich: resources are scarce, intermittent, unreliable and pathogenic. Meanwhile, golf courses and hotels frequented by western travelers often have special water facilities (Graham and Marvin, 2001: 172). This exemplifies the creation of 'premium network spaces' for global elites (Graham and Marvin, 2001: 389; Brenner, 2004: 244). This bifurcated material life is replicated, albeit less dramatically, in the west. Suburbs and gated communities receive new infrastructures while older, more spatially inclusive urban systems rust, corrode and decay. Many American cities, including New York, Chicago and Philadelphia, use drinking water mains which are between 90 and 150 years old (Phoenix, 2007: 512). Braudel's 'material life' might cover the earth, but it is increasingly segmented into privileged, technologically interlinked, islands of concentrated technology overlaying a landscape of older, gently crumbling infrastructures. In such circumstances, social differences become more reified than ever. The history of water networks offers an exceptional material history of uneven development, connecting the histories of global inequality and materiality.

Finally, ongoing mutation of this human-built hydrosphere has manifold environmental and geopolitical ramifications. By 1900, all but two of America's twenty-five largest cities used lead piping (Troesken, 2006: 10–11). The interaction of water and lead slowly poisoned significant numbers of people. Reservoirs have enormous, unpredictable environmental effects. Populations are displaced and resettled, while river flows are greatly altered, sediment accumulates, evaporation patterns change, ecologies are disturbed and tectonic activity magnified (L'vovich and White, 1990: 239). Control over water resources has major strategic significance. The Palestinian-Israeli conflict has been exacerbated by Israeli capture and control of water supplies in the Sea of Galilee and the West Bank (Pearce, 1992: 287). The destruction of water infrastructure has become a legitimate military objective. During the First Gulf War, US air strikes deliberately damaged most of Iraq's electricity grid. Water pumps and sewage plants failed, and raw sewage entered rivers from which people were forced to drink. This calculated cascading collapse of synergized material life generated a public health calamity causing at least 100,000 deaths (Graham, 2006: 255–258).

Meat and urban metabolism

For most foundational texts in urban sociology, the social realm was not merely opposed to the material, but also to the natural (Wirth, 1956: 143). If the history of 'society' was located in cities, then the history of 'nature' would be found outside them. Thus, when environmental history emerged in the 1960s and 1970s, its focus was ostentatiously non-urban, a view persisting into the 1980s (Worster, 1988: 292; for a critique see Melosi, 1993: 2). This focus was authoritatively dismantled by William Cronon, whose *Nature's Metropolis* (1991) used nineteenth-century Chicago to demonstrate how the metropolis and its putatively natural hinterlands were simultaneously co-produced through the construction of new technologies of circulation (railways, telegraphs) and the mass mobilization of physical substances (grain, wood, meat). To attempt to explain this in terms of straightforward 'urban' and 'natural' realms completely obscures the dynamic material reality of the urbanization process.

Nature's Metropolis offered a definitive history of how modern metropolises were formed from the acceleration and concentration of material and energy flows, or what is sometimes called *urban metabolism*. Metabolism is classically defined as the entirety of chemical reactions by which a living entity transforms raw materials into cells, tissues and energy. Today the word is used, not uncontroversially, to describe similar transformations of material streams operative at extra-individual scales (cities, ecosystems, societies), which stretches the concept beyond the purely biological (Fischer-Kowalski, 1998: 63). Very material analyses can calculate the quantity and quality of the material flow sustaining a city. Such material flow analysis (MFA) has, since the 1980s, been used to calculate the volume of toxins passing through cities or societies, or their total energy requirements (Bringezu, 2003: 22–23). Cities, it has been demonstrated, consume between 70 to 80 per cent of global resources (Baccini, 1997: 27). This emphasis on multiple material streams, rather than discrete, bounded domains, again demonstrates the redundancy of fixed domains like 'social' and 'natural' (Fischer-Kowalski, 2003: 45).

Food is a particularly germane substance through which to explore the history of this process. Industrialising western cities metabolized increasingly large quantities of food, which stretched the limits of their traditional resources, meaning that food was increasingly drawn from distant markets, distributed with greater speed via steam-powered transportation, and sold through a reorganized network of urban markets. This complex infrastructure provided an intensified flow of edible biomass, which was increasingly processed, refined, homogenized, commodified, standardized and, later, chemically enhanced and synthesized.

This material transformation could be approached by examining numerous foodstuffs, like wheat or sugar, but I will focus on meat. Urban meat consumption clearly rose as cities were themselves divested of farm animals. Modern urban dwellers generally consumed more meat than rural ones: in 1916, for example, Madrid's meat consumption was almost three times that of rural Spanish areas (Simpson, 1995: 186). Meat was increasingly associated with strength, virility and masculinity (Fiddes, 1991). Max Rubner, for example, described German urban workers adopting the 'cult of meat' (cited in Treitel, 2007: 55). This cult was manifest in rising consumption of cheap forms of meat (sausages, trotters, liver, sheep's head, black puddings, pies), a process given scientific validation by Liebig's argument that nitrogen in animal protein was essential for human health. Although Liebig's chemistry was discredited after 1850, the equation persists (Treitel, 2007: 52–53). Meat has considerable 'thing power'.

Such rising consumption required mass production and new infrastructures of production and circulation. This involved the creation of critical nodes (stockyard, abattoir, port, market, shop) linked by durable transportation networks (railways, steamships, trucks). Chicago's stockyards functioned like reservoirs supplying water to cities: raw materials were collected and concentrated, creating a giant reserve of nitrogenous and fatty matter to be liberated according to market demands (Cronon, 1991: 208–223). Modern abattoirs allowed amplified levels of production. Animals were killed in larger volumes, with increasing efficiency. In 1926, Argentina's seventeen meat factories could slaughter 27,500 cattle, 50,000 sheep and 4,000 pigs daily (Thévenot, 1979: 241). Like water systems, abattoirs and meat regulation increasingly fell under municipal control. Steamships and railways radically increased the speed and efficiency of distribution. Most importantly, organic decay was arrested by the development of mechanical refrigeration, which obviated the need to collect ice from rivers, ponds, mountains and glaciers. Refrigerated railway cars were first used successfully in America in the 1860s, and the first refrigerated abattoir was constructed in Texas in 1871. Cold stores spread across America in the 1870s and Britain in the 1880s. The temperature of the entire circuit of production and consumption could be regulated, forming 'cold chains' (Thévenot, 1979: 105). By the 1970s, some Japanese cold stores reduced temperatures to minus 55 degrees Celsius (Thévenot, 1979: 331).

The great rise in modern urban meat consumption, then, grew along with a new ecological system linking the city, via seamless cold chains, to a territorially discontinuous global hinterland. As with water, the circulation of potentially capricious matter was controlled and made predictable. Meat consumption increased in British, American, German and French cities, and, over the twentieth century, in most global cities with rising real incomes (Japan is a good example). This was not simply a technological achievement. It was also a major event in the history of what Alfred Crosby famously called 'ecological imperialism'. Crosby referred to the premium North American, Australasian, Argentine and Uruguayan farmland where cattle grazed as 'neo-Europes' (1986: 204). These spaces formed an agricultural archipelago which was technologically, economically and biologically knitted to Europe. Their temperate climates replicated Europe's. By the nineteenth century, they were teeming with transposed European biotic communities. By 1910, original Argentinian herds, themselves not indigenous, had been replaced with British pedigree herds (Perren 2006: 32–33).

Animals have a biological history which is not purely an evolutionary one. Darwin himself closely studied the effects of selective breeding in order to produce his theory of 'natural' selection. From the 1820s, British cattle breed societies began publishing herd books providing knowledge for farmers wishing to generate increasingly rotund animals. According to estimates, the average weight of cows increased from 500 to 800 pounds from the early eighteenth to the mid-nineteenth century, producing the fatty meat which made Victorians salivate (Turner *et al.* 2001: 209, 177). Fat, nineteenth-century experiments showed, increased more rapidly than the rest of the body. It could be created through selective breeding and careful, copious feeding (linseed and oilcake were popular), producing impressive levels of corpulence with unprecedented rapidity. Animals could be slaughtered at younger ages. John Morton, editor of the British *Agricultural Gazette*, considered the 'earlier maturity' of fattened beasts essential to increasing the meat supply. Appropriately fatty beef could be produced in two years, rather than four as previously (Morton, 1849: 362). The cow was not merely fatter than ever before, but its lifespan was dramatically telescoped. This trend towards fatty meat was reversed after 1950, when breeding and feeding dramatically reduced the fat content of cattle, sheep and pigs (Perren, 2006: 250).

Like water, meat has a material history which is simultaneously technological, political, environmental and physiological. There are around 1.5 billion cattle on earth today. Pasturing and feeding these animals uses vast quantities of resources, and their flatulence disgorges equally enormous amounts of methane into the atmosphere. Transporting chilled meat across the globe consumes large amounts of energy. This truncated, technologically-enhanced anthropocentric food chain demonstrates, according to MFA, the damaging environmental consequences of meat eating (Baccini, 1997: 34). Red meat has been regularly associated with heart disease. Meat is also an effective vector for numerous pathogens, from tuberculosis bacilli to BSE prions. The environmental history of meat binds methane, fossil fuels, water, refrigerants, saturated fats, bacteria and proteins (benevolent and malevolent) into a single nonlinear process. The inherent unpredictability of this process illustrates perfectly two critical lessons of environmental history: material complexity and the unintended consequences of technological systems (Radkau, 2008: 36, 135, 317; Blackbourn, 2006: 362).

Conclusion: rematerializing cities

Although urban sociology, Marxist urban studies, cultural theory and SCOT literature provided valuable insights into urban history, they relegated materiality to a limited repertoire of stock roles: background, outcome, medium, obstacle, text, symbol, determinant. The material world became an external environment within which analytically interesting action took place. New interdisciplinary work in phenomenology, science studies, environmental history and post-Marxist materialism has effectively reincorporated the material into the social, economic, cultural and political realms. This restoration of material immanence emphasizes the volatility, plurality and concatenation of the physical world. Indeed, 'materiality' itself might be too abstract a term to fully capture the rich and diverse array of qualities and capacities of the physical world. In conclusion, I will simply emphasize three things.

First, attention to materiality reveals its historicity, a historicity inseparable from other historicities. While historians have regularly focused on the emergence of classes, markets, identities and epistemological formations, they have seldom been so attuned to material transformation and emergence. Water, a substance basic to life itself, has undergone dramatic changes in its physical composition that are arguably as essential to 'modern' western life as democracy and freedom. Meat has been consumed throughout recorded human history, but today, it is produced in historically unprecedented volumes, and traverses great distances in a state of controlled gelidity. The consumption of nonrenewable fossil fuels, on which contemporary modern energy systems and petrochemical industries are based, has obviously risen dramatically since 1900 (Sieferle, 2001; Geiser, 2001: 43–45). Still more dramatic is the emergence of entirely new synthetic substances – polyester, polystyrene, Bakelite, celluloid, Teflon, superalloys – of which the everyday apparatus of contemporary life (antifreeze, cars, detergents, toys) is composed (Geiser, 2001: 21–88). These novel substances introduced specific forms of agency into the world: durability, catalysis, superelasticity, semiconductivity, flocculence. However, these materials have often been non-renewable and disposable, and, in combination with other materials, have sometimes produced damaging, unpredictable forms of agency: dissipation, corrosion, carcinogenicity, bioaccumulation, contamination, air pollution. Our history has a very real chemical dimension.

Second, it is clear that old analytic binaries (natural–social, urban–nonurban) no longer have much analytic purpose. To speak of, say, 'society' shaping 'technology' is to operate at a level of abstraction that obscures as much as it reveals. It introduces analytic partitions into a world typified by circulation and metabolism (Heynen, Kaika and Swyngedouw, 2006: 12). At no point on its journey from animal body to human stomach, for example, do the hydrocarbons and amino acids in meat suddenly cross a threshold dividing the 'natural' from the 'social.' Urban history focusing on how flows of particular substances are harnessed, channeled and metabolized can clearly be written without ossifying analysis into 'natural' and 'urban' elements (Cronon, 1991; Platt, 2005; Klingle, 2007). Instead, analyzing the flows themselves brings scholarship closer to the material transformations which have really defined the past 200 years: the dramatic exploitation of resources, the inefficiency of their use, the development of synthetics, the widening inequality of access to such resources, and the remarkable lack of concern for 'externalities' like air quality.

Third, abandoning some of the premises of twentieth-century social and cultural theory does not mean abandoning political analysis. Indeed, power has been central to my analysis here. There are enormous asymmetries of material life within the west, and between the west and much of the rest of the world. Control over, and management and distribution of, basic material resources is absolutely integral to the operation of distinct modalities of power (liberal, social, neoliberal). Materiality is not 'outside' power, any more than it is 'outside' the economic. Reintegrating it into political and economic analysis only mirrors what has been done in, for example, environmental economics and urban political ecology. Analysis of the velocity and intensity of particular material flows, for example, is integral to any comprehension of sustainable development (Geiser, 2001: 312–313). This allows us to study the historical emergence of big things like economies and cities without losing sight of either their molecular constitution or their turbulent, interactive nature. This is surely a vital move for anyone hoping to comprehend the history, nature and scale of today's 'environmental problem'.

Acknowledgements

The author would like to thank Tom Crook, Joanna Guldi, Patrick Joyce and Kristina Sessa for their generous and insightful comments on earlier versions of this paper.

Note

1 This position is, in all fairness, rarely stated so baldly. For softer, subtler examples, on Boston and Los Angeles respectively, see Warner, 1962 and Hall, 2002: 294–235.

References

Baccini, P. (1997) 'A city's metabolism: towards the sustainable development of urban systems', *Journal of Urban Technology*, 4 (2), 27–39.

Bakker, K. (2003) 'Archipelagos and Networks: Urbanization and Water Privatization in the South,' *The Geographical Journal*, 169 (4), 328–341.

Barlow, M. (2007) *Blue Covenant: The Global Water Crisis and the Coming Battle for the Right to Water*, New York: New Press.

Blackbourn, D. (2006) *The Conquest of Nature: Water, Landscape, and the Making of Modern Germany*, London: Norton.

Bonnell, V. and L. Hunt (1999) 'Introduction', in V. Bonnell and L. Hunt (eds) *Beyond the Cultural Turn: New Directions in the Study of Society and Culture*, Berkeley: University of California Press.

Bourg, D. and S. Erkman (eds) (2003) *Perspectives on Industrial Ecology*, Sheffield: Greenleaf Publishing.

Braudel, F. (1981) *The Structures of Everyday Life: The Limits of the Possible* (trans. Siân Reynolds), New York: Harper and Row.

Brenner, N. (2004) *New State Spaces: Urban Governance and the Rescaling of Statehood*, Oxford: Oxford University Press.

Bringezu, S. (2003) 'Industrial ecology and material flow analysis: basic concepts, policy relevance and some case studies', in D. Bourg and S. Erkman (eds) *Perspectives on Industrial Ecology*, Sheffield: Greenleaf.

Brown, B. (2004) 'Thing Theory', in B. Brown (ed.) *Things*, Chicago: University of Chicago Press.

Buiter, H. (2008) 'Constructing Dutch streets: a melting pot of European technologies', in M. Hård and T. Misa (eds) *Urban Machinery: Inside Modern European Cities*, Cambridge, Mass.: MIT Press.

Castells, M. (2000) *The Rise of the Network Society*, 2nd edition, Oxford: Blackwell.

Cosgrove, D. and S. Daniels (eds) (1988) *The Iconography of Landscape: Essays on the Symbolic Representation, Design, and Use of Past Environments*, Cambridge: Cambridge University Press.

Cronon, W. (1991) *Nature's Metropolis: Chicago and the Great West*, New York: Norton.

Crosby, A. (1986) *Ecological Imperialism: The Biological Expansion of Europe, 900–1900*, Cambridge: Cambridge University Press.

Dant, T. (2005) *Materiality and Society*, Maidenhead: Open University Press.

Daunton, M. (1983) *House and Home in the Victorian City: Working-Class Housing 1850–1914*, London: Edward Arnold.

Dear, M. and A. Scott (eds) (1981) *Urbanization and Urban Planning in Capitalist Society*, New York: Methuen.

de Landa, M. (1997) *A Thousand Years of Nonlinear History*, New York: Zone.

Deleuze, G. and F. Guattari (1987) *A Thousand Plateaus: Capitalism and Schizophrenia* (trans. B. Massumi), Minneapolis: University of Minnesota Press.

Donald, J. (1992) 'Metropolis: the city as text', in R. Bocock and K. Thompson (eds) *Social and Cultural Forms of Modernity*, Cambridge: Polity Press.

—— (1999) *Imagining the Modern City*, Minneapolis: University of Minnesota Press.

—— (2000) 'The immaterial city: representation, imagination, and media technologies', in G. Bridge and S. Watson (eds) *A Companion to the City*, Oxford: Blackwell.

Dyos, H. (1961) *Victorian Suburb: A Study of the Growth of Camberwell*, Leicester: Leicester University Press.

Engels, F. (1887; new edition 1993) *The Condition of the Working Class in England* (trans. F. Kelley-Wischnewetsky), Oxford: Clarendon Press.

Feenberg, A. (1999) *Questioning Technology*, London: Routledge.

Fiddes, N. (1991) *Meat: A Natural Symbol*, London: Routledge.

Fischer-Kowalski, M. (1998) 'Society's metabolism: the intellectual history of materials flow analysis, part I, 1860–1970', *Journal of Industrial Ecology*, 2 (1), 61–78.

—— (2003) 'On the history of industrial metabolism', in D. Bourg and S. Erkman (eds) *Perspectives on Industrial Ecology*, Sheffield: Greenleaf.

Fishman, R. (1987) *Bourgeois Utopias: The Rise and Fall of Suburbia*, New York: Basic Books.

Gandy, M. (2002) *Concrete and Clay: Reworking Nature in New York City*, London: MIT Press.

Geiser, K. (2001) *Materials Matter: Toward a Sustainable Materials Policy*. Cambridge, Mass. MIT Press.

Goubert, J-P. (1989) *The Conquest of Water: The Advent of Health in the Industrial Age* (trans. A. Wilson), Princeton: Princeton University Press.

Graham, S. (2006) 'Urban metabolism as target: contemporary war as forced demodernization', in N. Heynen, M. Kaika, and E. Swyngedouw (eds) *In the Nature of Cities: Urban Political Ecology and the Politics of Urban Metabolism*, New York: Routledge.

Graham, S. and S. Marvin (2001) *Splintering Urbanism: Networked Infrastructures, Technological Mobilities and the Urban Condition*, London: Routledge.

Gunn, S. (2000) *The Public Culture of the Victorian Middle Class: Ritual and Authority and the English Industrial City, 1840–1914*, Manchester: Manchester University Press.
Hall, P. (2002) *Cities of Tomorrow: An Intellectual History of Planning and Design in the Twentieth Century*, 3rd edition, Oxford: Blackwell.
Hamlin, C. (1998) *Public Health and Social Justice in the Age of Chadwick: Britain 1800–1854*, Cambridge: Cambridge University Press.
Hassall, A. (1876) *Food: Its Adulteration, and the Methods for their Detection*, London: Longmans, Green and Co.
Harvey, D. (1985a) *Consciousness and the Urban Experience: Studies in the History and Theory of Capitalist Urbanization*, Baltimore: Johns Hopkins.
—— (1985b) *The Urbanization of Capital: Studies in the History and Theory of Capitalist Urbanization*, Baltimore: Johns Hopkins University Press.
—— (1990) *The Condition of Postmodernity: An Enquiry into the Origins of Cultural Change*, Oxford: Blackwell.
—— (2001) *Spaces of Capital: Towards a Critical Geography*, Edinburgh: Edinburgh University Press, 2001.
—— (2003) *Paris, Capital of Modernity*, New York: Routledge.
Heidegger, M. (1927; first English edn 1962) *Being and Time*, trans. J. Macquarrie and E. Robinson, Oxford: Blackwell.
Heynen, N., M. Kaika and E. Swyngedouw (2006) 'Urban political ecology: politicizing the production of urban natures', in N. Heynen, M. Kaika, and E. Swyngedouw (eds) *In the Nature of Cities*, New York: Routledge.
Hughes, T. (1983) *Networks of Power: Electrification in Western Society, 1880–1930*, Baltimore: Johns Hopkins University Press.
—— (1987) 'The evolution of large technological systems', in W. Bijker, T. Hughes, and T. Pinch (eds) *The Social Construction of Technological Systems: New Directions in the Sociology and History of Technology*, Cambridge, Mass: MIT Press.
Hukka, J. and O. Seppälä (2007) 'Improvement of the lives of slum dwellers – safe water and sanitation for the future cities of the fourth world', in P. Juuti, T. Katko and H. Vuorinen (eds) *Environmental History of Water: Global Views on Community Water Supply and Sanitation*, London: IWA Publishing.
James, E. (1901) *Municipal Administration in Germany as Seen in the Government of a Typical Prussian City, Halle a/S*, Chicago: University of Chicago Press.
Jones, G.S. (1971) *Outcast London: A Study in the Relationship between Classes in Victorian Society*, Oxford: Clarendon.
Joyce, P. (2003) *The Rule of Freedom: Liberalism and the Modern City*, London: Verso.
Juuti, P., T. Katko and J. Hukka (2007) 'privatization of water services in historical context, mid-1800s to 2004', in P. Juuti, T. Katko and H. Vuorinen (eds) *Environmental History of Water: Global Views on Community Water Supply and Sanitation*, London: IWA Publishing.
Katznelson, I. (1992) *Marxism and the City*, Oxford: Clarendon.
Klingle, M. (2007) *Emerald City: An Environmental History of Seattle*, New Haven, Yale University Press.
Konvitz, J., M. Rose and J. Tarr (1990) 'Review essay: technology and the city', *Technology and Culture*, 31 (2), 284–294.
Latour, B. (1999) 'On recalling ANT', in J. Law and J. Hassard (eds) *Actor Network Theory and After*, Oxford: Blackwell.
—— (2005) *Reassembling the Social: An Introduction to Actor-Network-Theory*, Oxford: Oxford University Press.

L'vovich, M. and G. White (1990) 'Use and transformation of terrestrial water systems', in B. Turner, W. Clark, R. Kates and J. Richards (eds) *The Earth as Transformed by Human Action: Global and Regional Changes in the Biosphere over the Past 300 Years*, Cambridge: Cambridge University Press.

McFarlane, C. and J. Rutherford (2008) 'Political infrastructures: governing and experiencing the fabric of the city', *International Journal of Urban and Regional Research*, 32 (2), 363–374.

MacKenzie, D. (1990) *Inventing Accuracy: A Historical Sociology of Nuclear Missile Guidance*, London: MIT Press.

Marx, K. (1973) *Grundrisse: Foundations of the Critique of Political Economy*, Harmondsworth: Penguin.

Maurer, B. (2005) 'Does money matter? Abstraction and substitution in alternative financial forms', in D. Miller (ed.) *Materiality*, Durham NC: Duke University Press.

Melosi, M. (1993) 'The place of the city in environmental history', *Environmental History Review*, 17 (1), 1–23.

Miller, D. (ed.) (2005) *Materiality*, Durham NC: Duke University Press.

Misa, T. (1988) 'How machines make history, and how historians (and others) help them to do so', *Science, Technology and Human Values*, 13 (3&4), Summer/Autumn 308–331.

Mitchell, T. (2002) *Rule of Experts: Egypt, Techno-Politics, Modernity*, Berkeley: University of California Press.

Morton, J. (1849) 'On increasing our supplies of animal food', *Journal of the Royal Agricultural Society of England*, 1st ser. 10, 341–379.

Nead, L. (2000) *Victorian Babylon: People, Streets and Images in Nineteenth-Century London*, New Haven: Yale University Press.

Norton, P. (2008) *Fighting Traffic: The Dawn of the Motor Age in the American City* London: MIT Press.

Park, R. (1916) 'The city: suggestions for the investigation of human behavior in the urban environment', in R. Sennett (ed.) (1969) *Classic Essays on the Culture of Cities*, New York: Appleton-Century-Crofts.

Pearce, F. (1992) *The Dammed: Rivers, Dams, and the Coming World Water Crisis*, London: Bodley Head.

Perren, R. (2006) *Taste, Trade and Technology: The Development of the International Meat Industry since 1840*, Aldershot: Ashgate.

Philo, C. (2000) 'More words, more worlds: reflections on the 'cultural turn' and human geography', in I. Cook, D. Crouch, S. Naylor and J. Ryan (eds) *Cultural Turns/Geographical Turns: Perspectives on Cultural Geography*, Harlow, UK: Pearson.

Phoenix, L. (2007) 'Aging American urban water infrastructure', in P. Juuti, T. Katko and H. Vuorinen (eds) *Environmental History of Water: Global Views on Community Water Supply and Sanitation*, London: IWA Publishing.

Pickering, A. (1995) *The Mangle of Practice: Time, Agency, and Science*, Chicago: University of Chicago Press.

Platt, H. (2005) *Shock Cities: The Environmental Transformation and Reform of Manchester and Chicago*, Chicago: University of Chicago Press.

Radkau, J. (2008) *Nature and Power: A Global History of the Environment* (trans. T. Dunlap), Cambridge: Cambridge University Press.

Redfield, R. and M. Singer (1954) 'The cultural role of cities', in R. Sennett (ed.) (1969) *Classic Essays on the Culture of Cities*, New York: Appleton-Century-Crofts.

Rowlands, M. (2005) 'A materialist approach to materiality', in D. Miller (ed.) *Materiality*, Durham NC: Duke University Press.

Sennett, R. (1969) 'An introduction', in R. Sennett (ed.) *Classic Essays on the Culture of Cities*, New York: Appleton-Century-Crofts.

Schorske, C. (1961; new edition 1981) *Fin-de-Siècle Vienna: Politics and Culture*, New York: Vintage.

Sieferle, R. (2001) *The Subterranean Forest: Energy Systems and the Industrial Revolution*, Cambridge: The White Horse Press.

Simmel, G. (1903) 'The metropolis and mental life', in R. Sennett (ed.) (1969) *Classic Essays on the Culture of Cities*, New York: Appleton-Century-Crofts.

Simpson, J. (1995) *Spanish Agriculture: The Long Siesta, 1765–1965*, Cambridge: Cambridge University Press.

Smith, N. (1975) *Man and Water: A History of Hydro-Technology*, London: Peter Davis.

Stilgoe, J. (1988) *Borderland: Origins of the American Suburb, 1820–1939*, Yale: Yale University Press.

Thévenot, R. (1979) *A History of Refrigeration Throughout the World*, trans. J. Fidler, Paris: International Institute of Refrigeration.

Tisseron, S. (1999) *Comment l'esprit vient aux objets*, Paris: Aubier.

Treitel, C. (2007) 'Food science/food politics: Max Rubner and "rational nutrition" in Fin-de-Siècle Berlin', in P. Atkins, P. Lummel and D. Oddy (eds) *Food and the City in Europe Since 1800*, Aldershot: Ashgate.

Troesken, W. (2006) *The Great Lead Water Pipe Disaster*, Cambridge, Mass: MIT Press.

Turner, M., J. Beckett and B. Afton (2001) *Farm Production in England 1700–1914*, Oxford: Oxford University Press.

Verbeek, P.-P. (2005) *What Things Do: Philosophical Reflections on Technology, Agency and Design*, University Park, PA: Pennsylvania State University Press.

Walkowitz, J. (1992) *City of Dreadful Delight: Narratives of Sexual Danger in Late-Victorian London*, Chicago: University of Chicago Press.

Warner, S.B. (1962) *Streetcar Suburbs: The Process of Growth in Boston, 1870–1900*, Cambridge, Mass: Harvard University Press.

Winner, L. (1977) *Autonomous Technology: Technics-out-of-Control as a Theme in Political Thought*, Cambridge, Mass: MIT Press.

Wirth, L. (1956) 'Rural-Urban Differences', in R. Sennett, (ed.) (1969) *Classic Essays on the Culture of Cities*, New York: Appleton-Century-Crofts.

Worster, D. (1988) 'Appendix: doing environmental history', in D. Worster (ed.) *The Ends of the Earth: Perspectives on Modern Environmental History*, Cambridge: Cambridge University Press.

3 The matter of materialism

Literary mediations

Bill Brown

What better way of leaving reality behind than picking up a good book and settling into its fabrications, the fabric of its sovereign universe? Indeed, a novel's success no doubt depends on eliding itself as the object in hand – paperback or leather-bound – on behalf of providing access to its represented world, the world residing somehow within, somewhere beyond, the printed page. Yet the discipline of literary studies has nonetheless begun to suggest how literary texts register the material world, at times in excess of any agenda of representation, and how they can disclose aspects of material life, present and past, that are unlocatable in other archives. This critical task has been accomplished by a materialism that is irreducible to "Marxism": a materialism that may well grant Marx's discovery that abstractions ("exchange value," "total social capital") are "infinitely more concrete … than the objects one can "touch with one's hands" or "see with one's eyes" (Althusser, 1971: 76), but a materialism that nonetheless remains convinced that literature can enact a redemptive reification, demonstrating how visible and tangible objects can form and transform the life of human subjects. To avoid getting bogged down in discrepancies between the phenomenal and the material, this materialism settles for engaging the phenomenon of materiality, the *materiality-effect*, an end result of a process whereby you're convinced of the materiality of something. In the aftermath of various formalisms, deconstruction, and a wave of critical attention to the subject, this is a material turn that spotlights the role of objects in the drama of everyday life. In this chapter, as a way of illustrating how identities are mediated materially – mediated, that is, via objects – I will be tracking the experiences of a museum-goer in London, C.L.R. James, who would become one of the best known Marxist activists and writers of the twentieth century, but who was at the time (at age 31) part of a literary circle in Trinidad, and who had just finished writing his first novel. His encounters in London also provide an occasion for specifying "object culture" as a distinct field of scrutiny, and for marking the place of art objects within that field. I then turn to the current literary-critical history fascination with objects, accounting for it as something more than a frustration with the discipline. Finally, I concentrate on one novel, Theodore Dreiser's *Sister Carrie*, to illustrate what prose fiction can teach us about object culture, about the material constituents of that culture, and about the impact of material innovations on modern life.

Object culture and the art object

In one of his first "Letters from London" for the *Port of Spain Gazette*, written during his inaugural trip to England (1932), C.L.R. James reports on his "Visit to the Science and Art Museums". He begins the article with a sight which he was "knocked silly" by:

> [the] sight of the airplane in which Lieutenant Stanforth won the Schneider Trophy at a speed of 407 miles an hour; that is to say from Port of Spain to St. Joseph in one minute, quicker than the thoughts of many estimable people of my acquaintance.

He goes on to say:

> The plane is the most beautiful thing in the museum and one of the most beautiful I have seen in London … nothing superfluous, all cut and line … it looks so light … the body is like nothing so much as a long fish … the whole thing looks like a toy, and it is a thing for photographers to think about, that what has been built solely for utility turns out to be so beautiful.
>
> (James, 2003: 3–4)

His fascination with the object has little to do, finally, with this moment of Corbusian appreciation. It has to do, rather, with his recognition of how "scientific knowledge goes forward" provoked by competitiveness and the seemingly irrational dedication to "mere speed" , for instance. It has to do with his estimation of how such public displays – the museum's combination of historical artefacts and elaborate models – can serve to inspire a next generation of inventors. "So Galileo must have looked at the pendulum," James writes, "noting how evenly it swung" (9). And it has to do, too, with a sense of lack and of longing: "Why haven't we got such a place at home?" (1). "We, in Trinidad, know what the answer to any such effort … [would] be. No money, and probably a hint that, 'Oh, the people will not be interested,' 'the people this and the people that' " (10). To his readers back in the West Indies, James describes a perverse projection (of what "the people" can't appreciate) and the distinction between wealth and poverty, extraordinary access ("Everything free") and inaccessibility (10), center and periphery, metropole and colony. My interest lies in the way that – for a writer who was to become one of the twentieth century's best known analysts of "civilization" and its colonial, class, and race relations – a particular and particularized object occasions this cultural comparison and charged complaint. The Stanforth plane both embodies technological sophistication and passion (a physical manifestation of a physical triumph) and serves as an allegorical object that stands for those opportunities presented by the twentieth century, and those denied.

As a point of departure in his account of this foreign yet familiar land, James focuses not on behavioral, ideological, or economic facts but on his confrontation with an object that fairly well overwhelms him. You could chalk up this decision to rhetorical skill (a novelist's recognition that successful travel writing depends on concrete detail), but I want to emphasize how James registers the importance of objects – indeed, their hyperpresence – within the psychological, social, and political dynamics among modern human subjects. The account of Stanforth's plane is a brief yet theatrical example of how objects mediate our sense of ourselves, as individuals and as collectivities, and our sense of others. Spotlighting the role of the inanimate object world within culture, as culture, and as a means of apprehending culture, James has found (if I may paraphrase Lévi-Strauss), a "thing to think with" (1966: 36).

How might we describe this thinking – this field of thought? Whether he is detailing the wretched boarding houses of London or the private homes of the suburbs, a fourteenth-century "clock from Wells Cathedral" (7) or the Stanforth plane, James inadvertently produces as his object of address and analysis the *object culture* of London. By *object culture* I mean to designate the objects through which a culture constitutes itself, which is to say, too, culture as it is objectified in material forms. A given object culture entails the practical and symbolic use of objects: the ways in which inanimate objects (buildings, toys, tools, clothes, etc.) mediate human relations, the ways in which humans mediate object relations (generating differences of value, significance, and permanence among them), and the systems (material, economic, symbolic) through which objects become meaningful, or fail to. The dimensions of an object culture vary geographically, chronologically, and sociologically: we should be able to speak of the object culture of post-war America, of Weimar Germany, of the Pennsylvania Dutch, of fifth-century Athens as well as of twenty-first-century Shanghai, and of the local kindergarten. Of course, more so than James's foreign correspondence, the novel, in particular the realist novel from the nineteenth century (say Dickens, Balzac, Zola, Dreiser) dedicated itself to rendering object culture legible and to making objects metonymically meaningful. Indeed, as Jacques Rancière has put it, while Marx taught us how to decipher the commodity, Balzac taught us to decipher objects for the social histories within them; a new "aesthetic regime" honors the commonplace; "things" become newly legible and newly audible (Rancière, 2004: 33; 2007: 13). Moreover, two sociologists from the end of that century (in the inaugural era of sociology), Thorstein Veblen and Georg Simmel, demonstrated the ways that object culture can be analyzed, whether attention is paid to particular objects (Veblen's attention to the corset, the lawn, etc.) or to the display of objects (Simmel's attention to the Berlin Trade Exhibition) or to the "culture of things" more generally (as when Simmel writes of the "widening gap between the culture of things and personal culture," and the impossibility of "absorb[ing] into our lives all those things, which multiply as if in obedience to an inexorable fate indifferent to us" [Simmel, 1997: 101].) As Habermas put it, Simmel "was the first, despite all psychologistic idealism, to accomplish the return of philosophy to concrete objects, which remained canonical for all who were not drawn to the banging of the critique of knowledge and of spiritual history" (Habermas, 1996: 406). The case of James proves both intriguing and exemplary because, devoted though he is to providing an account of events and of English character, his discursive encounter begins with concrete objects.

Although the term remains uncommon (however commonsensical), in fact the analysis of *object culture* has many genealogies. Among those who heard Simmel lecture, Ernst Bloch, Walter Benjamin, and Sigfried Kracauer each in their way pursued his engagement with object culture, that pursuit achieving its most compressed and best known realization in Benjamin's exposé of the *Passagen-Werk*, "Paris, capital of the nineteenth century" (1935), where he imagines how object culture, "from enduring edifices to passing fashions," stores "the unconscious of the collective" (Benjamin, 1935: 34). Whereas Marx recognized a history of human labor that lay congealed in every human artefact (accounting for its value), Benjamin recognized multiple histories congealed there together: a history of production but also of circulation and consumption and use, thus also a history of fascination, apprehension, aspiration. Still, insofar as ethnology developed the culture concept as such through the rearrangement of objects on exhibition – displaying a given basket not within one grand technological history of basket weaving but within a diorama, a local scene of its use – the field of cultural anthropology remains (historically and currently) the privileged site in which object culture becomes visible (see Brown, 2003: 91–99). From the museum work of Franz Boas to Mauss's work on the gift in the 1920s, Lévi-Strauss's analysis of masks in the 1970s to Nicholas Thomas's history of "entangled objects" in the 1990s, anthropology has consistently centralized objects. But that consistency has been riddled by an ongoing recognition of how, within the study of object culture, the "density of objects," in Annette Weiner's (1994) words, remains overlooked – on behalf, say, of culture. More than a decade after Arjun Appadurai edited and published *The Social Life of Things* (1986), meant to interrupt the functionalism inherited from Mauss, the field was working urgently to prevent itself from "overlook[ing] the material properties of things," to recognize how those properties complicate or compromise "semiotic deployment" (Meyers, 2001: 22). The "very materiality of objects," Webb Keane argued, in 2001, "means that they are not fully arbitrary signs." Describing the socio-political ramifications of a torn banner among the Anakalangese (of West Sumba), Keane insists that "however semiotically" we may wish to treat such cultural artifacts, "they remain material objects and thus vulnerable to all that can happen to things." He adds:

> This would be so obvious as to go without saying were it not for a curious artifact of the polarization between symbolic and materialist approaches to society in the 1960s and 1970s, a tendency to reduce objects to being either economic and utilitarian goods or semiotic vehicles.
>
> (Keane, 1997: 32)

Meanwhile, a "general renaissance in the topic of material culture studies" meant that Daniel Miller (introducing an anthology of essays, *Material Cultures*) could say that "the point that things matter can now be argued to have been made," the ongoing task being one of balancing general theorization with a "strategy that looks to the specificity of material domains and the way form itself is employed to become the fabric of cultural worlds," culture itself now appearing not as text but as textile (Miller, 1998: 3, 6).

But even as it makes obvious sense to track the analytic history of object culture within anthropology and material culture studies (let alone archeology), I don't want to pretend that there is anything genuinely ethnographic about James's essay; indeed, as his aesthetic attention to the Stanforth plane anticipates, he concludes his letter on the museums not with inventions (culture) but with a work of art (Culture), and not with some metonymically or metaphorically English piece (like the clock), but with a sculpture by Rodin: *John the Baptist* – "a statue of a naked man walking, that's all" (12). "I was dreadfully tired out but the thing made me fresh again" (13). The refreshment prompts (if it is not prompted by) a brisk proliferation of other affiliations, identifications, interpellations. Suddenly, James writes about what "we" of the twentieth century will be able to say to the ancient Greeks – to the ancient Greek who could sit with James and stare at the statue "with much the same eyes and feelings" as would in fact "a wanderer from the West Indies" seeing the statue of the man walking "three thousand years from now" (14). While the Stanforth plane would be "meaningless" to the Greek, and dismissed by the future West Indian "as one of a crowd of obsolete designs" (14), the Rodin "cannot grow old. It cannot go out of date. It is timeless" (14). The object prompts an unanticipated sequence of first person plurals – *we* moderns, *we* humans, *we* West Indians present and future – and it is as though the object suddenly releases James from the confines of modernity, including its colonial history. The "timelessness" that James projects onto the object is in fact a timlessness he himself experiences, at one with the ancient Greek and the future West Indian. However scripted this experience may be by the science/art binary and by aesthetic ideology, Schiller might say that James here experiences a specific type of humanity. In step with Schiller, Jacques Rancière might say that James here occupies a "region of being" where the asserted equivalence of experience eventuates in an unexpressed afterthought on behalf of the material realization of a common humanity (Rancière, 2004, 24–27; and see Rancière, 2006).

The acts of identification elicited by London's object culture – the Rodin statue and the Stanforth plane – occur within a more general dynamic by which human subjects depend on inanimate objects to establish their sense of identity, dynamics described most persuasively not by anthropologists but by philosophers. John Locke, among others, imagined that identity was an effect of remembering thoughts and actions, but Hannah Arendt came to argue that our sense of ourselves and what we call identity stabilize foremost in relation to concrete objects. She wrote:

> Things of the world have the function of stabilizing human life and their objectivity lies in the fact that – in contradistinction to the Heraclitean saying that the same man can never enter the same stream – men, their ever-changing

> nature notwithstanding, can retrieve their sameness, that is, their identity, by being related to the same chair and the same table.
>
> (Arendt, 1958: 137)

But most things of this world – food and clothes, computers and cars – are eminently consumable, fungible, disposable; far from interrupting the transience of our lives, they illustrate ephemerality at its most banal. This is why Arendt distinguishes between labor and work, between human effort which disappears without a trace (consumed commodities) and that which results in reification, some more enduring product that is the material externalization of human will (as Marx would say in the 1844 manuscripts). Arendt underscores the "outstanding permanence" of artworks as the quality that makes art such a significant part of the human condition. "Nowhere else," she argues, does the "thing-world reveal itself so spectacularly as the non-mortal home for mortal beings. It is as though worldly stability had become transparent in the permanence of art" (168).

It is not difficult to imagine all sorts of objections to Arendt's claim, but she helps to elucidate the case of James in London and, without resorting to any esoteric ontology, she productively specifies the role of particular objects (what we call art, what we understand or experience as art) within object culture, even though this particularity is a historical product of the same systems (material, economic, symbolic) that particularize other kinds of objects (food, kitsch, trash, etc.). Her assertion helps to dramatize the oddity of any emergent "new materialism" within literary studies given that (if it is not pursuing the crudest history of the book) such materialism proceeds by isolating one very distinct kind of object within an object culture in order to render that object culture (other objects within that culture) newly apprehensible. (Imagine staring at the Rodin statue in order to learn more about the plane and the clock.) This is a literary criticism that depends on one kind of object relation – reading – to explore other object relations; a criticism that engages an object of relative permanence to perceive the transient; a criticism necessarily in the thrall, let us say, of an object (say a novel) that, utterly consumable and disposable as it is, works to establish itself not beyond the market, but beyond the laws of decay, precisely by holding the decaying object world within a kind of stasis, as though transfixing it in amber.

Given that oddity, why bother with the novel? When it comes to apprehending object culture, why not stick with historians (say Simon Schama, in *An Embarrassment of Riches*, his account of Dutch culture in the Golden Age) or ethnographers (say Paul Stoller, in *The Taste of Ethnographic Things*, his account of the Songhay of Niger)? What is the attraction to the object culture within literary representation, and what is the attraction to instrumentalizing literature on behalf of learning how subjects constitute themselves in relation to the inanimate object world?

Though my response to such a question remains provisional, I'm willing to propose some telegraphic speculations that are at once phenomenological, epistemological, and psychological. Whenever we speak of material culture or of materiality as such, this is a constituted and mediated materiality, a materiality apperceptively produced, as it were. This is one reason why "materiality" can prove to be such an elusive term, and why materiality might best be understood as a series of materiality-effects. (What are the materiality-effects that convince you that you're holding a book?) It may be that literature grants us access to such a process – and thus to the temporality of materiality – precisely because a text must obviously (self-consciously, and at times ostentatiously) work to fabricate a material world for its reader. Moreover, as one of the great (albeit recently neglected) phenomenologists of reading has put it, "objects represented in a literary work are derived from purely intentional objects projected by units of meaning," which is to say that, whether or not we ask about the significance of one object or another in a novel, it is significance (meaning) that has generated the object in the first place, making novels an obvious site for parsing the dynamics of object/meaning (Ingarden, 1973: 218). Finally, because even novelistic realism "imposes raw presence to the detriment of the rational sequences of the story" (Rancière, 2004: 24), we can isolate an historical, materialist phenomenology from history-as-usual; and because the relation between any represented object and the "extensive objective whole" remains underdetermined in any novel (Ingarden), we can foreground the question of determination, by which I mean, simply, the question of how (within novels and outside of novels) we understand how a particular object fits within a more expansive material field, how it fits within what I've been calling object culture.

A new materialism

In fact, though, addressing some kind of "new materialism" within the field of literary studies amounts to consolidating rather disparate work. Still this is work that, despite different objectives and different reading practices, shares: 1) an effort to think through (into and beyond) the familiar anti-ontologizing orthodoxies, wherein things must be regarded as the unsightly residues of some naiveté we overcame long ago; 2) an effort to rethink those accounts of the social or discursive construction of the subject (the subject interpellated or performed, the subject rendered abject or constituted intersubjectively, the subject gendered, raced, sexualized, ethnified, nationalized, creolized, hybridized) that assiduously neglect the role of material constructions and physical constraints; 3) an effort to put more meat on the bones of the highly textualist historiography generated by many (but not all) new historicists; 4) a willingness to re-energize a number of philosophers (Simmel, Bergson, Bachelard, Merleau-Ponty) who were displaced by a new wave of "continental theory" (Lacan, Derrida, Foucault); and 5) a fascination with Benjamin.

For some time now, there has been a kind of shorthand with which to differentiate (the now waning) new historicism and cultural materialism: the former is American, the latter British; the former depoliticizes the act of criticism, the latter remains political; the former eschews any Marxist account of determination and embraces a Foucauldian understanding of power, the latter remains engaged by Marx (the term "cultural materialism" having appeared first in Raymond Williams's *Marxism and Literature*); the former tends to textualize culture, the latter does not. When Clifford Geertz's methodological emphasis on "interpretation" and on "writing" (in *The Interpretation of Cultures* [1973]) energized the field of literary criticism, it had an unanticipated effect that squared, however unpredictably, with the logic of deconstruction. For if it seemed possible to find – within a literary text – some generative structure or dialectic that explained the culture at large, that is because culture at large seemed newly explicable through the act of "close reading" that Geertz analogized to the kind of textual analysis practiced by literary critics. All told this somewhat circular trajectory could result in the dematerialization of culture; as Kiernan Ryan explained about the apparent discrepancy between the New Critics and new historicism, "despite the violent differences between them, both approaches contrive to make material history vanish: the one by severing the work from the world, the other by reducing the real to the written" (Ryan, 1996: xiv). Textualizing history was the enabling condition for new historicism's august productivity and insight, the epistemological move that could homogenize literary and non-literary discourse, text and context, and different cultural spheres (law, literature, political economy, medicine, government,etc.).

By the mid-1980s new historicism was thriving, and by the mid-1990s – say 1996, the year Ryan published a Reader entitled *New Historicism and Cultural Materialism* – some other materialism appeared on the horizon. I tentatively mentioned the term – "what might be called a new materialism" – within my introduction to *The Material Unconscious* (1996), a book that tried to show how material culture remains subliminally present within literary texts (no matter how apparently insignificant or underdetermined the references to it), and that tried to demonstrate how an "engagement with literature can produce an alternative space of elaboration wherein ephemera that have yet to attain historicity" might complicate one or another master narrative (of modernity, or consumer culture, of US Imperialism) on the microhistorical scale, dramatizing the material everyday as something irreducible to one or another "cultural logic" (1996: 18, 5). On the one hand, then, I meant to produce a grittier understanding of the American 1890s. On the other, I meant to produce for literature a different unconscious from that elaborated by Pierre Macherery and Fredric Jameson. A more "material" unconscious (within which one could not necessarily detect some regnant ideology or a class-conflict narrative) was the product of "the pressure" that the material world "exerts on literary texts" and the "formalizing pressure" those texts exert on the "heterogeneity of lived life" (Brown, 1996: 4). However utopian (or, say, patently Benjaminian), the project focused on material practices – children playing with the new iron toys, the popular use of the new Kodak camera, the thrill of new roller coasters – where one could glimpse an alternative sociality and thus recognize the noninevtitability of history.

In 1996 as well, in a different historical field, a group of essays anthologized in *Subject and Object in Renaissance Culture* (De Grazia, Quilligan and Stallybrass, 1996) showed how productive the concentration on objects can be while pointing out how assiduously the field had elided objects on behalf of representing the

Early Modern era as the period that gives birth to the modern subject, that "long and monotonous history of the sovereignty of the subject" or the other narratives "we have been telling ourselves over and over again: the rise of subjectivity, the complexity of subjectivity, the instability of subjectivity." "[R]enaissance studies have been doubly instrumental in sustaining this obsessive teleological history," the editors wrote in their introduction, "by keeping the subject out of touch with the object and by staging this exclusion as the beginning of the Modern." Concerned to show "how objects have a hold on subjects," how "material things – land, clothes, tools – might constitute subjects who in turn own, use, and transform them," they imagined provisionally reversing the Aristotelian form/matter relation: "it is the material object that impresses its texture and contour upon the noumenal subject" (Stallybrass, 1996: 5–11). Although the collection included central figures within New Historicism (Stephen Greenblatt and Stephen Orgel, for instance), and though New Historicism itself had certainly worked to stage a new relation between literature and "the real" (Gallagher and Greenblatt, 2000: 54), the contributors highlighted the material constituents of culture: "Renaissance England was a cloth society" (Stallybrass, 1996: 289).

In a subsequent book on Renaissance clothing, Stallybrass and Ann Rosalind Jones express their frustration with those scholars who, working on one or another aspect of object culture, apologize for their fetishistic engagement with the material world as though the engagement threatened to replicate the fetishisms of capitalism. As the authors put it, those scholars thus fail to recognize that Marx addressed "the fetishism of the *commodity*, not of the *object*." They point to Daniel Miller who, in his book on *Material Culture and Mass Consumption* (1987), still seems (in their view) "embarrassed before actual objects," embarrassed on Marxist grounds. And yet "no one," they argue, "has been less embarrassed by material markings than Marx. Marx's critique of capitalism is not a critique of materialism." They go on to say that "it is because things are not fetishized that, in capitalist societies, they remain theoretically lifeless" (Jones and Stallybrass, 2000: 7–8). Fetishism thus looks like the answer to the problem, not the problem itself.

Indeed, among some of the more avant garde anthropologists (James Clifford and Michael Taussig, for instance) fetishism had been adopted as a passing analytic strategy in the 1980s, somewhat prefiguring the ways in which what I'm calling a new materialism (engaged with Marx or not) responds to a phenomenon described by Marx and repeatedly voiced within the Marxist tradition – what Lukács called the loss of the character of the "thingness of things" that results from the saturation of society with the commodity form (Lukács, 1968: 92). Although the question of what that thingness might be has been answered very variously, my point is simply that drawing attention to object culture should be recognized as an effort (conscious or unconscious, successful or not) to interrupt the abstraction effected by capital, just as it should be recognized as a way to punctuate those materialisms without matter of which Lukács's body of work provides the best example. More simply, the study of object culture might be understood as an effort to overcome the paradox pointed out (in 1968) by Harold Searles, the rare psychoanalyst (along with Winnicott) for whom "object relations" were not reducible to relations between subjects (where the inanimate object stands in for a human). Searles argued that,

> In our culture, a conscious ignoring of the psychological importance of the nonhuman environment exists simultaneously with a (largely unconscious) *overdependence upon* that environment. I believe that the actual importance of that environment to the individual is so great that he *dare* not recognize it. Unconsciously it is felt, I believe, to be not only an intensely important conglomeration of things *outside* the self, but also a large integral *part* of the self.
>
> (Searles, 1960: 395)

A new materialism thus "dares" to bring that importance into consciousness.

Having made those generalizations, let me briefly name some of the recent books of literary criticism that could fall under the rubric of "new materialism." In *The Tears of Things* (2006), Peter Schwenger shows how modern art and poetry dramatizes the melancholic relation of humans to the object world, the ways we invest our emotions in them, and the ways they fail to provide sufficient return on those investments. In *The Prose of Things* (2006), Cynthia Wall charts the transformation of the description of objects in the English novel of the eighteenth century. And Mark Blackwell has published a collection of essays, *The Secret Life of Things: Animals, Objects, and It-Narratives in Eighteenth-Century England* (2007), where the contributors treat the curious genre of the object autobiography not as an illustration of commodity fetishism, but as a means of thinking through a new object culture and the human relations it mediates. In *The Sense of an Interior: Four Writers and the Rooms that Shaped Them* (2004), Diana Fuss examines how the sensuous apprehension of interior space (doors, windows, chairs, etc.) provided Emily Dickinson, Sigmund Freud, Marcel Proust, and Helen Keller with the grounds for imagining psychic interiority. In *Persons and Things* (2008), Barbara Johnson, a prominent psychoanalytic and deconstructive critic (and one of Derrida's translators), produces a discursive collage that stages and restages that ontological ambiguity; on the one hand, she reminds her readers that Derrida's first course at Yale was entitled "The Thing;" on the other, her own purview encompasses puppets,Barbie dolls and computer games. Even these one-line descriptions make it clear how divergent these projects are, from one another and from the Marxist literary-critical tradition. Other work resides within that tradition, however idiosyncratically. In *Ideas in Things: Fugitive Meaning in the Victorian Novel* (2006), Elaine Freedgood focuses on particular objects – the mahogany furniture in *Jane Eyre*, the calico curtains in *Mary Barton*, the Negro Head tobacco in *Great Expectations* – and both provides a history of these objects and tracks the hermeneutic policing whereby the Victorian novel works to contain the significance of the objects it represents, teaching us, as it were, to ignore the object culture on which realism depends. In *Portable Property: Victorian Culture on the Move* (2008), John Plotz tracks the way in which novels investigate a world of fungible objects where certain things could be at once portable and inalienable, holding transcendent value, able to preserve an owner's familial, religious, or national identity.

All told, I'm inclined to argue that those of us who end up working on objects, on object cultures, on things, may think of ourselves as reacting against, within literary-critical discourse, inflated and exhausted accounts of the subject, the textualization of culture, a fixation on image culture (let alone, say, the "materialism without matter," as Derrida defined Paul de Man's deconstruction). Yet I suspect that if there is a material unconscious at work in this material turn it might be regarded as some response to (or as some compensation for) what the archeologist Colin Renfrew has called the "dematerialization of material culture." Because "the electronic impulse is replacing whatever remained of the material element in the images to which we became accustomed," he writes, the "engagement with the material world where the material object was the repository of meaning is being threatened … [P]hysical, palpable material reality is disappearing" (Renfrew, 2003: 188–189). Just as the flourishing history of the book might be read as a reaction formation to the book's rapid transformation – or its disappearance into something other than the object-form we call a book – so too I imagine that the proliferating histories and theories of things implicitly serve as a retaining wall to prevent Renfrew's "material reality" from being washed away. At the very least, this attention to things may seem to promise some newly stable ground, some grounding in the visible, the olfactory, the tactile, mediated though it may be by the act reading. But it is such mediation that helps to prevent the study of object culture from retreating into empiricism, that enables materiality to arrive here not as an answer, but as the provocation of new questions.

Literature and the matter of substance

Distinctions between one kind of literary-critical approach and another are not so easy to fathom in the abstract, so let me begin reading a well-known American novel, *Sister Carrie* (1899), both to illustrate how literature might mediate our apprehension of object culture as material culture, and to realize an ambition that has emerged within the study of material culture itself. In his contribution to an anthology of essays on material culture, *History from Things*, Robert Friedel points to what Aristotle designated the "first cause" of things – the material cause, as that which has been elided in studies of material culture that emphasize instead the design, the maker, and the purpose (to continue with Aristotle). "It is ironic," he writes, "that studies of material culture should so neglect the actual materials that go into creating culture" (Friedel, 1993: 42). Using the example of two teapots – one manufactured from tin, the other blown glass – he insists on what might be considered obvious: that only by considering the material of each object can one begin to understand the cultural significance of each. What one might call materialist readings of *Sister Carrie* have been keenly attuned to class distinctions, constructions of gender, consumer culture, the desire sustained by capitalism, and the urbanization of America. Far from wishing to interrupt those readings,

I simply want to focus on how the text dramatizes the material mediation of the transformations being charted.

When Carrie Meeber secures her first job, she's not just relieved. She is also, despite being disappointed by her weekly wage ($4.50), somewhat titillated: "This was a great, pleasing metropolis after all. Her new firm was a goodly institution. Its windows were of huge plate glass. She could probably do well there" (29). The apparent *non sequitur*, where glass seems somehow integral to success, bespeaks Carrie's anticipation, her naiveté, and her infatuation with windows, the more evident when, reporting her success to her sister, she celebrates the fact that "it seems to be such a large company" with "great big plate-glass windows" (31). Yet the illogic makes considerable sense of both the character and her context because windows had indeed become a new measure of an institution's status in Chicago, and because Carrie's own status in the modern city – her embarrassment, her unwitting success in attracting the attention of Drouet and Hurstwood, and her success on the New York stage – depends on a visual economy. When Drouet takes her to dinner, he sits by the window in order "to see and to be seen" (58). But as Carrie's peripatetic search for work has established from the outset of the novel, this reciprocal looking is no mere opportunity; it is also, more simply, a new urban condition, the condition that humiliates her as she walks though the wholesale district: "As she contemplated the wide windows and imposing signs, she became conscious of being gazed upon and understood for what she was – a wage-seeker" (18). This is a gaze that quickly becomes ubiquitous, fundamentally internalized. When, through another "window [she sees] a young man in a grey checked suit," she can't determine whether or not he has "anything to do with the concern," and yet, "because he happened to be looking in her direction her weakening heart misgave her and she hurried by, too overcome with shame to enter" (18). The gaze may be fictitious; the abjection is real. The city's vitreous culture has produced a regime of visibility, both real and phantasmatic, that can frighten as intensely as it fascinates. Although Carrie will ultimately succeed within New York's theater world, it is the glass-mediated theatricality of everyday life that she enters as, stepping off the train at Chicago, she enters modernity. Indeed, the theater (windowless and darkened) might be said to provide a residual institutional containment of vision, where the dynamics of seeing have been regularized, and where Carrie can capitalize on being the object of visual attention.

In Chicago, she occupies an expanding field of visibility that extends from the worlds of amusement and consumption to the worlds of production and circulation. She can see – through the factory windows across the Chicago river – the "figures of men and women in working aprons, moving busily about" (17). Portraying the city's world of glass in these opening chapters, Dreiser adopts his historian's mode, at pains to underscore the novelty. "The large plates of window glass, now so common, were then rapidly coming into use, and gave to the ground floor offices a distinguished and prosperous look. The casual wanderer could see as he passed a polished array of office fixtures, much frosted glass, clerks hard at work, and genteel business men in "nobby" suits" (16). While windows still had the basic function of illuminating the workplace with natural light, they also served to exhibit a concern's success, made manifest in the floors and ceilings, the desks and chairs. When Dreiser himself first found the *Globe-Democrat* building in St. Louis, "a prosperous eight-story brownstone and brick affair," he stood and "stared at it in the night, looking through the great plate glass windows at an onyx-lined office and counter" (2000: 106–107). The scene is repeated over and over again in Chicago, where he stares at the "glowing business offices" that always seem "so far removed from anything to which [he can] aspire" (5). For Dreiser, as for his most famous character, the plate glass window has become an optical mechanism that generates a dialectic of proximity and distance which structures the "drag of desire" (23), as he calls it in *Sister Carrie*. The more completely one sees (or sees into) the object world of success the more desperately one feels one's remoteness from it, wanting what one sees but cannot touch. As Rachel Bowlby put it, in her study of Dreiser, Gissing, and Zola, this is the world of "just looking," a world that depends on glass (1985: 15).

The "large plates of window glass" became considerably cheaper and better in the 1890s: more colorless and flawless, more transparent. But the ubiquity of glass in Chicago was really a product of the 1871 fire that destroyed the city's center. The task of rebuilding the commercial and industrial districts became an opportunity for experimenting with new building techniques and thus for accomplishing on a vast scale what no other city could accomplish: the extensive use of iron and the new Bessemer steel, meant to protect the buildings from subsequent fire, but also to diminish the load-bearing function of the masonry walls, which were increasingly thinned to mere facades. Skeleton construction promoted modular, multi-story building (the nation's first skyscrapers), and enabled architects to devote floor after floor to expansive windows, what soon became known as the "Chicago Window" (Condit, 1964: 79–94; Giedion 366–394; Jordy, 1972: 1–82). The introduction of the electric elevator in the late 1880s further liberated vertical ambition: the Manhattan building (1891) rose to 16 stories, the Masonic Temple (1892) to 22. As Louis Sullivan put it, "In Chicago, the tall building would seem to have arisen spontaneously" (Sullivan, 1924: 314). Travelers to the city were inevitably in awe of both the height of the buildings – "they scale the very heavens" – and the expanse of glass, the "innumerable windows" (Paul Bourget [1895] quoted by Jordy [1972: 52–53]). With the amplified use of both gas and electric light (Marshall Field introduced electricity to his store in 1882), the new buildings produced a luminous city, which is why, when Carrie and Drouet walk late in the evening on Adams street, they walk in a world lit up. "The lights in the stores were already shining out in gushes of golden hue. The arc lights were sputtering overhead, and high up were the lighted windows of the tall office buildings" (76). The field of visibility had extended not just spatially, but also temporally, far into the night.

Among the innovators who wove this new urban fabric, William Le Baron Jenney stands out as the "founder" of the Chicago school of architecture that thrived from the late 1870s until 1893, when the *beaux arts* tradition triumphed at Chicago's Columbian Exposition, and when an economic "crash" retarded new commercial building. *Industrial Chicago* (1891) celebrated the "science" of his second Leiter Building (1889) as something comparable to the science devoted to "a steel railroad bridge of the first order"; the "giant structure" was a "commercial pile in a style undreamed of when Buonarroti erected the greatest temple of Christianity" (205). Jenney's design for "The Fair" (1891), one of Chicago's new department stores, was a vast (55,000 square feet), 11-story steel and iron rectangle (running along Adams Street, between State and Dearborn), with its first two stories devoted to glass. Built for the renowned sum of three million dollars, "The Fair" drew attention as the latest example of I-beam construction and tile fireproofing, but it stood out above all as the latest chapter in the story of Chicago's commercial ambition – a monument *of* and *to* retailing. Dreiser's choice of "The Fair" (1891) as the department store that figures so prominently in the development of Carrie's materialist longing (in 1889) is anachronistic. But its notoriety helped him make much of the novelty of the retailing phenomenon.

> The nature of these vast retail combinations, should they ever permanently disappear, will form an interesting chapter in the commercial history of our nation. Such a flowering out of a modest trade principle the world had never witnessed up to that time.
>
> (Dreiser, (1994 [1899]): 22)[1]

Much of the genius of the department store lay in the invitation to browse (as opposed to the proscription against loitering), which is the recognition that the task of the store was not simply to sell goods but also to incite and generalize consumer desire. Whereas shopping once included the ritual of bargaining, the department store's fixed prices transformed the act of consumption into a relation between the consumer and the merchandise, between people and things (see Benson, 1986; and Leach, 1993: chs 1–8). And the things themselves, theatricalized within display cases and shop windows, assumed the rhetorical burden of persuasion. "Fine clothes to her were a vast persuasion," Dreiser writes, "they spoke tenderly and Jesuitically for themselves. When she came within earshot of their pleading, desire in her bent a willing ear. The voice of the so-called inanimate! Who shall translate for us the language of the stones?" (97). It is tempting to read such animation as the phenomenal illustration of Marx's notion of commodity fetishism, where things assume lives of their own. But Marx's point is about the deceptively autonomous value that seems to inhere in objects (a value that in fact depends on their relation to other objects, and that derives from human labor). The scene is more explicable according to Walter Benjamin's translation of "commodity fetishism" into a visual, erotic fascination with the material object world, the "sex appeal of the inorganic" (Benjamin, 1935: 7). But the elaborate personification of things in *Sister Carrie* most simply enacts the very achievement sought by the new window dressers who managed the exhibition of objects. Stewart Culin, the exhibit coordinator for John Wannamaker's department store in Philadelphia, wrote of "trying to coax and arrange" objects so they would tell their "story to the world" (quoted by Bronner,

1989: 231). For Frank Baum, author of *The Wizard of Oz* (1900) and one of the nation's foremost window dressers, the fundamental goal of window displays was to make objects "come alive" (86). Within a realist register Dreiser makes it clear that modernity, far from disenchanting the material world, has re-enchanted it by other means.

The prominence of the show window within the history of this re-enchantment has prompted analysts of film to argue that the cinema screen (which was the genuinely new cultural phenomenon of 1900) "incorporated and displaced" the shop window as the frame that energized objects before the captivated spectator (Friedberg, 1993: 66). Among its other accomplishments, then, *Sister Carrie* reads as a discursive transition point between the shop window and film, prefiguring what Vachel Lindsay called film's power to transform a "non-human object" into a "hero," to grant furniture a personality, to render things human (Lindsay, 1922: 35, 32, 33). But the ubiquity of glass in Dreiser's cityscape anticipates not just a mass-cultural phenomenon, but also a modernist one: the "glass-covered dwellings" built by Loos and Le Corbusier, which, as Benjamin wrote, were imagined by Paul Scheerbart (in 1913) as adumbrating a new "culture of glass." Developing a "positive concept of barbarism" (when, in 1933, it was barely sill possible to do so), Benjamin relied on Scheerbart's sense that glass was "in general, the enemy of secrets': "The new glass milieu will transform humanity utterly," he quotes; "and now it remains to be wished that the new glass-culture will not encounter too many enemies" (Benjamin, 1933: 731–736). Within Dreiser's novel, those moments where Carrie can *see into* the world of labor and the world of management might be said to register the potential for glass to effect a democratized visibility and what Scheerbart called the "absence of illusion." However, those moments are overwhelmed, within the novel, by the intensity with which glass generates and sustains illusion. This is a modernity "haunted," as Anthony Vidler would say, "by a myth of transparency," a myth repeatedly debunked and resurrected (Vidler, 1992: 217); and it is a modernity in which the realist novel, to the degree that the genre itself says "Look!" (Bal, 1996: 5), plays an obvious role, as do those science and art museums that James visited (the year before Benjamin championed the new culture of glass). But suggestive as it is to imagine how Dreiser prefigures an emergent mass culture and an emergent modernist utopia utterly compromised by modernity, it might be more important to sense how Carrie herself, notoriously passive and insubstantial, assumes something of the double character of glass, if not transparently disclosing the culture around her (rather than some inner self), then merely reflecting, with her "innate taste for imitation" (157), the taste of others. It may be true, as Fredric Jameson has suggested in a reading of Sartre's fiction, that "glass is a kind of figure for consciousness in that it cannot exist by itself but must show its surroundings through itself" (Jameson, 1984: 84), but there are few characters in fiction whom one *sees through* so completely as Carrie, who have so little opacity of their own, and with whom there seems to be no separation between interior and exterior (as Giedion [1965: 514] said of Le Corbusier's glass houses), which is to say no psychic interiority.

Coda: The matter with materialism

In this brief account of a long novel, I've tried to show how *Sister Carrie* makes Chicago's vitreous culture visible, and how Dreiser dramatizes the role of plate glass in changing both the relation among human subjects, and the relation between those subjects and inanimate objects. The new window is an object that manifests social relations and mediates them – an object within object culture that transforms that culture utterly. But though I've concentrated on the matter *of* materialism, trying to stage modernity in the register of historical phenomenology, I want to close with the potential matter *with* this materialism. It is a problem vehemently voiced by Fredric Jameson, who draws attention to the way that Simmel's "phenomenological commitment to the concrete" – to particularity and empiricity – "forestalls concept-formation" and results in an inability to move "towards the absolute of universal or abstract ideas" (Jameson 1999: 269, 281, 271). As Habermas puts it, Simmel "was a creative although not systematic thinker – a philosophical diagnostician of the times with a social-scientific bent rather than a philosopher or sociologist" (Habermas, 1996: 405). From Jameson's point of view, the limit of Simmel's thought, which becomes the limit of Benjamin's thought, is, in a phrase, the unwillingness to theorize, by which he means the unwillingness to totalize. For Jameson, of course, the plea to "always historicize," as he put it, is a plea to totalize, which means to allegorize: to transcode the phenomena at hand into the terms of the modes-of-production and stages-of-capital narrative, the barely perceptible telos of which is the democratic socialization of the means of production. But it is precisely the translation of the object at hand into those terms that threatens *not only* to deny it phenomenal specificity (on behalf, say, of diagnosing a dominant spatiality or temporality) *but also* to forestall other (not necessarily alternative) accounts of how object culture forms and transforms human life. Seeking a way through the fundamental impasse – the Scylla of mere phenomenality and the Charybdis of mere conceptuality – I'd say that literature provides especially good navigation points, organizing the non-human environment and its human inhabitants in a manner that can disclose dynamics, recognizable and abstractable, in the midst of what can seem the excesses of realism. As Raymond Williams put it, there is a "changing materialist content of materialism." For the "materialist enterprise ... defines and redefines its procedures, its findings and its concepts, and in the course of this moves beyond one after another 'materialism' " (Williams, 1980: 122). A book of prose fiction, precisely because it must elide its physical self on behalf of representing the physical world, highlights the phenomenon of materiality: materiality understood as an effect registered by the human body and the human psyche.

Note

1 The air of novelty is somewhat overdrawn, for the Bon Marché (1852) in Paris is generally considered the first department store, and, based on the Bon Marché, Émile Zola's

Au Bonheur des Dames (1883) had already demonstrated how the *grand magasin* could become a topic for fiction.

References

Althusser, Louis (1971) *Lenin and Philosophy and Other Essays* (trans. Ben Brewster), London: Monthly Review Press.

Appadurai, Arjun (1986) *The Social Life of Things: Commodities in Cultural Perspective*, Cambridge: Cambridge University Press.

Arendt, Hannah (1958) *The Human Condition*, Chicago: University of Chicago Press.

Bal, Mieke (1996) *Double Exposures: The Subject of Cultural Analysis*, New York: Routledge.

Baum, Frank L. (1900) *The Art of Decorating Dry Goods Windows and Interiors*, Chicago: National Window Trimmers' Association.

Benjamin, Walter (1933) 'Experience and poverty' (trans. Rodney Livingstone), *Selected Writings Volume Two 1927–1934*, Cambridge, Mass.: Harvard, 1999.

—— (1999 [1935]) 'Paris, capital of the nineteenth century', *The Arcades Project* (trans. Howard Eiland and Kevin McLaughlin), Cambridge, Mass.: Harvard University Press.

Benson, Susan Porter (1986) *Counter Cultures: Saleswomen, Managers, and Customers in American Department Stores 1890–1940*, Chicago: University of Illinois Press.

Blackwell, Mark (ed.) (2007) *The Secret Life of Things: Animals, Objects, and It-Narratives in Eighteenth-Century England*, Lewisburg: Bucknell University Press.

Bowlby, Rachel (1985) *Just Looking: Consumer Culture Dreiser, Gissing, and Zola*, London: Routledge.

Bronner, Simon J. (1989) 'Object lessons: the work of ethnological museums and collections', *Consuming Visions: Accumulation and Display of Goods in America, 1880–1920* (ed. Simon J. Bronner), New York: Norton, 217–254.

Brown, Bill (1996) *The Material Unconscious: American Amusement, Stephen Crane, and the Economies of Play*, Cambridge, Mass.: Harvard University Press.

—— (2003) *A Sense of Things: The Object Matter of American Literature*, Chicago: University of Chicago Press.

Condit, Carl W. (1964) *The Chicago School of Architecture: A History of Commercial and Public Building in the Chicago Area, 1875–1925*, Chicago: University of Chicago Press.

De Grazia, Margreta, Maureen Quilligan and Peter Stallybrass (1996) 'Introduction', *Subject and Object in Renaissance Culture*, Cambridge: Cambridge University Press, 1–13.

Dreiser, Theodore (1994 [1899]) *Sister Carrie*, New York: Penguin.

—— (2000 [1922]) *Newspaper Days: An Autobiography*, Boston: David R. Godine.

Freedgood, Elaine (2006) *Ideas in Things: Fugitive Meaning in the Victorian Novel*, Chicago: University of Chicago Press.

Friedberg, Anne (1993) *Window Shopping: Cinema and the Postmodern*, Berkeley: University of California Press.

Friedel, Robert (1993) 'Some matters of substance', *History from Things: Essays on Material Culture* (ed. Steven Lubar and W. David Kingery), Washington, DC: Smithsonian Institution Press, 41–50.

Fuss, Diana (2004) *The Sense of an Interior: Four Writers and the Rooms that Shaped Them*, New York: Routledge.

Gallagher, Catherine and Stephen Greenblatt (2000) *Practicing New Historicism*, Chicago: University of Chicago Press.

Geertz, Clifford (1973) *The Interpretation of Cultures*, New York: Basic Books.
Giedion, Sigfried (1965) *Space, Time and Architecture: The Growth of a New Tradition* (4th edn), Cambridge, Mass.: Harvard University Press.
Habermas, Jurgen (1996) 'Georg Simmel on philosophy and culture: postscript to a collection of essays' (trans. Matthieu Deflem), *Critical Inquiry* 22 (3) (Spring), 403–414.
Ingarden, Roman (1973) *The Literary Work of Art* (trans. George G. Grabowicz), Evanston: Northwestern University Press.
James, C.L.R. (2003) *Letters from London* (ed. Nicholas Laughlin), Port of Spain: Prospect Press.
Jameson, Fredric (1984) *Sartre: The Origins of a Style*, New York: Columbia University Press.
—— (1999) 'The theoretical hesitation: Benjamin's sociological predecessor' *Critical Inquiry* 25 (2) (Winter): 267–288.
Johnson, Barbara (2008) *Persons and Things*, Cambridge, Mass.: Harvard University Press.
Jones, Ann Rosalind and Peter Stallybrass (2000) *Renaissance Clothing and the Materials of Memory*, Cambridge: Cambridge University Press.
Jordy, William H. (1972) *American Buildings and their Architects. Progressive and Academic Ideals at the Turn of the Twentieth Century*, vol. 4, New York: Oxford University Press.
Keane, Webb (1997) *Signs of Recognition: Powers and Hazards of Representation in an Indonesian Society*, Berkeley: University of California Press.
—— (2001) 'Money is No Object: Materiality, Desire, and Modernity in Indonesian Society', *The Empire of Things: Regimes of Value and Material Culture*, ed. Fred R. Myers (Santa Fe: School of American Research Press).
Leach, William (1993) *Land of Desire: Merchants, Power, and the Rise of a New American Culture*, New York: Pantheon Books.
Lévi-Strauss, Claude (1966) *The Savage Mind* (trans. John Weightman and Doreen Weightman), Chicago: Chicago University Press.
—— (1988) *The Way of the Masks*, trans. Sylvia Dodelski, Seattle: Washington University Press.
Lindsay, Vachel (1922) *The Art of the Moving Picture*, New York: MacMillan.
Lukács, Georg (1968) *History and Class Consciousness Studies in Marxist Dialectics* (trans. Rodney Livingstone), Cambridge, Mass.: MIT.
Mauss, Marcel (1990) *The Gift*, trans W.D. Halls, New York: Norton.
Meyers, Fred R. (2001) 'Introduction: The Empire of Things', *The Empire of Things: Regimes of Value and Material Culture*, ed. Fred R. Myers, Santa Fe: School of American Research Press.
Miller, Daniel (1998) 'Why some things matter', *Material Cultures: Why Some Things Matter* (ed. Daniel Miller), Chicago: University of Chicago Press, 3–24.
Plotz, John (2008) *Portable Property: Victorian Culture on the Move*, Princeton: Princeton University Press.
Rancière, Jacques (2004) *The Politics of Aesthetics* (trans. Gabriel Rockhill), London: Continuum.
—— (2006) 'Thinking between disciplines: an aesthetics of knowledge' (trans. Jon Roffe), *Parrhesia* 1: 1–12.
—— (2007) *The Future of the Image* (trans. Gregory Elliott), London: Verso.
Renfrew, Colin (2003) *Figuring it Out*, London: Thames and Hudson.
Ryan, Kiernan (1996) "Introduction." *New Historicism and Cultural Materialism* (ed. Ryan), London: Arnold, ix–xviii.

Schama, Simon (1987) *The Embarrassment of Riches: An Interpretation of Dutch Culture in the Golden Age*, New York: Vintage.

Schwenger, Peter (2006) *The Tears of Things: Melancholy and Physical Objects*, Minneapolis: University of Minnesota Press.

Searles, Harold F. (1960) *The Nonhuman Environment in Normal Development and in Schizophrenia*, New York: International University Press.

Simmel, Georg (1997 [1909]) 'The future of our culture' (trans. Mark Ritter and David Frisby), *Simmel on Culture* (ed. David Frisby and Mike Featherstone), London: Sage.

Stallybrass, Peter (1996) 'Worn worlds: clothes and identity on the Renaissance Stage', *Subject and Object in Renaissance Culture*, 289–320.

Stoller, Paul (1987) *The Taste of Ethnographic Things: The Senses in Anthropology*, Philadelphia: University of Pennsylvania Press.

Sullivan, Louis H. (1924) *Autobiography of an Idea*, New York: AIA Press.

Thomas, Nicholas (1991) *Entangled Objects: Exchange Material Culture, and Colonialism in the Pacifics*, Cambridge, Mass.: Harvard University Press.

Vidler, Anthony (1992) *The Architectural Uncanny*, Cambridge, Mass.: MIT Press.

Wall, Cynthia Sundberg (2006) *The Prose of Things: Transformations of Description in the Eighteenth Century*, Chicago: University of Chicago Press.

Weiner, Annette (1994) 'Cultural difference and the density of objects', *American Ethnologist*, 21 (2) (May), 391–403.

William, Raymond (1980) *Problems in Materialism and Culture*, London: NLB.

Zola, Émile (1883) *Au Bonheur des Dames*, Paris: Charpentier.

Part 2

Assembling the state

4 The unintended state

Chandra Mukerji

> Although I might have no authority to seek a means of ameliorating the misery of the people of this state, and that I might be perhaps the least likely man in the realm to have the qualities necessary to accomplish such a thing, I have not stopped working at it, persuaded that there is nothing that an active and enduring application could not bring to pass.
>
> — (Vauban, *La dîme royale*, 1968, p. 60, translated by the author)

The modern state is traditionally understood in social theory as an apparatus or structure of power. Its formation is treated as either teleological – the result of historical forces unfolding in an interruptible, but inevitable way – or as part of a process of political rationalization pursued to empower the institution itself. The "fully" modern state is equated with a Prussian-style bureaucracy – a set of offices ordered like an army but turned to administrative purposes. The goal of the state, by such accounts, is to manage the interplay of political forces, adjudicating conflicts, and embodying the power of and over the collectivity. Historically, it is assumed that when those in power *can* invent a more modern state, they do so (or have to do so) to institutionalize their advantages and make their regimes more robust.

The problem with these theories is that they treat the state only as a system of social relations, and ignore that it is also a social institution of territorial governance with vast powers over the material wellbeing of its people. Theorists generally do not consider the importance of the natural world to governmental power – even though militaries defend territories, social hierarchies are related to the allocation of land, and famines, floods, and infrastructural failures are destabilizing political events. Theories that assert that modern states control territories nonetheless generally do not attribute any distinct power to the administration of the countryside – just an availability of resources and a domain for assessing taxes. Assuming that materiality must concern economic relations, they do not recognize power over land as a political tool, missing the ways that state infrastructure, land use practices, and regulations of resources affect the social order in subtle but consequential ways. Built environments exert powers, silently changing the ground on which political struggles take place and defining the conditions of possibility for collective life (Bowker and Star, 1999).

The centrality of territorial engineering to state power is clearly visible in the history of state formation in seventeenth-century France (see also Mukerji, 2009), In that time and place, natural knowledge and engineering were self-consciously used as tools and measures of government, giving the administration greater powers vis-à-vis the nobility. The king took land from local estates to "improve" his kingdom, changing the material bases of local life by physical means. Working on French infrastructure also affected those involved, including the three architects of the French state that are the focus of this analysis: the Chevalier de Clerville, Pierre-Paul Riquet and Sébastien Le Prestre de Vauban. The development of France's infrastructure was so palpably consequential both locally and for the administration that engineers who engaged in one project were stimulated to consider others and think about the kingdom's welfare as their political goal, forgetting that their primary duty was to obey the king. They became early technocrats, whose technical abilities both served the king, and defined a kind of power outside of monarchical will.

France before the period of Louis XIV was a kingdom in which local nobles dominated land use practices because the monarchy was weak. The wars of religion illustrated and exacerbated the problem. The king's religious convictions could neither define the beliefs of his people, nor quell religious dissonance. Major noble families in many parts of the kingdom were drawn to the new religion in part for the freedom from royal authority it offered, making France an even weaker state and land control a matter of local political processes (Baumgartner, 1995: 211–237; Holt, 2005: 99–101). This instability helped spur early infrastructural improvements in the kingdom to help protect its borders. Italian engineers were brought to France by the state to refortify border cities which were now seen as vulnerable to invasion not only because of cannon warfare that was making old defenses useless, but also because of the palpable weakness of the state itself. Still, the new defenses had to be sponsored and carried out locally by towns that feared for their safety because there was no money in the treasury for such work, so the material powers of the state were not extended through this work (Blanchard, 1979: 50–55). France remained more a set of independent (and warring) principalities than a political state, and the land was degraded by war. Henri IV and his minister, Sully, tried to change this, reducing religious warfare and uniting the kingdom around a program of territorial improvement. They wanted engineering efforts to be a major element of public administration, defining stewardship over the kingdom as the moral role of the king. But the early death of Henri IV stopped this work, and his reign was followed by a regency that left the state in Church hands–igniting more antagonism towards the state from Huguenots. Louis XIII, when he claimed his throne, became a warrior for the Church, not a steward of the land. And his untimely death again left a regency before Louis XIV ascended to the throne. Throughout this period, the monarchy had little money or power over the lands and people of France, and only patrimonial rules of law to define the king's power (Beik, 1985).

The political world that the engineers, Clerville, Riquet and Vauban, helped construct for Louis XIV was startlingly new and effective. It was also seductively modern in its materialism. It was a system of impersonal rule – rule through natural knowledge and material transformation. (Latour, 1999; Callon and Latour, 1992; Mukerji, 2008: 203–228) This was a form of power that seemed a simple extension of the culture of political stewardship initiated and promoted by Henri IV, but it created a form of mute power which was not expected to have such potency or politically transforming effects. It produced an unexpected state.

Organizing the French state around territorial administration became a surprisingly effective form of government, but also one that Louis XIV had reasons to fear. He could not control the landscape with his will alone, and those who could control it wielded powers that had the potential to rival his own. Both the king and his minister tried to limit the damaging effects of territorial governance by experts by asserting the ongoing authority of the king's will. This finally required turning against the major architects of the French state, and publicly discrediting them for lack of proper obedience.

Jean Baptiste Colbert, minister of the treasury, navy, and the king's household under Louis XIV, is often said to have invented the modern state by rationalizing the tax and legal systems, giving his administration greater financial and legal powers over the kingdom. The minister in fact did make the administration powerful, but what he did and how he did it has been sorely misunderstood. He explicitly avoided the social rationalization of offices associated with Weber's bureaucracy to avoid threatening the patron–client ties cemented in offices, and pursued instead policies of territorial improvement that gave the state new control over French lands that had been freely used by local nobles in the past.

The idea that the French state gained power in this period through bureaucratic reform defies the historical record. First of all, competitive hostility between Colbert and the Minister of War, Louvois, made bureaucratic integration completely untenable in France before Colbert's death. Also many important offices were held by powerful nobles, making fundamental change politically dangerous. Still, a shift of political relations began in this regime (Mettam, 1988: ch. 5). The shared interest of the king and his ministers in territorial expansion and land stewardship stimulated experiments in material power. This small opening had radical effects. It created political possibilities that surpassed the will of the king and Colbert. The modern state was an accident on the road to Louis XIV's presumed empire.

Territorial engineering made ideological sense for Louis XIV's regime because his political ambition was to make France a new Rome, an empire in the classical tradition. Using engineering projects to do this seemed appropriate. A powerful and showy infrastructure could make France appear more Roman, using technologies of power that the ancients deployed to assert military authority over their colonies. There was no reason to think that building roads, digging canals, enclosing ports and fortifying towns would change the political landscape in a profound way, but it introduced a pattern of material politics that was more consequential than expected and too effective to be completely abandoned.

Politics under Louis XIV was meant to be mainly patrimonial – not designed to change the institution of government. To secure his power in the provinces, Louis XIV appointed *intendants*, creating a new network of loyal public servants who could deal with provincial nobles and their local political institutions. Building a glittering court at Versailles was similarly important as a magnet for the aristocracy, binding them to the king (Elias, 1998). Both these strategies were ways of rearranging patron–client alliances through royal favors and flows of information to keep the king at the center of patrimonial networks (Kettering, 1986).

Clerville, Riquet, and Vauban all entered this system as clients of the king, working to promote his glory. They won wars, created ports, cut canals, and elaborated fortresses that were monuments to his reign as well as tools of territorial control. But they came to see the powerful effects of their engineering on social life, and this inspired them to dream of further "improvements" they could make in the kingdom. They started to treat France as though it was their land to imagine and manage, thinking like a king and acting like functionaries in a modern state. But France was not politically modern under Louis XIV, and the monarch insisted on doing his own thinking. He responded to their hubris by acting willfully, limiting or destroying their careers.

It is well known that the aging king attacked previously trusted agents of the crown, but the motives have usually been treated as personal. Saint-Simon (1990) thought the king a self-centered man who demanded strict obedience to his desires and tastes, cutting off those who crossed him. This psychological portrait of the king might have been correct, but it does not itself explain why men like Clerville and Vauban, who were used to placating the king, would start exercising their own judgment. Their political fall resulted not from individual characteristics, but something more sociological: changes in the administration that reconfigured the imagination and reasoning of its agents. Surprising acts of political independence were unintended consequences of a new form of politics that was seductive to those who engaged in it: the material redesign of the landscape to affect the wellbeing of the country and its people.

Louis XIV was clear that service was obedience, and asserted his will to demonstrate that his agency, not the abilities of engineers, was the foundation of French power. This political technique demonstrated his final authority, but could not erase the obvious effectiveness of administrative stewardship and territorial engineering. The new infrastructure in France continued to shape local life, marking the boundaries of the kingdom and defining lines of communication and commerce. Even after the engineers who built the infrastructure were dead, their physical ordering of French life remained a part of local existence and a reminder of the powers of the state even in provinces far from Versailles.

Louis XIV and Colbert had no inkling that territorial politics might become as significant and problematic as it did. The king was more interested in war than infrastructure, and Colbert was more concerned with controlling the nobility than changing the landscape. Machiavelli (1966) explained the problem with French internal politics. He argued that monarchs in that kingdom had never overwhelmed great noble families. Local aristocrats often had loyal followers, who would obey them before the king. So, nobles of high standing depended little on their monarch, and could ignore his wishes, or stymie his policies. Their loyalty had to be explicitly solicited with ongoing acts of respect, favoritism, and generosity: the tools of patronage politics (Kettering, 1986).

For Louis XIV and Colbert, this situation was intolerable. As a boy, the king had witnessed the Fronde, an uprising against the crown and its agents by nobles and wealthy urban merchants. As much as the young monarch did not want to stay in Paris among potential adversaries, he did not want to witness a similar turn of events (Mousnier, 1979: 12, 611–630). So, he moved his court to Versailles and gave specific political attention to the great families of France. By spreading favors and financial opportunities at Versailles the king also made nobles more dependent on his largesse, but this would not assure his power (Mukerji, 1997: 198–247).

So while the king built his patrimonial networks, Colbert pursued a program of territorial politics to empower the administration and constrain the power of local nobles. Following the precedent of Henri IV's minister, Sully, he defined the state as a great estate, and promoted programs to "improve" the king's lands, positioning Louis XIV as a good Christian steward of his domain (Mousnier, 1979: 17; Murat, 1984b: ch. 3; Ranum, 1979: 259–272; Meyer, 1985: 71–84). Patterns of provincial life were changed by the new infrastructure and regulations of natural resources that Colbert installed. Nobles lost lands by indemnification for these "improvements," and the new roads, ports, canals, bridges, and forests set up across the countryside changed quotidian forms of life that had served noble privilege.

Territorial politics could be politically successful during this period in large part because of its moral foundations. Stewardship was seen as a Christian duty and moral measure. Good Christians were expected to make the best use of the gift of Creation, and restore the land to the perfect form it had in Eden. This meant that landholders in seventeenth century were obliged by religious conviction to take stewardship seriously. And in the estate-based system of power, they also had to respect the king's claim to be steward of his own lands (Mukerji, 2009: ch. 2; Mukerji, 2007: 227–253).

Territorial politics based on stewardship principles, then, directly confronted noble claims to land. If the kingdom could be improved by building an infrastructure of ports, roads, canals, arsenals, and citadels, their lands could be confiscated to do it. If the army or navy needed timber, they had to protect the forests to supply it for the king. If a fortress had to be built on their land, they had to accept the loss – even if they complained about it. And if a canal crossed their fields, cutting off their granaries from local mills, all they could do in the end was to agitate for a bridge.

Territorial politics empowered the state by both extending its authority and undermining patrimonial networks, serving the administration by threatening the foundation of noble power. This was fine as long as the king's personal rule was not also victim to this turn to impersonal politics, and that technocrats did not start taking personal responsibility for the kingdom. At first, Clerville, Riquet, and Vauban were obedient to the king and good clients of Colbert, and they expected to make the king glorious with their imposing fortresses, grand waterways, and technological finesse. Meanwhile, they also extended the reach and responsibility of the administration by taking land for state projects and leaving an infrastructure in the countryside as marker and means of state government. But each of them eventually took stewardship of the kingdom too personally. They ruined themselves by confusing their abilities to improve France with the king's will to do so. They made manifest the dangers of stewardship politics, and were slapped down to contain the risk they posed.

Following Saint-Simon, Louis XIV's outbursts against Clerville, Riquet, and Vauban could be taken as fits of temper, but they were more precisely assertions of monarchical singularity in the face of the rise of technocratic power, railing against and trying to contain a shifting political landscape – the creation of a modern state administration that he did not intend.

The Chevalier de Clerville

The Chevalier de Clerville was the first of the architects of the French state to be attacked for political hubris for his dedication to territorial governance. He was *commissaire general des fortifications* from 1658 to 1673 when he was eclipsed, if not replaced formally, by his more famous successor, Sébasiten Le Prestre de Vauban (Vérin, 1993: 188). Ongoing exchanges of letters between Colbert and Clerville documented the events that both propelled and finally ended Clerville's career. It shows that the military engineer did not fall from the king's grace because he made technical mistakes or acted as a bad client to his patron, but because he took on administrative authority not granted by the king to exercise his stewardship over the province of Alsace where he was working (Clément, 1979: 23–36, 43–53, 58–59, 71, 81–84).

As *commissaire des fortifications*, Clerville served Colbert well before 1673. In turn, Colbert protected him and advanced his interests (Clément, 1979: 11). Clerville, for his part, was an obedient servant to his patron, writing him frequently, speaking honestly, working assiduously, and taking on whatever duties were asked of him. He would build the France that the king desired and Colbert required.

If his technical success alone had been what the engineer needed to serve his patron, Clerville's career and relationship with Colbert would have been over in December 1669 when a large portion of the facing for a wall at Château-Trompette collapsed. Clerville immediately wrote to the minister, describing the disaster, and Colbert responded as follows:

> I strongly fear that [we have] done with this [project] some thing that is completely against good sense in putting stone for sculptures and inscriptions on the face of the bastion … and a multitude of similar sites[.] I am deeply fearful, I tell you, [because Perrault, who rebuilt part of the Louvre] says [there is] so little solidity that all the construction is not good … If this is true,

> believe me, the entire building of Château-Trompette will fall into pieces; what has not fallen this year will fall the next and so on.
>
> (Clément, 1979: 23–25)

Clerville responded with proper deference, and technocratic moves. He did studies, called meetings of experts, and wrote back to the minister with a plan:

> It gives me great displeasure, Monseigneur, to find myself obliged to tire you so much, … while you work to sustain the greatest portion of a great state … But … after the last tests that I had made of the foundations of the wall that fell, after the observations I made … concerning the state of the platforms, and after the last conferences I've had with the architects that I have had come on site … [who are] the most capable of this region, [I tell you] that the repairs of this wall can be made … as described in the plan below.
>
> (Clément, 1979: 25)

Colbert responded positively:

> After examining all the reasons you have given me for enclosing the [broken wall] with new masonry, everyone [here] is in agreement that your advice is the best; that is why it is necessary to follow it absolutely, and to apply yourself to reestablish [the structure] in such a way that there is no reason to fear that a parallel accident will occur.
>
> (Clément, 1979: 25–26)

Clerville's engineering failure at Château-Trompette did not ruin him because he was a man who knew how to act properly with his patron. He knew it was his job to serve the minister loyally and with all the thoroughness and assiduousness he could. In return, Colbert would protect him, and trust him to repair the damage.

Clerville's fall came later when he was supervising construction on the fortresses at Philipsbourg and Brisach in Alsace. Surprisingly, it did *not* result from tensions between Clerville and Colbert when Colbert's cousin was made the local *intendant* for Alsace. This made the situation delicate, but Clerville understood the problem, and was discrete about the cousin's failings. The minister saw the danger in the situation as well, cautioning his cousin that building Brisach and Philipsbourg was a test of whether he could serve in the administration or not. His success depended on Clerville.

The problem with Colbert's cousin was that he was fond of an inexperienced entrepreneur, the sieur Saint-André, and awarded his friend the contract for both these jobs. The older Colbert immediately objected, saying that Brisach and Philipsbourg were too important and difficult to build to be given to a single entrepreneur. But the *intendant* refused to hire any of the other entrepreneurs that the minister sent to him for this purpose. Colbert, as minister, insisted that Clerville personally oversee construction of the foundations for the forts. It was clear from Château-Trompette that the success of the construction depended on how the foundations were built. The plans for construction were also drawn up by Clerville and approved by the king (Clément, 1979: 23–36). As expressions of the king's will, they had to be followed exactly.

Still, the situation did not improve. Saint-André had accounting problems, and huge unexplained costs. Without open bidding on the project and with disorder in the books, there was no way to be sure that the entrepreneur was acting honestly. So, the minister turned to Clerville again, asking the military engineer to check the costs, and to sort out the growing confusion both about the quality of the work, and the expenses of the project (Clément, 1979: 33–36, 43, 47, 49–53). Finally in September 1671, the king discharged Saint-André from the project, and a year later, appointed a new *intendant* for Alsace, M. Poncet de la Rivière (Clément, 1979: 58–59, 71).

It seemed that Clerville had weathered a bad political storm, using his skills in patronage politics to offset the technical and financial deficiencies of Saint-André. But in May, Clerville wrote to Colbert that the new entrepreneur appointed by the *intendant* was disregarding his plans for the work (Clément, 1979: 81–83). Colbert continued to be sympathetic to his frustration, but without warning, the king lashed out. Clerville was reprimanded, and never recovered the king's trust. Colbert explained in a letter dated June 10, 1673:

> I received your letter from last month about which I must explain the true sentiments of the king, which I have not explained to you forcefully enough until now. In your letters, it seems that you have assumed to be or appointed yourself as the financial officer [*contrôleur public*] for the *intendant*. You find ways to speak for all that he does; you criticize and examine how he regulates the *corvées* [labor taken as tax payments from peasants]; you want him to raze the butte d'Eckersberg, against the orders and intentions of the king; you want him to supervise the entrepreneur [subcontracting for the work] and his wife, and ask that he determine the house that they must occupy; you also want him to account to you for all the expenses that he orders, and all he does.
>
> I am obliged to tell you that all of this is not in any way your authority; since the king has chosen an *intendant*, his majesty has judged him worthy of his confidence both in the disposition of the taxes he collects and for everything else on which he depends, and that you have no authority to act as his *contrôleur public*. It is true that if you see that the king is manifestly mistaken [in his trust of the *intendant*], you must advise the *intendant* about this, honestly and civilly, so that he can take care [of the problem]; and in case that he does not remedy the abuses that you have discovered, all that you should do is to keep memoirs [of what you have seen] to alert the king, which his majesty could reflect on if he wanted to do so.
>
> (Clément, 1979: 84)

The terms of this letter revealed the political line that Clerville had crossed. He had usurped powers that were not his to take, trying to supervise the *intendant* who had been appointed by the crown. Clerville, of course, did not see this. He was continuing to supervise the engineering – assuming that his job was to make sure it was done correctly. He even changed the plan for the fortress "against the orders and intentions of the king" (Clément, 1979: 84). Razing part of the butte d'Eckersberg was a technically effective way to expand the fortress and was eventually done, but in Colbert's terms, "all of this is not in any way your authority" (Clément, 1979: 84). The king had to approve all the engineering decisions so that the fortresses in Alsace would be expressions of his will.

The *intendant* had authority over Clerville because the *intendant* was the king's client and Clerville only worked for Colbert. It did not matter if the military engineer was more competent to build fortresses because "his majesty has judged [the *intendant*] worthy of his confidence" (Clément, 1979: 84). The king could have misjudged the *intendant*, but that did not mean that Clerville should administer the province's projects independently. It was Clerville's job to make the king's choice of an *intendant* a worthy one: "if you see that the king is manifestly mistaken … you must advise the *intendant* about this, honestly and civilly" (Clément, 1979: 84). It was not Clerville's duty to assure the *intendant*'s stewardship of Alsace.

Clerville assumed that executing his work well would be appreciated since he saw the fortresses as assets of the king, but that was focusing on the landscape and its improvement, not the king's will and its expression. The military engineer remained the supervising engineer for the Alsatian fortresses, and continued to do work for Colbert. But he had fallen out of the king's favor, and Vauban stepped in to become the leading military engineer in France. Clerville's career as an esteemed client of the king effectively came to an end.

Pierre-Paul Riquet

Another man involved in building the French infrastructure in this period, Pierre-Paul Riquet, fell from grace in a different way. He was a tax farmer from Languedoc who contracted with the king to dig a navigational canal across his province. He lacked Clerville's courtly manners and connections at Versailles, and he lacked engineering credentials as well, but he was a wealthy financier who could help shoulder the expense of the enterprise, so Colbert promoted him for the job.

The Canal du Midi cut across Languedoc just north of the Pyrenees, joining the Atlantic Ocean through the Garonne River at Toulouse to the Mediterranean Sea at the port of Sète. Built from 1662–1684, it was a huge enterprise, stretching more than 168 kilometers and requiring a hundred locks as well as a vast array of bridges, aqueducts, dams, water intakes, drains, and ports. It had to cross rivers, weave through mountains, and tap the waters of high mountain sources to float ships across southwestern France. (Bergasse, 1982–1985; Conseil d'Architecture 1992; Maistre, 1968; Rolt, 1973).

Riquet seemed an unlikely person to supervise such a vast undertaking. He was the *commissaire generale* of the salt tax for Languedoc and Rousillon, not an engineer, and had little experience of infrastructural contracts with the crown. (Rolt, 1973: 69) But he had supplied the army in Roussillon with meat and successfully met his contractual obligations to the treasury for the salt tax. Locally, he was also well connected to the Catholic clergy. His patron was the incoming archbishop of Toulouse, d'Anglure de Bourlement, a man with whom Colbert wanted to strengthen his ties. (Mukerji, 2008).

This huge enterprise was successfully completed, but Riquet nonetheless ended up despised by Colbert and alienated from the king. He became a bad client as he became a good steward of French land, failing to recognize his debt and duty to the king and flaunting his own newfound abilities.

Because he wrote Colbert frequently, explaining his feelings and actions, we can follow his psychological transformation in detail as Riquet began to alienate himself from the minister and monarch. He thrilled at his intellectual growth as his technical knowledge expanded, gaining an inappropriate sense of his personal importance both to the enterprise and to the administration. Riquet confided in Colbert, recounting his dreams of more improvements he wanted to make in Languedoc, too. Although he argued that he wanted to do these things to serve Louis XIV, he never understood that service to the monarch was first and foremost obedience to his will (Mukerji, 2009: ch. 7).

Because Riquet's letters reveal so clearly the seductions of material efficacy that lured him away from his patrimonial duties to personal pursuit of political territoriality, they help reveal the underlying social psychological forces that may have swayed Clerville and Vauban, more seasoned engineers and political actors, to alienate themselves from the king, too. All three ended up focusing on technical problem-solving more than social obedience. Riquet was an extreme case, so naïve that he did not censor himself when he started talking about the province as his to improve – thinking like a king – a form of hubris that was untenable politically. The entrepreneur even routinely disobeyed Colbert and by extension the monarch, attributing his technical successes to God and relying on his own decisions (Mukerji, 2009: ch. 7).

Riquet started the enterprise playing patrimonial politics, when he sought out the support of d'Anglure de Bourlement. He invited the then-future archbishop to his estate at Bonrepos to show him a model of the canal with a miniature water supply, weirs, locks, and other technical elements. He also took the cleric to the part of Languedoc where he thought he could cut the canal. Riquet did not simply argue for the feasibility for the project, but sought patrimonial allies for it (Rolt, 1973: 37–38). Riquet then wrote to Colbert, saying:

> It was a while ago that [the archbishop] did me the honor to come here [to my estate] … and to those places near Castres where he could see the possibilities [for the canal]. With the company of the bishop of Saint Papoul and other people of standing, [we] did this, and he saw things the way I had explained them to him … If you take the trouble to read my relation of this visit, you will agree that it is true that the canal is feasible, that it is mainly difficult

> because it would be expensive, but given the good that would result from it, the expenses should be of minor consideration.
>
> (Rolt, 1973: 40)

But while Riquet used his networks to get the project to the attention of Colbert, he also used the logic of stewardship politics to assert the technical feasibility of the project. Writers on stewardship politics, such as Oliver de Serres, argued that the state could be treated as the great estate, and made more abundant and peaceful with territorial improvement. Letting his estate serve as a microcosm for the macrocosm of the state, Riquet presented the canal as an enterprise that would work for stewardship of "the great estate" of France. (compare to Mukerji, 1997)

The dual strategy of patrimonial networking and stewardship demonstration was persuasive. The archbishop threw his substantial weight behind the construction of the Canal du Midi, and Colbert followed suit (Rolt, 1973: 38). Still, Colbert did not entirely trust Riquet's engineering judgment. So, he asked the Chevalier de Clerville to verify the plan with a commission of high-born gentlemen and technical experts, who could assess its political and technical feasibility and develop the specifications for the project. (Malavialle, 1891: 286–289; Adgé, 1985: 174)

Building the Canal du Midi turned out to be more difficult than anticipated because it was in fact technically beyond the formal engineering knowledge of the period. In the first few years of the project, one technical disaster followed the other as the channel and locks both experienced dramatic failures near Toulouse. The entrepreneur became more and more difficult for Colbert to deal with as the former acquired massive debts, meanwhile lying to the minister about the technical problems. Colbert was sure Riquet was also siphoning off funds, which he was not, but the bonds of trust needed for patrimonial politics were strained. Riquet focused more on getting the technical work done well, and Colbert focused more on improving his standing at court, both pursuing opposite forms of politics and moving farther away from each other. By1670, the canal was beginning to be finished in some places and soon put to use, but the ties between Colbert and Riquet remained strained and were never repaired. (Mukerji, 2009, ch. 4)

The break between Colbert and Riquet is usually portrayed either as a conflict of personalities, or as a product of differing views of how to build the canal. (Murat, 1984a) But on closer inspection, it illustrates Riquet's growing independence from patrimonial networks, and Colbert's reaction to his disobedience. Riquet began the canal project as a subservient and docile client, but ended up imagining himself to be more the monarch's ally and God's agent than Colbert's client.

Riquet had become infatuated by his newfound engineering capacities, and the power of transforming the regional infrastructure. More than Colbert, he could see the significance of what he was doing for local life, and this made him feel important. By mixing more with engineers, architects, masons, and laborers, Riquet also began to think more about the technical aspects of the canal. He had ideas about changing the walls of the channels to make them more stable, how to design locks doors, where to route the channel toward the sea, and how to design a new port on the Mediterranean – subjects he had never entertained before. Like Menocchio in *Cheese and the Worms* (Ginzburg, 1980), he found himself surprised by and enchanted with the workings of his own mind.

> I am beginning to realize that I am the one who knows more than others … I am at the moment a kind of experimenter and [designing] new implements is easy beyond my dreams, so that [for the lock doors] a single man without the aide of any mechanical device can open and shut them. A machine [for such work] is simple and ordinary. These [doors] are the best … Even more, I provided for myself, among these implements, novelties that with their aid can fill and empty the locks with incredible speed.
>
> (Riquet à Colbert, March 27, 1670, ACM 23-16)

Riquet felt blessed by God, and able to serve the king because he had been chosen to do so. He also thought of himself as a martyr, too, because he was losing his family fortune building the canal. Riquet tried to explain all this to Colbert in a letter written on the March 27, 1670.

> God has inspired me with thoughts that I call sacred, since with them my works will be advanced, and I will not lose [my way]: it is in truth, Sir, a philosopher's stone which gives to all and misses no one … from dreams, I've found such miraculous expedients for the advancement of the canal. My apprenticeship has cost me dearly, and my ruin will follow if one does not make available my funds.
>
> (Riquet à Colbert, March 27, 1670, ACM 23-16)

Talk of his own divine inspiration was no way to address a patron whose authority was founded on the king's divine right. The hubris of presenting himself as God's agent in Languedoc made the tax farmer seem dangerous to Colbert. The minister had no doubt that Riquet had advanced the project and was devoted to making it work, but he felt that the entrepreneur now saw himself as too important. Riquet did not understand that it was the king's generosity and powers that had allowed him to build the Canal du Midi, and instead thought of the enterprise as his personal accomplishment.

The depth of Colbert's impatience became clear in 1669. The canal project had been divided into two parts. The first section was to be dug from the Garonne to the Aude River. In Riquet's original proposal, the Canal du Midi was to connect the two waterways, but the Aude was not appropriate for shipping. This meant that another section of canal had to be built to the Mediterranean. To his surprise, Riquet's proposal for this "second enterprise" was not accepted immediately by Colbert. The minister insisted that Clerville draw up the plan and the *intendant* put it up to bid. It was not clear whether the minister really expected that a different entrepreneur could or would complete the Canal du Midi (Maistre, 1968: 69–71), but he made it clear to Riquet that the tax farmer was not unquestionably entitled to the new contract. Riquet had become a difficult man and a political burden to Colbert, and the minister, in all likelihood, did indeed wish to end his patronage.

Surprisingly, there were some other bidders for the second enterprise. Jean Farrand of Montpellier offered to do it for 6,232,000 livres over eight years. Louis Ponthier proposed a bit less, 6,182,000 livres. Riquet came in with the lowest bid of 5,832,000 livres, but excluded from his bid some parts of the plan. Begrudgingly, Colbert approved the new contract, and the Arrest was posted in June of 1669 (Archives du Canal du Midi (ACM) 07-12; Maistre, 1968: 69–72).

Still, when Riquet was finally given the contract for the second enterprise, Colbert sent a new engineer to Languedoc, the sieur de la Feuille, to supervise the work, keep the books, and correspond with the minister about the canal's progress (Murat, 1984a: 105–122). The minister wanted a more reliable client in Languedoc to supervise work on the Canal du Midi:

> I have sent to Languedoc the Sieur de la Feuille who will bring you this letter to [authorize him to] be incessantly at your work[sites], to take care with you for their conduct, and to make sure that all the estimates and specifications of the chevalier de Clerville and the [innovations] that you have made with him would be well executed, so once more I can have complete faith in you about the success of this great enterprise. It will be always good and advantageous for you to have someone from the side of the king on the worksites to be an ocular witness of all you do and to take into account the warmth and zeal with which you execute this great enterprise. In this way, the king will be more precisely informed, and I can assure you that this will augment his satisfaction which his majesty has already of all you have done until now. Give [La Feuille] your complete confidence and let him know all you do as you would to myself, so that his efforts and presence might be useful.
>
> (Colbert to Riquet, June 9, 1669, ACM 22-18)

For Riquet, this was a terrible slap in the face. His patron had abandoned him, and his claims about his personal contributions to the canal had been rejected. He wrote in 1671:

> As I am the inventor of this canal now being constructed in Languedoc and the one who studied it the most, I am beginning to realize that I am also the one who knows it better than anybody else. My venture is the dearest of my children; I see the glory, your satisfaction, and not the profit. I want to leave honours to my children, and I do not pretend to leave them any big amount of money.
>
> (Riquet quoted in Rolt, 1973: 83–84)

To Riquet, the canal was his legacy to give to his children, not a feat of the regime that anyone could build. Colbert rarely wrote detailed letters to Riquet again or asked for his news. When the minister wanted information about the canal or to express his or the king's views on the project, he corresponded mainly with the sieur de la Feuille.

Riquet was at first bereft. Naïvely, the taxman had assumed that Colbert would be enthusiastic about his new ideas, and happy to use the amazing capabilities he had been granted by God. When he realized that this was not true, Riquet started to act more independently, assuring himself that if he improved the land in Languedoc, he would be serving both God and the king. He changed the route of the canal north in spite of Clerville's opposition. He tunneled through a mountain even though Colbert tried to stop him. He was going to make the project work no matter what anyone said. God was his guide and patron now.

Colbert was horrified by Riquet's independence and lack of respect, and wrote to the *intendant* of Languedoc, d'Aguesseau, in 1677:

> You have penetrated more deeply [into] the conduct of M. Riquet and the source of his views on the matter of the vast range which he has given his imagination. Although it might be best to treat him as ill, we must, nevertheless, apply ourselves with care in order that the course and strength of his imaginings does not bring on us a final and grievous end of all his works … This man does as great liars do who, after telling a story three or four times, persuade themselves it is true … It has been said to him so many times, even in my own presence, that he is the inventor of this great work that in the end he has believed he is in fact the absolute author. And, on the greatness of the work he has founded [the idea of] the grandeur of the service he renders to the state and the greatness of his fortune. It is for this that he has made his son a Master of Requests, and which has given to his spirit, regarding the establishment of his children, a vast career and an inflation which hasn't any proportion or relationship with what he is or with what he has done.
>
> (Colbert quoted in Rolt, 1973: 9)

Riquet was seen as dangerous and delusional because he did not follow the rules of patron–client relations, taking stewardship politics as more important than obedience to his superiors. His independence was based on his sure sense that he could engineer a canal in Languedoc that others could not, and that the waterway would empower France by improving the countryside. His recognition and championing of territorial politics was disruptive to the patronage system, so he was ejected from the social network he had yearned to enter at the beginning of the project. He had become a technocrat for a government that still was dominated by patrimonial politics.

Sébastian Le Prestre de Vauban

It would be easy to dismiss Riquet's actions as those of a naïve dreamer from the provinces, but the most respected French engineer of the seventeenth century, Sébastian Le Prestre de Vauban, also gave free range to his imagination and fell from grace. He had been hailed for dreaming of France as a territory expanded through war into a rectangle, and protected by a border of fortresses. He was even forgiven for treason in his youth. But when he had the audacity to propose a tax reform – one that even suggested taxes on the nobility – and argued it was a rational way to ensure the wellbeing of the kingdom and its people, he was lost. He must have seemed to the king and Colbert as delusional just like Riquet. The language he used to advocate his "dîme royale" indicated instead his vision of stewardship. More than Clerville and Riquet, Vauban thought about the wellbeing of the kingdom (Vauban, 1992).

Vauban did not start that way. He began his career as a soldier for and client of the Prince de Condé during the Fronde. He went into exile after the frondeurs had lost power, but returned, and the Cardinal Mazarin, who was minister during Louis XIV's minority, forgave Vauban to take advantage of his military skill. The engineer switched his political allegiance, and began to serve in the French army (Lynn, 1997: 15–17; Blanchard, 1996: 75–85).

Vauban was valued early in his career for his skills in siege warfare. He was interested in the design of battlements to protect fortresses, and he also knew how to tunnel toward citadels, and through defensive walls to attack a city under siege. He worked under the Chevalier de Clerville in the siege of Sainte-Menehould, and was put in charge of repairing the fortress after it had been successfully taken by France. He continued to conduct many sieges – at Stenay, Clermont, Landrecy, Condé, Saint-Guillain and Valenciennes. He was wounded at Stenay, and almost fatally again later at the siege of Montmédy. His most celebrated siege was of Maëstricht, in 1673 (Langins, 2004: ch. 2). He had become a master of techniques of attack, and was celebrated just as Clerville fell from the king's grace.

Vauban worked in a tradition of formal military engineering. Men such as Jean Errard de Bar-le-Duc, a military engineer for Henri IV, had argued that engineers needed to learn geometry because formal methods were the most efficient means for communicating plans and strategies. They were equally vital to technical innovation, scheduling, and good masonry – the responsibilities of his job (Langins, 2004: 23–35, esp. 34–35). Vauban's success as an engineer was based on his mastery and innovative uses of this art.

The formal techniques used in sixteenth-century France were imported from Italy during the wars of religion. Italian military engineers showed the French how to design star-shaped bastions, partly derived from Vitruvius (1960), to withstand sieges using cannon fire (Rosenau, 1959; Morris, 1979). Brought to France by the king as *ingenieurs du roy*, the Italians in turn hired Frenchmen to build the new structures, teaching fortress engineering techniques and siege strategies to the French military (Blanchard, 1979: 42–43, 47–49, 53–54).

Vauban acquired his knowledge of engineering both from experience and reading. He studied the classics, learned the literature on Italian fortress design, and was trained in mathematics. He came to insist that soldiers in his engineering corps do the same. As the head military engineer of the French army, he started testing soldiers for their mathematical abilities before allowing them to enter his service (Langins, 2004: 81). He even asked Joseph Sauveur, a mathematician and *membre associé* of the Académy des Sciences, to help him examine candidates for the engineering corps. Military engineering under Vauban became not only a military role, but also an area of study (Langins, 2004: 81; Vauban, 1968: 89–95; Duffy, 1985: 23–42; d'Aiglun, 1972: 379–380).

Vauban was most famous for his proposal to build a system of fortresses along the border of the kingdom to make France a *pré carré*, a rectangular and defended territory that symbolized its perfection in its form. He felt that France was naturally regular, and had borders that were mainly defined by geographical features like the Alps, the Pyrenees, the Atlantic, and the Mediterranean. His plan was to complete the figure that had been set out on the earth. By razing internal citadels and building border defenses to house the king's army, he could make France a more perfect and defensible kingdom (Blanchard, 1996: 197–201; Pujo, 1991: 99–109).

Vauban, like Clerville and Riquet, also worked on the Canal du Midi. He was asked to inspect and perfect the waterway after Riquet and Clerville had died. Although he had been previously dismissive of the project because of his competition with Clerville, now he saw it as a marvel that needed additional work. Even though he was much more of an intellectual than Riquet and Clerville, he too was seduced by the power of moving earth and water with stone and timber. The benefits of it were palpable, and he thought long and hard about improving French life through these efforts (Blanchard, Adgé and Bergasse, 1984: 186–218); Blanchard, 1996: 133–139, 155, 162, 265–267; Clément, 1979: xcix–c).

Given Vauban's career in battle and interests as a military engineer, it may seem odd that toward the end of his life he would have proposed a new tax system. But taxes were a form of material politics. They were ways of extracting the natural wealth of the land, and putting it into the treasury. He hoped to rationalize the tax system, and correct the inequities that made taxes such a burden on ordinary people. He wrote:

> The itinerant life that I have lived over more than forty years has given me the opportunity to see many times and in many fashion the bulk of the provinces of this realm … I have often had occasion to give free reign to my thoughts and to notice the good and bad [rich and poor] lands … It is certain that the poor are pushed to excess, and that, if this is not remedied, the people will fall into an extremity from which they will never recover, the great roads of the country and the streets of towns and villages becoming full of beggars chased from their homes by hunger and lack of clothing. According to all the research that I've been able to do over many years, I have noticed that close to a tenth of the people [of France] are reduced to begging and beg for a living; of the other nine parts, there are five that are no in a position to give alms to them because they are themselves impoverished, not far from this unhappy condition [themselves]; of the four other parts that rest, three are plagued with debt and legal problems; and in the tenth one finds all the nobles of the sword, the robe, ecclesiastics and laity, all the high nobility, the most distinguished noble families and the men in charge of the military and civil authorities, the wealthy merchants, well-off bourgeoises [One] cannot count [among them] more than one hundred thousand families, and I think I am not lying when I say

> that there are not among them more than ten thousand, lowborn or noble, that one could say were at ease [financially]; and leaving out the business men and their allies or followers covert and overt that the king sustains with his favors, some merchants, etc. … I am sure that the rest would be a small number.
>
> (Vauban, 1968: 58–59)

Vauban's observations were extraordinary for their simplicity, social acumen, rational form, and tenderness toward French men and women. They were the outcome of careful observation and calculation, precisely the attributes that had made Vauban so useful to the army. The program seemed idealistic, but for Vauban, the dîme royale was no more utopian a dream than his plan to make France into a *pré carré* (an idealized battlefield) with his fortresses. The latter had been embraced for all its idealism. Vauban may have expected something similar for his tax proposal.

Vauban approached the king carefully, showing his awareness of the rules of patronage politics. He did not tell his patron how to organize his tax system, but wrote a "memoir" about his observations (Vauban, 1968: 75, 143). He said:

> According to this system, [a tax of ten percent, or *dîme royale*] should be imposed in all the revenue districts of the kingdom, no matter what kind they are [or their historical patterns of taxation] so that none would be exempt, like a mobile ground rent [*une rente foncière mobile*], required by the state, which will be the biggest, more certain and most noble that has ever been, since it will be paid in preference to all others, and that the funds will be inalienable and inalterable … One must admit that if it would come into being, nothing would be more grand or larger; but one must at the same time take care not to exclude from imposing it on the most high.
>
> (Vauban, 1968: 66, 68)

Thinking more mathematically than politically, Vauban treated all the people of France as the same – equally indebted to the king and beneficiaries of the state. But as Machiavelli made clear and Louis XIV understood well, they were not. The exemption from taxes for nobles was an important part of what kept the nobility docile and great families at the top of the social order. The king's patrimonial powers depended on the tax system that Vauban proposed to change.

Vauban was a smart and educated man who usually was no fool about politics, but failing to see the tax system as a technique for the reproduction of social rank, he made himself seem crazy. As a good steward of the kingdom, he wanted to gain revenues without spreading misery, and he did not recognize how this might compromise the king's authority. (Vauban, 1968: 61, 157–158, 250–251). He stated, "I am a Frenchman very attached to my country and very aware of the graces and bounties which the king in his good will has bestowed on me for a long time" (Vauban, 1968: 57).

Vauban was a mareschal of France when he fell from the king's favor. He had won many wars for his patron, and saw himself as a good servant who had given good service. He did not, like Riquet, create enemies with his imaginings by considering himself in direct connection with God. He was trained to look clearly and rationally at the material conditions around him, and to address difficult circumstances without flinching. He was a better soldier because he would tell the truth about what he saw, and act on reliable information in a rational way. He proposed a tax system that he thought would be reliable, too, and realistic given the condition of the French people. His abilities were honed against the world in its material fullness, not the limited social relations at court. But Vauban offered his patron a tax system that would ensure Louis XIV's political demise by alienating the nobility. The aging soldier, no longer a good servant of his monarch, was not allowed to talk to the king again (Rebelliau, 1962: 272–274; Pujo, 1991: 300)

The unintended state

The three men described in this chapter served Louis XIV and his administration well, realizing many of the monarch's political desires, but in the end suffered rejection by the king and Colbert for exercising the same kind of skills that had made them useful. They mastered the logics of stewardship politics, and advanced the powers of the administration vis-à-vis the nobility through material politics. They helped to redesign the landscape to define France as a territory, not just a kingdom by name but a material formation that revealed publicly the abilities of French people to improve the earth in the name of the monarch.

Clerville, Riquet, and Vauban were very different men who all promoted territorial stewardship as a political strategy but carried out their duties in distinctive ways. They had varying engineering abilities, different analytical styles, and diverse levels of desire and ability to engage in court politics. Still, their political falls were similar. They were publicly disgraced not because of their personal weaknesses or individual mistakes, but because they took stewardship of the kingdom too seriously. Louis XIV did not attack them simply because of his tyrannical nature. They were victims of a clash of political logics. They treated the material management of the kingdom as more important than obedience to their betters, and the king used his will to show they were wrong.

In Colbert's struggle to make the administration more powerful, their skills were useful, but for the king, their political logic was dangerous, taking material management of the land and its people as the measure and goal of government – not the king's will. In spite of their differences, each of these men was transformed by territorial politics, becoming a new kind of political agent who imagined the kingdom as his responsibility. They became civil servants serving a state more than clients serving a king. As they veered too far from their patrimonial duties, the danger of their political trajectory became more palpable. The king reacted willfully, trying to forestall the development of what they and their territorial practices had started to produce: a powerful, modern state governed by experts.

This story of state formation in seventeenth-century France provides a useful case for considering the character and workings of material power. It demonstrates the surprising and threatening powers that territorial engineering posed in the period. Land control through infrastructural improvement turned out to be a very effective means for renegotiating social relations, and one that startled those who recognized its potential.

It is important to note that the engineering that transformed French politics was not designed primarily for economic purposes, although the building of ports, canals, roads, and bridges had obvious economic effects. Even the Canal du Midi was not meant to be a piece of economic infrastructure, although it was certainly expected to facilitate trade. Its main strategic purpose was to take French warships between the two seas, avoiding Gibralter, and bring a state presence to the province of Languedoc that was famous for its dissidents. The waterway avoided towns rather than tried to connect them, a sure sign that trade was not its purpose (and perhaps also an indication that local hostility to the project could be inflamed if the canal came too near). Even though he was finance minister and promoting industry in France, Colbert at first protested when Riquet asked to change the route to reach Castelnaudary and build an inland port for that town. He only consented because the city fathers promised to pay for it, and Riquet needed money for the project.

The story of French infrastructural work also suggests that the material transformation did not gain its value primarily from its symbolic significance. Although engineering was used to help promote France as a new Rome, demonstrate stewardship by the king, and turn the countryside into Vauban's *pré carré*, its political power lay more in land control than its symbols. Territorial engineering was used to make the land of France serve the king more than the nobility. Land control in itself was a potent political weapon, and yielded powers that were hard to articulate but visible on the ground.

The new infrastructure not only transferred land from noble landholders to the king, but also changed daily life in areas of France far from court, and made manifest the interests and will of the king in concrete terms. The new infrastructure also came under government regulation, multiplying the supervisory powers of the administration. Wherever the hands of the state went to change the environment, the eyes of the administration followed. The administration became more modern as a result in the sense that its powers were not simply derived from the will of the king, the tradition of monarchical singularity, and divine right, but also embedded in impersonal forms – the engineered landscape and natural knowledge. The state became a place not only ruled by the king, but also governed by forestry practices, port regulations, communication systems, post roads, botanical gardens for medicines, military installations, arsenals, and ship-building facilities. Surveyors and engineers as well as laborers and artisans who knew how to work the land gained a political importance that had previously not existed.

The novelty of modern administrative power lay in material governance for political effect. As Clerville, Riquet, and Vauban exercised stewardship over the kingdom using engineering and the wellbeing of the land and its people as measures of their worth, they became both important to the state and dangerous to the political tradition of monarchical rule. They assumed that policies that "worked" on the ground were also good. Deriving administrative powers from material expertise and not relying on personal will alone, they turned a political corner, creating a new, impersonal form of power: a modern territorial state.

References

Adgé, Michel (1985) 'Chronologie des Principaux Évènements de la Construction du Canal, 1662–94', in *Le Canal du Midi*, ed. Jean-Denis Bergasse, Cessenon: J.-D. Bergasse, vol. 4: 173–192.

Baumgartner, Frederic (1995) *France in the Sixteenth Century*, New York: St. Martin's Press.

Beik, William (1985) *Absolutism and Society in Seventeenth-century France: State Power and Provincial Aristocracy in Languedoc*, Cambridge: Cambridge University Press.

Bergasse, Jean-Denis (ed.) (1982–85) *Le Canal du Midi*, vols 1–4, Cessenon: J.-D. Bergasse.

Blanchard, Anne (1979) *Les Ingénieurs du Roy de Louis XIV à Louis XVI*, Montpellier: Université Paul-Valéry.

—— (1996) *Vauban*, Paris: Fayard.

Blanchard, Anne, Michel Adgé and Jean-Denis Bergasse (1984) 'Les Ingénieurs du Roy', in *Le Canal du Midi*, vol. 3, ed. Jean-Denis Bergasse, Cessenon: J.-D. Bergasse, 181–194.

Bowker, Geoffrey and Susan Leigh Star (1999) *Sorting Things Out*, Cambridge, MA: MIT Press.

Callon, Michel and Bruno Latour (1992) 'Don't throw the baby out with the Bath School!', in Andrew Pickering, ed. *Science as Practice and Culture*, Chicago: University of Chicago Press, 343–368.

Clément, Pierre (1979) *Lettres, Instructions et Mémoires de Colbert, vol. 5*, Liechtenstein: Klaus Reprints.

Conseil d'Architecture, d'Urbanisme et de l'Environment de la Haute-Garonne (1992) *Canal royal de Languedoc: le partage des eaux*, Caue: Loubatières.

d'Aiglun, Albert de Rochas (1972) *Vauban, sa famille et ses écrits, ses oisivetés et sa correspondance: analyse et extraits*, Geneva: Slatkin Reprints.

Duffy, Christopher (1985) *Siege Warfare: The Fortress in the Early Modern World, 1494–1660*, London: Routledge and Kegan Paul.

Elias, Norbert (1998) *The Court Society*, New York: Pantheon.

Ginzburg, Carol (1980) *The Cheese and Worms*, trans. J. & A. Tedeschi, Baltimore: Johns Hopkins University Press.

Holt, Mack P. (2005) *The French Wars of Religion, 1562–1629*, Cambridge and New York: Cambridge University Press.

Kettering, Sharon (1986) *Patrons, Brokers and Clients in Seventeenth-Century France*, New York and Oxford: Oxford University Press.

Langins, Janis (2004) *Conserving the Enlightenment: French Military Engineering from Vauban to the Revolution*, Cambridge, MA: MIT Press.

Latour, Bruno (1999) *Pandora's Hope: On the Reality of Science Studies*, Cambridge, MA: Harvard University Press.

Lynn, J. A. (1997) *Giant of the grand siècle: the French army, 1610–1715*, Cambridge: Cambridge University Press.

Machiavelli, Niccolo (1966) *The Prince,* ed. and trans. D. Donno, NY: Bantam Dell.

Maistre, André (1968) *Le Canal des Deux-Mers: Canal Royal du Languedoc, 1666–1810*, Toulouse: E. Privat.

Malavialle, L. (1891–92) 'Une Excursion dans la Montagne Noire', *Société Languedocienne de Géographie Bulletin*, vols 4, 5, 7, 8, 9, 14, 15.

Mettam, Roger (1988) *Power and Faction in Louis XIV's France*, London: Basil Blackwell.

Meyer, Jean (1985) 'Louis XIV et Colbert: les relations entre un roi et un ministre au XVIIe Siècle', in *Colloque pour le tricentenaire de la mort de Colbert, sous la direction de Roland Mousnier, Un nouveau Colbert*, ed. Jean Favier and Roland Mousnier, Paris: Éditions Sedes, 71–84.

Morris, A. E. J. (1979) *History of Urban Form: Before the Industrial Revolution,* London: George Godwin Ltd.

Mousnier, Roland (1979) *The Institutions of France under the Absolute Monarchy 1598–1789: Society and the State*, trans. Brian Pearce, Chicago: University of Chicago Press.

Mukerji, Chandra (1997) *Territorial Ambitions and the Gardens of Versailles*, Cambridge: Cambridge University Press.

—— (2007) 'The Great Forest Survey of 1669–71', *Social Studies of Science*, 37 (2), 227–253.

—— (2008) 'French *Mesnagment* Politics and the Canal du Midi: Labor and Oeconomy in 17th-C France', in Lissa Roberts, Simon Schaffer and Peter Dear *The Mindful Hand: Inquiry and Invention from the Late Renaissance to Industrialization*, Amsterdam and Chicago: Edita Press and University of Chicago, 169–188.

—— (2009) *Impossible Engineering: Technology and Territoriality on the Canal du Midi,* Princeton: Princeton University Press.

Murat, Inès (1984a) 'Les rapports de Colbert et de Riquet: Méfiance pour un homme ou pour un système?' in *Le Canal du Midi*, vol. 3, ed. Jean-Denis Bergasse. Cessenon: J.-D. Bergasse, 105–122.

—— (1984b) *Colbert*, trans. Robert Cook and Jeannie Van Asselt, Charlottesville: University Press of Virginia.

Pujo, Bernard (1991) *Vauban*, Paris: Albin Michel.

Ranum, Orest (1979) *Paris in the Age of Absolutism: An Essay*, Bloomington: Indiana University Press.

Rebelliau, Alfred (1962) *Vauban*, Paris: Fayard.

Rolt, L. T. C. (1973) *From Sea to Sea: The Canal du Midi*, London: Allen Lance.

Rosenau, Helen (1959) *The Ideal City: Its Architectural Evolution*, Boston: Routledge and Kegan Paul.

Saint-Simon, Louis de (1990) *The Age of Magnificence*, ed.Ted Morgan, New York: Paragon.

Vauban, Sébastien Le Prestre de (1968) *A Manual of Siegecraft and Fortification,* trans. George A. Rothrock, Ann Arbor: University of Michigan Press.

—— (1992) *La dîme royale*, ed. Le Roy Ladurie, Paris: Imprimerie Nationale.

Vérin, Hélen (1993) *La Gloire des Ingéneurs: L'intelligence techniques du XVIe au XVIIIe siècle*, Paris: Albin Michel.

Vitruvius (1960) *The Ten Books on Architecture*, trans. M.H. Morgan, New York: Dover.

5 Filing the Raj

Political technologies of the Imperial British state*

Patrick Joyce

> The security and quality of government lies in the (government of the) whole of India being carried on in writing, so that it will be held to account in the United Kingdom. It is not to be governed by public opinion, which neither knows nor cares.
>
> John Stuart Mill

When the state is written about it still tends to be in the familiar terms of its constitutional and administrative manifestations, its social and economic role (welfare, educational and economic policy for instance), or in terms of ideas or experiences of the state. The state is in such understandings decidedly an "it". Much the same applies as regards the chief conceptual schools of understanding the state. This is so whether these be the liberal and pluralist ones which envisage the state as the autonomous and neutral regulator of society and of its rights and obligations, or Marxist and 'elite'-based notions which see the state as the projection or instrument of interests and classes.[1]

Recent historical work that has engaged with the nature of materiality has called this conception of the state in question. This work has had a number of influences, which are very much operative in this collection, in particular science studies, the history of science and technology, and the field of governmentality studies. The consequence of this conjunction of influences is that the relationship between scientific and technological forms of knowledge and practice, and forms of power, has become an increasingly close one in the recent literature (for two excellent recent historical examples of the conjunction of an interest in science, material power and the political, see Otter, 2008, and Vernon, 2006). This bears a great deal on the question of material power and the state. These recent approaches, which emphasise dispersal and networks alongside the local and 'micro', tend to call in question the idea of the state as a stable, unified entity. Logically, given their conceptions of power, post-Foucauldian positions in particular have served to problematise traditional accounts of the state by questioning the status of all unified subjects, individual and collective, the latter for example class or the state. This is evident for instance in the work of Timothy Mitchell on what he calls the 'state effect' (Mitchell, 2002).

I

In this chapter I want to draw on a book I am currently working on, with the title *The Soul of Leviathan: Political Technologies of the Imperial British State.* In the book I argue that from around the middle of the nineteenth century in Britain the domain of the 'technical' attained a new and critical mass, the state itself in turn becoming increasingly 'technical', both as the cause and effect of these changes. At this time, the things of the state began to form themselves into a state of things. By the term technical I denote the received sense of science and technology, obviously in the ascendant at the time, the technological of the railway and factory for example. However, I also employ the term in a wider sense, that of the proliferation of techniques and technologies of power of all sorts, and involving the emergence of experts and expertise in many fields, themselves increasingly linked into the state. For example, it is around this time that in Britain we see the final separation of administration and politics, so that in the form of a new 'professional' civil service administration itself becomes 'technical', a matter of all sorts of new techniques and technologies operating not only upon the governed but upon the bureaucratic self (on the formation of the bureaucratic self understood in the context of material powers see Becker and Clark, 2005, and for some previous work in this field, see Joyce, 2003: ch. 3).

However, the state has always been 'technical', and the change in the nineteenth century was one of degree rather than of kind. And, when one looks more closely at the relationship between the state and the material world at the time, the sort of 'technical' that often mattered most was low-tech rather than high-tech, and slow paced and superficially undramatic in its patterns of change, contrary to so many present-orientated accounts (in which for example the telegraph and the telephone play an exaggeratedly large role). Characteristically, and in fact very similar to the contemporaneous 'industrial revolution' itself, change was very often a matter of the hand and the body, of skill and strength, rather than science and technology in more sophisticated forms. To be more precise, again like contemporary industrial changes, which have been characterised by the term 'combined and uneven development', old and new forms of the technical might be combined, the temporal and spatial differences between the two being highly complex (see the seminal Samuel, 1977, and for an overview Joyce, 1991). Indeed, the very designation 'old' and 'new' needs caution: the seemingly 'old', here in the form of producing and managing paperwork through the time-honoured form of the human hand and its extension in the form of the pen, turns out on closer inspection to be characterised by continual innovation and a very high level of micro-technical change. At the very zenith of the British Imperial state, in which the governance of India was the central element, hand technology in the form of writing continued to be crucial, just as it had always been for the state (Clanchy, 1992).

Partly in line with some of the theoretical and methodological emphases evident in this collection, a good deal of the historical literature on empire and colonialism has come to be interested in networks, flows, dispersal and connections, so that the contingency of empire is highly marked in many accounts. However, the central questions of how flows and disposals are coordinated, and connections are made and stabilised over space and time, still remain somewhat opaque, so that the technics of stabilisation do not seem to have received as much attention as the parallel and of course inseparable emphasis on contingency. It is important therefore in this sense to de-provincialise Europe after its recent provincialisation (Chakrabarty, 2007). It is also important to provide paper- and bureaucratic system-driven accounts of Empire alongside information-driven ones for if the empire was only as good as the information it had, the systems by which it assembled and processed this information undergirded the nature and quality of the information itself (for a very influential information-driven account see Bayly, 1996). The systems themselves, their material forms, were anything but neutral tools employed by a directing governmental intelligence. They had their own part to play, their own agency, indeed their own autonomous role. The recent work of Miles Ogborn on the British East India Company, *Indian Ink*, enables us to begin thinking along these new lines:

> The shape and politics of the growing and changing British empire from the seventeenth century onwards is not adequately captured by simple models based upon the assumed centrality of Britain within a hierarchical set of relationships to discrete overseas colonies, territories, and trading zones. Instead, alternative models of 'networks' or 'webs' seek to explore a different geography that allows a range of competing and contradictory relationships to come into view. These alternatives emphasise the vulnerability of empire as well as its dynamism … Investigations of this complex whole refuse, both as impossible and undesirable, calls to provide totalising accounts of this reconceived British empire, or the global geography of which it was a part. Instead the focus is on analysing and tracking particular sites, connections, and movements. As Kathleen Wilson puts it, 'In one sense, empire as a unit was a phantasm of the metropole: all empire is local.'
>
> (Ogborn, 2007)

However, by the same token it could be said that all empire is central, the important thing in fact being, as Miles Ogborn refers to the matter, to find ways to 'treat metropole and colony in a single analytic field.' (Ogborn, 2007). The analytic fields that I point to, in terms of the major theoretical influences at work in this volume, do in fact provide very important elements of this field. In order to consider these influences at work in empirical and historical terms, in the rest of this chapter I shall draw upon the example of the India Office itself, the government department set up in 1858 which replaced the governance of the commercial East India Company. As such, the India Office represented a new phase of colonial intervention in the form of direct political government from London.

Paper and writing were especially important in the government of India, given that this involved governance at a distance, indeed multiple distances, so that the India Office in London ostensibly governed all of 'India', from the central parts of the imperial administration – first in Calcutta and then in Delhi – to the individual political units that made up the complex political formation that was India (Presidencies, Provinces, and so on). This complexity marked the whole edifice of British rule, down to the level of the individual District Commissioner, indeed the village itself as a political structure. Given the complexity and the distance of the British governance of India, the supposed head office in London often had relatively little if anything to do with the actual governance of India on the ground (on the political and administrative structure of India, Moir, 1988; Kaminsky, 1986; Potter, 1986).[2] The (white, British) execution of power in India depended not only upon the various bureaucratic organs of the Government of India, and the shock troops of the incongruously minute number of officers in the Indian Civil Service itself, but upon a myriad of local intermediaries and arrangements, as well as a vast numbers of Indian civil servants in the lower ranks (Joyce, 2003: ch. 6). How, then, did empire cohere, in the face of these profound centripetal tendencies? In short, how was the imperial show kept on the road in the first place?

Almost as great a question as this was how what was known at the time in India as the 'monster of correspondence' was to be controlled, a monster much less apparent at home, but a threat there too. In India there was always more of a premium on writing than in Britain. This was for a variety of reasons, including the multiple levels and institutions of governmental organisation in India, the distances involved – making personal communication difficult – and the calibre and status (non-gazetted) of lower level recruits in India,[3] which Lord Curzon, then Viceroy of India, complained of in 1898 as in comparison with their British equivalents not being part of the practical knowledge created by daily interaction in a coherent department with a spirit and identity of its own. As a consequence these lower bureaucrats were always inclined to put things in writing, becoming addicted to writing at length, in part necessarily so given the conditions, one of which was also that writing was in India one of the main criteria for promotion. Curzon, like many before and since saw this loquacity as the curse of the British Empire.[4]

Almost immediately after his arrival in India he confronted the terrible face of the correspondence monster: in India he came upon 'prodigious files which start almost from the commencement of time', some being almost a foot high. He also wrote, in his usual laconic, patrician fashion of being in a 'wilderness of diverse opinions', in which he was subject daily to 'the dismal ordeal of irresponsible loquacity', in which the purpose of the file was entirely lost to view, becoming 'mummified in the Departmental tomb'. File circulation he likened to badminton and tennis, the purpose being to keep things always in the air.

As this picture indicates power did indeed work itself out at local points in unexpected and often contradictory ways, but in order to operate at all British power had to be articulated at particular sites. Such a site was the India Office. The most important site of all other sites, it served to articulate the government of India in India with the institutions and processes of the central British state, something which was not only an administrative but also a political and constitutional necessity. I concentrate here on the first necessity, mindful of the other two nonetheless. The governance of India was indeed governance at a distance. However, in one way or another, government can be regarded as *always* involving 'action at a distance'. This is a term frequently found in the work of Bruno Latour, where it serves to illuminate understandings of how material objects and processes, for example 'immutable mobiles' such as navigation devices and maps, operate to coordinate and command dispersed entities, making them in the process governable entities. In this sense, 'centres' can be understood to be what Latour calls 'centres of calculation' (for definitions see Latour, 1999: 304, 307, 311). As an Indian Office memorandum of 1910 indicates, keeping open the channels of information from India meant the fullest possible extension of government by writing, something which was central to what was called the 'superintendence of control'. The India Office was therefore very much a centre of calculation, or as John Stuart Mill put it, a centre in which the *accounting* of power through the means of writing could be carried on.

Centres are however more than locations of calculation alone, however capacious the definition of calculation, extending amongst other functions to matters of decision and execution as well. All these were functions of the India Office, which was deliberately fashioned as a centre of empire at the time. However, it will be apparent that I extend the sense of 'centre' beyond orthodox understandings (usually denoting the centre as the active, directive and sentient source of policy formation and enactment). Clearly, it is difficult to find a single term that describes the multiple functions of the India Office as a centre.[5] If one were forced to choose, perhaps it might be called a centre of connection, or of 'connectivity', a term now in vogue, but one nonetheless useful and not anachronistic in denoting the capacity to connect (in contemporary infrastructure provision connectivity is treated almost like a commodity, or indeed a utility, like water or electricity).

The origins of this can in fact be traced back quite precisely to this time, the mid-Victorian period witnessing the rapid expansion of the railway and telegraph systems, in the US just as in the UK. This brought with it a fusion of business organisation, communication and information, so that what can properly be called communication *systems* emerge, alongside the emergence of what has been called 'systematic management' (Yates, 1993). 'Connectivity' therefore, can be understood in terms of the new importance of securing the free flow of information in and through the means of a 'system'. 'Systematicity' and 'connectivity' were and are central to infrastructure of all sorts, and they also have a particular relation to liberal governance, one I have elaborated upon previously in terms of the history of the city (Joyce, 2003: ch. 2). In *The Soul of Leviathan* I explore what was still the most significant communications system of them all, the Post Office (Joyce, 2008). However, communication flows had to be regulated, and systems given a centre.

As a centre articulating all other centres, the India Office helped to make a bureaucratic *system* a reality, and, a variation on the same theme, make bureaucracy a *systematic reality*. Because, under the pressure of rapidly escalating demands upon imperial governance, it slowly and unevenly became such between the mid-nineteenth century and the First World War, it does not at all follow that this guaranteed control, least of all, as we have seen, control on the ground in India. Nor was the emergence of this new system by means of this new centre of connection the only reality of imperial governance. Quite often, just like the immediacies of power on the ground, it might not matter at all; very often what mattered was talk, informal connection, the talk of gentlemen, and this is why in the work in progress book, *Soul of Leviathan*, of which I speak I go on to analyse these 'informal' dimensions of governance in some detail, including the pedagogic materialities by which these gentlemen and their talk were formed.

Nonetheless, the system mattered, and with it the material forms that made it up. What then in practice was this system? It, and therefore the very notions of 'centre' and 'connection', turn above all on the material forms and operations of writing. Writing had to deal with what were already the abstractions of administration and governance (reports, minutes, memoranda, and so on) in an even more abstract way, so that questions to do with the systematisation and division of information and knowledge became crucial. The operations of this centre of connection worked at a *systemic* level, but it can also be said to have worked at a *symbolic* one, involving in the case of the India Office what might perhaps better be called the *performance* of its functions, a performance to the various 'publics' involved in Britain, India and the empire more broadly.[6] Through its operations, in the display of the putative efficiency, coherence and eventually the openness of its paperwork systems, it can be said not only to have performed its functions to these publics, but also to have functioned as a technology creating them in the first place. This in the sense that the institution itself had a key role in its public presentation and thereby shaped the various constituencies perceiving it. This production of the institution through paperwork spoke to other constituencies also: first and foremost to bureaucrats themselves, then to its various political constituencies (especially Parliament), to the press, and eventually to its scholarly, especially historical, constituency (so that this chapter is to some degree framed by that paperwork).

A proper consideration of this performative aspect requires an examination of paperwork management extending far beyond the organisation of the file itself, as indeed does a full understanding of the systematic dimensions of the India Office's operation as the centre of connection upon which I concentrate here. Aspects such as paperwork registration and archiving were of central importance, and I return to these briefly later, present limitations of space confining me mostly to the organisation of the file itself. However, file organisation was of quite fundamental importance, in that the file can be considered as the basic unit, the primordial cell, of the whole system. In considering the file, it is necessary first to turn to the nature of writing itself.

II

At the most basic level bureaucratic authority, and hence the state, rests upon writing. Foucault recognised the central place of writing in this regard.

The 'disciplinary power' which he saw emerging in the seventeenth and eighteenth centuries depended upon institutions – armies, prisons, hospitals among others – and in turn institutions rested upon writing (Foucault, 1991: 'Docile bodies', especially pages 189–190). The central place of the particular and individual 'case' was inconceivable without the keeping of files, the writing of reports, in general the keeping of records, whether or not the case in question was that of an individual, a body of medical symptoms, or an institution itself. As such, as Foucault saw, bureaucracy and writing were part of a new 'economy of visibility' prior to the nineteenth century, in which power radiated from the centre and was no longer massed there, as in the old state of the royal will (where power, as Foucault put it, was immanent and expressed in "what was seen, what was shown"). This new power was in contradistinction to previous forms of monarchical power, which hinged upon display, and upon the projection of 'majesty', earlier in the form of the monarch's body, and then in the Court of the monarch, as in the Gardens of Versailles (Foucault, 1991: part one, 'Torture'; Kantorowicz, 1997). This new emphasis on a radiating power, from the centre, led to a retreat from the subjectification of the monarch and a new emphasis on the objectification of that which was now to be governed, something made possible above all else by writing.

All discursive authority is obtained by citational practice, either by revelation (of an author) or by its opposite non-revelation, as demonstrated *par excellence* in the case of the bureaucrat. In resting upon writing, bureaucratic authority inheres however in a special sort of writing, one that is 'reiterative', dependent on repetition and rule.[7] In this sense bureaucratic writing, and bureaucratic practice in general, can be said to be self-referential: for instance, the authority of the file, rests upon its relationship to other files and its place in a system of files. Only secondarily does the authority of bureaucratic writing rest upon something outside the system of which it is a part, even when that something is the state itself. Therefore it is not possible ever to recreate the full authority of the file, unless we have access to the plenitude of other files and documents of which it is a part, something which the selectivity of the archive always militates against, as will become apparent (Feldman, 2008: 34–40). We might then properly speak of the authority of bureaucracy as obtaining before its legitimacy, contrary to Weber, who maintained that all authority was legitimated domination. It is always at one remove that bureaucratic writing stands for the 'something else' of the state, for its authority depends upon its systemic properties, hence the invariable bureaucratic anxiety about tracking papers removed from files, and files transferred from one system to another. Thus, in the very nature of bureaucratic writing, we see emerging the origin of the systemic qualities of the particular kind of 'centre' which I consider here, just as of all other centres of the bureaucratic function.

The nature of the link between bureaucratic authority and the state was therefore contingent, for the authority of bureaucratic writing only secondarily rests upon something outside the system of which it is a part, even when that something is the state itself. This is especially apparent in the case of weak states, but applies generally. In the case of a weak state, describing the history of twentieth-century Gaza under its various administrations, including the British mandate over Palestine, Ilana Feldman has shown how bureaucratic authority can survive detached from the state, so much so that the bureaucracy in Gaza perpetuated its own autonomous authority from the state by actively not drawing attention to the regimes of which it was a part (Feldman, 2008: ch. 2–3). In strong states the link to the state was correspondingly stronger, but still inherently contingent and conditional.

Reiteration, rule following, systemic regularity, all make for the authority of the file, and hence form the basis of all bureaucracy. They are conducive to discipline and conformity of course, but by the same token productive of the often remarked ossification of bureaucracies. Also, by establishing authority in the way they do, in terms of regularities of rule, they make possible challenges to this authority, based upon the perceived absence of system should this occur. In fact, they entail rights as well as enforce discipline. Because it is self-referential, the authority of bureaucratic writing seems autonomous from political institutions, seems to inhere in autonomous 'system'. This autonomy conveys authority and is an integral part of those processes whereby the state has come in the modern world to be naturalised. Bureaucratic writing thus minimises the agency of the bureaucrat and bureaucracy, who do not appear as its personal authors. Bureaucracy in fact depends heavily on the extinction of the individual personality of the bureaucrat and its replacement by what is designed to be regarded as the neutral, and therefore autonomous, personhood of the bureaucrat.

This autonomy of bureaucratic writing, resting upon its systemic, self-referential character, is more though than a question of 'appearance' only, and of simply 'seeming' autonomous. Bureaucratic authority is of course related to particular institutional regimes, in this case state ones, and therefore from one perspective is clearly not autonomous. In writing of Muslim society, Brinkley Messick's example of Yemen is one quintessentially based upon writing and textuality, those of Sharia law, so much so that the author speaks of the 'calligraphic state' (Messick, 1993). Correspondingly, it is clearly difficult to speak of the autonomy of writing in cases like this, the link to the particular state structure being so transparent. While the nineteenth-century British state cannot be considered a calligraphic state as such, what Messick calls 'textual domination' was apparent there, in the sense that the authority of the pen certainly concerned the conveyance of the message of 'ruling ideas' and of the state, the hegemony of which was initiated and supported by other state institutions, such as the education system.

However, authority did not only *seem* autonomous, in the sense of being naturalised, it was autonomous, in the sense that the systematicity of the file and filing organisation, contained in the materialities of writing, comprised their own non-human agency, their own material powers in fact. This agency was in turn reinforced through the operation of the underlying structural characteristics reproducing these systemic properties, which might be beyond the comprehension and control of human actors. As Messick describes the mechanics of this systematicity,

> A textual habitus, a set of acquired dispositions concerning writing and the spoken word, and the authoritative conveyance of meaning in texts was reproduced in homologous structures and practices across different genres and institutions. It was the resulting, partly implicit, experience of coherence amid diversity, the reaffirming of basic orientations with multiple forms and sites of expression, that enhanced the natural qualities of the dispositions themselves. From domain to domain, the quiet redundancies of discursive routines were mutually confirming.
>
> (Messick, 1993: 251–252)

In the case of bureaucratic writing and authority, in Britain and elsewhere, homologous structures and practices across different institutional sites within the greater institution of bureaucracy itself (cross-institution departmental structures say, and their common filing or registering practices) similarly reproduced the experience of coherence, and indeed inevitability, that constituted not only what was 'natural' about bureaucracy, and hence the state, but also a material agency that was non-human as well as human in its operation.

There was thus a very close correspondence between what we might call the logic of the state and the logic of capital, a logic behind the naturalisation of both. Each in large measure depended on controlling writing in a new way. In this regard Ogborn's study of the operation of writing systems in the East India Company is again illuminating: he indicates how new accountancy systems in Company factories served to naturalise the operations of capital in such a way as to make them seem inevitable, something with their own logic. As Ogborn writes,

> The aim was to construct a controlled space for writing and calculation which would seek to ensure the accessibility of the books, the orderly conduct of accountancy, the absence of the selfish interests of factory chiefs, and all that depended upon it. Understanding this specific and small-scale geography of writing and writing practices as an ordering of the relationships between power and knowledge in the making of global trade, means recognising the social and cultural relationships that lie right at the heart of the economic arrangements of mercantile capital. It is also the case that if the 'logic' of capital was felt by those engaged in these forms of exchange as a 'logic' – as an impersonal, inexorable, and determining force – then that was exactly the effect achieved by the separations, hierarchies, and controls instituted in the factories' writing offices as the sites of local practices of abstraction and standardisation performed upon chains and compilations of inscriptions and reinscriptions … It was within these restricted public spaces, and only within them, that the English East India Company could turn their concerns into an objective and controlling profit-seeking force external to their servants' private interests, into the 'logic' of capital.
>
> (Ogborn, 2007: 102–103)

By the same token, and recognising what was by the middle of the nineteenth century already an old debt on the part of the state to the non-state capitalist economy, in this case in the form of the East India Company, the India Office itself can be understood as a new sort of controlled space for writing and calculation, involving accessibility, order, the absence of selfish interest, also the absence of the political, newly stigmatised as the political was as a kind of selfishness by the institution of a rapidly emerging 'professional' civil service at this time. Therefore, we can say that the authority of bureaucratic writing served to 'format' not only the institution of bureaucracy, and hence the state, but also the bureaucrat himself or herself, at the time of course – and central to that bureaucratic ethos – overwhelmingly the former. Writing achieved this de-personalisation although obviously it was not the only means (the powers inherent in the material forms of offices, the buildings that housed these offices, the garb and demeanour of the bureaucrat were other means).

III

In order to explore the systemic, self-referential nature of the authority of bureaucracy I turn now to the file. The file is the central unit by which information is assembled and knowledge produced, knowledge that enabled the institution to know and control itself as well as that which it governed. However, this is not a matter of files in the abstract, for the powers of the file were indeed material powers, resting upon such matters as the spatial organisation of documents, the physical nature of writing, and in particular the paper, pens and other means of communication that were used. I can do no more here than advert in passing to crucially significant advances in technologies of handwriting at the time, and their increasing popular purchase from the 1830s and 1840s, so that the period indeed does see that very considerable acceleration in the coming of the 'low-tech' technical referred to earlier: the first half of the century witnessed an interrelated series of technological and industrial changes that ended for ever the millennia-old technical hegemony of the quill pen, a technology as cumbersome as it was ancient. This was above all apparent in new, mass-produceable versions of the steel pen, this wonder of the age being to contemporaries 'the knitting needle of civilisation'. Alongside the steel pen, new kinds of paper and new kinds of ink were developed, making huge advances in the legibility and durability of writing, obviously essential to bureaucracy.[8] In the wake of these devices was the development of a vast range of new machines and processes to do with the office in general, and the file in particular.[9] Of the latter, of particular importance, a veritable landmark in this little world of technology, was the surprisingly late development between 1900–1914 of the horizontal systems of filing which we take so much for granted. 'Flat' systems of filing themselves only developed from around the 1880s.

The file itself can in fact be understood in terms of the phenomenon of 'black boxing' described in the science studies literature, the process of framing, and hence harnessing and redirecting, the various agencies of persons and things so as to give them new form, and hence a new capacity for action in the world

(Latour, 1987; 2005: 178, 181). Files are therefore concerned with excluding as much as including things, the 'engineering out' as well as the 'engineering in' of knowledge production and capacities for action. Hence the emphasis in science studies on how science and technological change is not a matter of cumulative progress but a series of stabilisations of agency that may be quite arbitrary (on agency see Pickering, 1995), or at least arbitrary in the sense that these reflect the particular dispositions of power and resources evident at the time.

Thus while the file is a means of controlling matters and hence stabilising the institution and its works, it is also always a contingent and to some degree arbitrary framing of the world. Also, often an unstable one. There was, and is, nothing necessary or inevitable about the ways in which files were composed and how information got into files and became knowledge, so that it becomes necessary to look in some detail at this business of how a file is made. This in two senses, first that of the arduous and decades-long process of invention and trial and error that marked the evolution of the file, file engineering as it might be called, something almost invariably developed by relatively low-level bureaucrats, who were in fact the unsung engineers of empire. It is indeed the case that the business of becoming in any way an effective 'centre' was dearly bought and constantly undermined by the contradictions of different forces at work inside offices, in terms of individuals, departments, institutional traditions, and so on. In a sense, therefore, one can speak of different and often contradictory 'centres' within the greater 'centre' itself. Although a measure of uniformity of practice within and across government departments in Britain emerged in the last couple of decades of the nineteenth century, heterogeneity was always marked.

While a discussion of the historical sense of file making is beyond the scope of this chapter, I shall discuss the second sense, , that of what a file actually is, its makeup. Because of this continuous process of file engineering the choice of any particular example becomes a little arbitrary. However, it is necessary here to be quite concrete and look at a single file, one taken from the year 1900, when the file system of the India Office had developed a certain degree of sophistication and stabilisation (prior to further destabilisation and attempts at a new stabilisation later when, post-First World War, the British government of India took on the new direction of the 'Indianisation' of the service). The importance of the file, and the degree of historically cumulative expertise that had come by this time to mark its construction is evident in the extraordinary level of attention given to questions of methods of arranging and submitting papers in the 'India Office Procedure' of 1910.[10] The first and fundamental law of the arrangement of files in this document was as follows:

> The papers in a file submitted under the Office Procedure Rules should be so arranged that the file, if read from top (the latest papers) to bottom, will present the history of each stage of the case in this Office in strict chronological order.

Therefore, each file was a sort of miniature history that made up a 'case'. What the file black boxes is 'the case', and each case is strictly arranged not only in temporal but also in spatial form – from top to bottom – just as in temporal form, 'in strict chronological order' (the horizontal filing system had not yet been invented). The chronological order in fact reproduces what is historical ordering, so that the primary model here is in fact History itself, this at a time when taxonomies of knowledge had taken on very powerful historical forms, ones organised around linear and progressive ideas of time, notions emerging with particular force from the early nineteenth century. However, in practice 'each stage of the case in this Office' involved the active intervention of the Office itself, in that files were put together at different times and by different hands, so that 'each stage' (and the very idea of a 'stage' itself) was a *post facto* creation, something constructed over a time period the stages of which did not run in strict chronological order at all.

The other model of the file was the legal dossier or file, for minutes and the proposals had to be accompanied by the papers and the letters to which they referred, so that the 'evidence' that supported a particular line of action was supplied, again in strict chronological order. Of course, just as was the case with the historical model, the 'evidence' in this legal model was highly selective, for there was again a very high degree of *post facto* choice of documentation, dictated by the strict imperative to always manufacture a developmental path, a historical way, so as in turn to create a 'case' or "subject", and so justify the final course of action, the so-called 'decision'. More than this, file construction involved the fabrication of 'policy' itself, which was not a spiritual emanation of either wise or stupid heads but in part the creature of file construction itself, one that altogether left out of the account, and indeed deliberately suppressed, the complex trail of paper and of circumstances that had actually led to proposals.

The file I shall look at for the purposes of this study is 2101/1900 of the Judicial and Public Committee of the India Office, concerning – as it is put on the top page of the file – 'Subject. ICS Final Examination Proposed Inclusion of Indian History among Compulsory Subjects' (to be found in India Office Records/ PJ/6/554, Part One). Files varied greatly in their size and content matter, which to some degree impacted upon their basic structure. For example, there were many files of a 'technical' nature, in the received science and technology sense of the term, in which the principal points of the subject were merely summarised, and vast amounts of information of a supposedly technical character were hived off into appendices, replete with statistics and tables.[11] However, almost all of this information in practice involved the making of 'policy', the fact that it was such being secured by the designation of the technical as natural, part of the rule of experts in the ascendant at the time, a rule that seemed not to be rule at all, just part of how things were (Mitchell, 2002, *passim*). However, variation among files notwithstanding, as the 'India Office Procedure' of 1910 indicates, the basic structure of files by this time was fairly uniform.

Looking more closely at file 2101/1900, 1900 refers to its year, the first number to the file's place in a chronological sequence over that year. The arrangement of the file follows the pattern of the 'India Office Procedure' of 1910, which is as follows:

(I) (Top Paper). The submission docket.
(II) (a) Departmental minute.
(b) One or more blank foolscap sheets, when necessary.
(III) Draft letters, telegrams or despatches with half margin.
(IV) The despatch or other documents with which the file originates.
(V) 'Previous' papers, among or below which (and not among papers I to IV) any papers added in the course of inter-departmental reference should be placed.

The physical layout of the file is therefore itself a self-ordering device, for the first page (see Figure 5.1, the top paper as described earlier – the 'submission docket' – was in fact page 2 of the actual file) in addition to including the subject also makes reference to previous files, as well as the 'next file' in the system. It also indicates what papers were included from outside the file itself. As can be seen from the illustration, there is also reference to paper 791.2101 of 1900. Already the composition of the file is complex, for it includes *another file*, 791/1900, so complicating considerably the whole process of tracing files and combining their contents. The file number on the top paper is an immediate reference to other files and file numbers, in relation to which its existence depends, so that the business of accurately relating it to other files in an overall system is crucial. The role of handwriting is already evident here in the referencing notations on the top paper, and comes dramatically into its own in the submission document (see Figure 5.2).

In this the self-ordering form of the file becomes clear again in that the left-hand column is reserved for the use of the Secretary and the Secretary of State, while that on the right is set apart for a synopsis showing briefly the progress of the proposal submitted (under the heading of 'Subject'). Here 'the case' has already taken on the form of action as a 'proposal'. The file has become that which actions the world, the paper form of doing things, which if not the actual form in which these things necessarily got done, is the form without which nothing could have got done at all. On the right-hand side, 'the first entry will be made by the initiating Department at the time of putting forward the file; it should state in terms as brief and precise as possible the nature of the action proposed'. The 'file' can be seen as indeed a *post facto* creation, because someone in the department concerned (normally the Head) had decided it will become such, after the event of the initiating papers, which might be numerous.

The file as a self-ordering system is however most of all evident in what was called at the time 'the ladder' (see Figure 5.2). This took precedence at the top of the page, above these left- and right-hand divisions. The right-hand division below the heading 'Subject', can be seen to be the actual file minute *in extenso*, running in rough, unamended handwritten order starting beside the space reserved for the major Office officials, and then continuing over two columns thereafter.

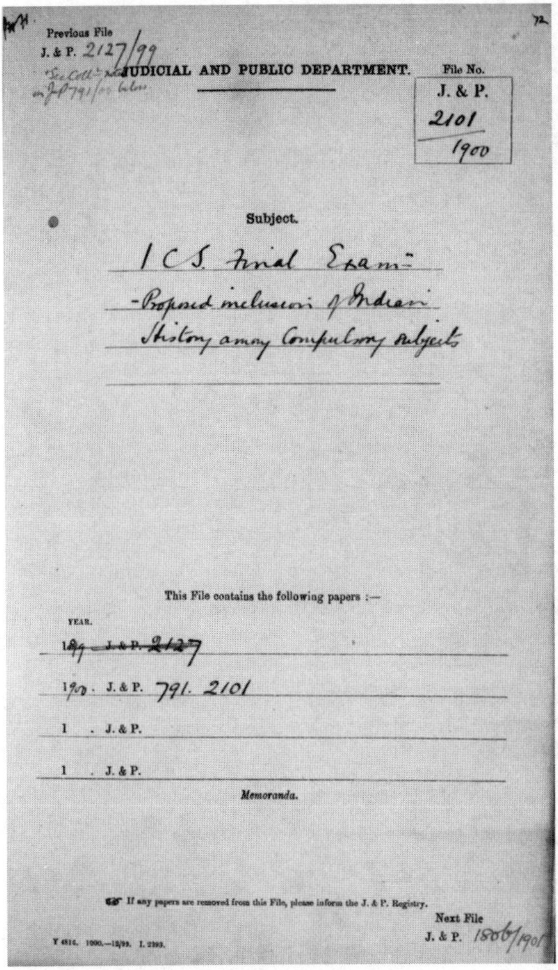
Previous File
J. & P. 2127/99
JUDICIAL AND PUBLIC DEPARTMENT.
File No.
J. & P.
2101
1900
Subject.
I.C.S. Final Exam:
- Proposed inclusion of Indian
History among Compulsory subjects
This File contains the following papers :—
YEAR.
~~1899. J. & P. 2127~~
1900. J. & P. 791. 2101
1 . J. & P.
1 . J. & P.
Memoranda.
If any papers are removed from this File, please inform the J. & P. Registry.
Next File
J. & P. 1806/1901

Figure 5.1 Top page of file 2101/1900.

The 'India Office Procedure' guidelines here were elaborate, being concerned with the perennial problem of the length and prolixity of minutes so the order was that 'minutes should invariably be as precise and brief as possible. Every minute should conclude with a definite statement as to the nature of the proposal for which the approval is sought'. The use of micro-tools of management is evident, for instance 'flags of stiff paper' to indicate particular papers referred to in a file, or the 'yellow slips' in the front of files to indicate to which department a file had been referred to should it leave the 'home' department (Note by the Under Secretary of State, 'India Office Procedure', 1910, India, p.11). The routing of documents in the India Office was tracked by many such tools – 'flags' not only

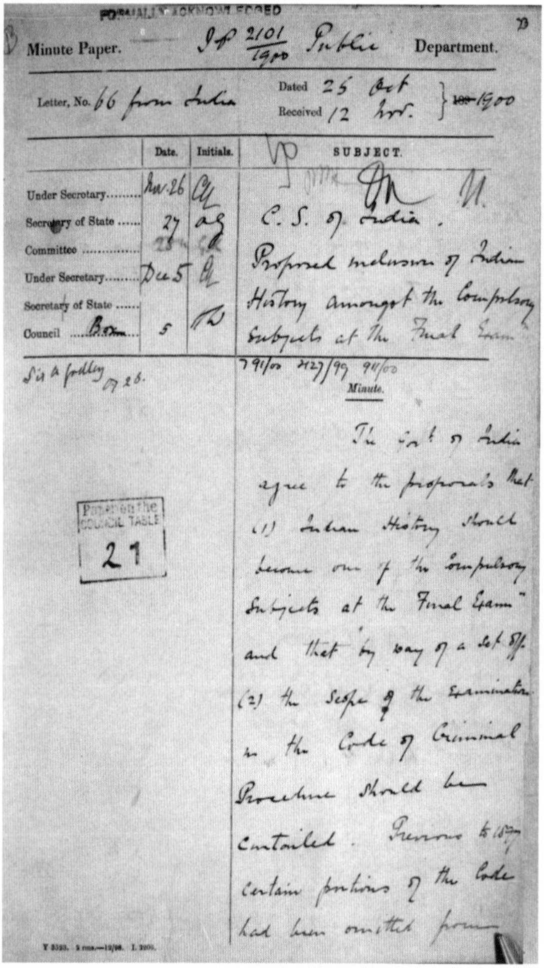
Minute Paper. I&P 2101/1900 Public Department.

Letter, No. 66 from India. Dated 25 Oct, Received 12 Nov. 1900

	Date.	Initials.
Under Secretary	Nov 26	
Secretary of State	27	
Committee	28	
Under Secretary	Dec 5	
Secretary of State		
Council Box	5	

SUBJECT.

C. S. of India.

Proposed inclusion of Indian History amongst the Compulsory Subjects at the Final Exam.

Minute.

The Govt of India agree to the proposals that (1) Indian History should become one of the compulsory subjects at the Final Exam" and that by way of a set off (2) the scope of the examination in the Code of Criminal Procedure should be curtailed. Previous to [illegible] certain portions of the Code had been omitted from

Papers on the COUNCIL TABLE 21

Figure 5.2 The second page of file 2101/1900.

marked places in files, but could also carry directions – for example 'Action', 'Paper under Consideration', 'Draft for Approval', 'Important' and 'Immediate', would be in different colours.

The ladder itself was comprised of the names of the Under-Secretary and Secretary of State, the Committee (of Council), and then again the Under-Secretary and Secretary, followed by the Council (the reference here is to a box number, box 5, boxes containing documents being left on the Council table for consultation should the Council want this (on the role and function of the Council see Moir, 1988). The fact that the Council committee minutes were not included on files, nor the deliberations of the Council itself, is very striking. Even more striking is the fact that these committee minutes were in fact not even retained by the India Office archival systems: the models of evidence that served the historical and legal models of file construction are again seen as highly arbitrary, and very far from the complex and meandering passage of paperwork through the Office. A contemporary estimated that paperwork spent 90 per cent of its time circulating around the office, and 10 per cent of its time divided between the direct attention of officers.

The 'ladder' that helped construct this vision of order had strictly to be followed, so that the movement of the file could be traced from date to date, and person to person. It was therefore another device within the device of the overall file itself. Another such device, in hindsight seemingly quite obvious and inevitable, but in fact elaborated over what seems in retrospect an inordinately long period of time, was the registry document, whether that of the Central Registry, or of the Registry of particular departments. In the case of number 791, the passage of papers and the history of the file was traced now in horizontal fashion, compared to the vertical of the ladder, only now in much more detail – the Judicial and Public Register, for instance follows the passage of paper from reception in the sub registry (on 26 April 1900) to the resulting dispatches to India, via its passage through the authorities of what was now in effect a horizontal 'ladder'.

However, these mini tools of knowledge production need always be considered beside the original and still immensely powerful tool of handwriting itself. The profusion of handwriting will be apparent in the illustrations so far: the rough, much amended copies of letters themselves, the frequent use of initials as themselves devices for marking the passage and the history of paper, the marginalia, and above all the extended handwritten letter and note. This use of handwriting concerned the employment of the body, the personal imprint, in the form of a signature that had a known author. Handwriting played a complex role within British bureaucracy at the time.

Its use in this document is in fact evidence of the distinction within the relatively newly reformed civil service between auxiliary/low/mechanical labour and primary/high/intellectual work. This model as Agar has recently shown was built into the subsequent technical information systems of the British civil service itself, becoming apparent eventually in the construction of the modern computer (Agar, 2003). For while the lower ranks of the civil service had to be anonymous, the higher ranks could be, and in fact had to be, anything but anonymous. Hierarchies of the bureaucratic self were essential to the production of bureaucracy; in particular the differences and the transitions between the monitored and the self-monitoring self, the former in the shape of the lower levels of bureaucracy which had to be *directly* disciplined and monitored, and so were minutely policed by rules and regulations. These involved not being able to employ their hands and so divulge their identities. In this regard a great many office practices and material forms, from the most humble aspects upwards – pens that worked, handwriting styles, ruled paper – were in fact means of cutting out room for mistakes, but also room for manoeuvre, latitude, and initiative on the job.

Looking more closely at file 791.2101, it begins with a (handwritten) letter from R. Palme Dutt, a former senior Indian civil servant, then teaching history at University College London. Palme Dutt was a very significant Indian political intellectual and activist, and of great significance in the history of Indian nationalism. In the retrospectively conceived file system his letter is followed by the handwritten letters and notes of leading figures in the Office, including Godley and the head of the relevant department, who consult each other and conduct a sort of conversation via these means, making their own judgements on the proposal (not always complimentary to Palme Dutt), liberally deploying initials and handwritten dates on their own and other documents.

After this exchange the file contains the handwritten form of a much cross-referenced standard, page 2 'docket', with a succession of dates indicating that it had gone through the 'the ladder' vetting system between May the 1st and the 15th. However, what this burgeoning file indicates – it is already quite lengthy and full of detailed information about past precedents concerning Indian Civil Service (ICS) examination subjects – is the actual 'birth' of a file, in this case a fairly rapid one after the initial letter. The next in order in the file is the draft, handwritten form of a long letter from the Secretary of State George Hamilton to the Governor General of India in Council, which capitalises on and develops the previous information. This on the first page is festooned with many signatures, comments, and in the top left-hand corner a hastily assembled handwritten 'ladder'.

The critical point here is that the file simply does not produce any evidence of what must have been the very considerable amount of labour involved in getting this subject information together, itself involving a great deal of paperwork, which was either not retained at all, or very rapidly got rid of (rather like the unretained Council committee minutes). The file therefore frames or 'black boxes' a greatly complex series of happenings. Some of the labour that went into the next stage of the file, which was the printed version of this handwritten draft letter to the Governor General, where 2101 bisects with 791 in fact, is at least indirectly indicated in the draft, by means of marginalia. However, the effect of the printed version of the draft is to further erase the labour that went into the printing, most of all the great deal of work within departments, flattening out into a retrospective unity the many exchanges, personal and oral as well as written, that went into file making, including the labour and written documentation that would have supported the initial round of 'conversational' handwriting between the high officials of the office.

However, the departmental head was by no means the only one involved in file making, for it was the case that the file was the construction of many hands, the role of the departmental head being not as magisterially directing as one might think, and in fact more one of coordinating, even controlling and curbing different inputs, some of which might be from a low level in the organisational hierarchy. Evidence from the Provincial Governments in India, as well as other government departments in Britain, makes it apparent that despite constant initiatives to expunge autonomy and initiative at the lower levels of bureaucracy such room for manoeuvre continued to exist, and indeed would always exist given the reliance on a subdivision of administrative labour in which in practice the line between upper and lower divisions, and different mental faculties, was so often blurred.

In the government of India within the borders of India itself when a letter was received at a particular Provincial departmental secretariat, it was first registered and then given to a Reference Clerk. He read it, noted all the references mentioned in the letter, and retrieved all the files in which those references were found, placing a slip at each reference. As mentioned earlier, this aspect of recording and registration, and many other aspects such as indexing, can only be adverted to in passing. Therefore, even before the 'birth' of the file there was a great deal of mostly hidden activity, as well as a fair measure of clerical initiative. The Reference Clerk then passed the papers on to another clerk, who composed a note on the gist of the letter, which was to set out and explain the connections between it and previous notes and papers on the matter, referring to any precedents that applied or might be relevant to the question at hand. The clerk was forbidden from making criticisms or comments, though in simple cases he was permitted to make a suggested course of action known. Nonetheless, these prohibitions notwithstanding, the various clerks involved had a decided input into file construction. This input continued further up the clerical chain, the papers then being passed to a Superintendent Clerk (a superior officer in charge of a section of the office but still not regarded as a high level, 'intellectual', labourer) who would have read the note and then been responsible for editing it/passing it on/revising it/rewriting it, as he saw fit. The file would then finally go forward to the highest levels, crossing the supposed boundary between manual and intellectual labour and ending up with the Under Secretary or other very senior figure (Blunt, 1937: 158–159).

When a decision had been made at senior level, a similar process is again evident in the execution of that decision. As one eminent Indian civil service officer put it,

> The clerk who writes [the reply] must always reproduce the sense, and if possible the words, of the order. Occasionally he overdoes verbal fidelity with disastrous results, for notes are sometimes expressed in terms more lucid than polite; or in his anxiety to make sure that nobody can mistake the meaning, he will reiterate the same phrase again and again. He rarely uses a short word if he can use a long one; and, by the time his draft reaches the under-secretary, it is often a mass of 'grandiloquent and redundant verbiage' as he himself would call it.
>
> (Blunt, 1937: 159)[12]

The Under Secretary might then have to amend/redraft/rewrite the draft before either issuing it or not.

In the light of this, we might consider imperial governance in terms of what has been called 'collective' or 'distributed' cognition, the production of action being distributed between many authors themselves arranged in many forms and layers of, in this case, collective governance (Mukerji, 2009). If the lower levels had undoubtedly the subordinate agency, the force of this agency if limited was real enough. The manifold distributions of agency involved produced incoherence as well as coherence. Within the paper empire itself, at all levels but especially in India, the sources of incoherence were systemic, that is to say they were inherent to the paper world of administration. The systemic qualities of centres of connection were therefore dysfunctional as well as functional, these two aspects being reciprocally connected. Sources of instability were a constant, in that the impetus for change and the reform of systems was driven by its own success, in the shape of the increasing volume of paper communication, which constantly threatened to overwhelm existing arrangements. As new systems were put in place to handle change they invariably ran up against the limits of the very changes they had instituted, or these changes were productive of unforeseen outcomes which generated more complexity and incoherence.

One very good example of this was the in-context major development that led from the old folded system of papers to the new open or flat file system around the 1880s. This changed the age-old procedure whereby an incoming letter itself formed the file on its subject, being folded into four so that the blank front of the letter became the place on which the docket and minutes were written. In the instance of the Home Office (the 'India Office Procedure' developed in much the same way around this time) only in 1885 did new papers begin to be put away flat in white jackets, the front of which formed the first minute, to which extra sheets could be added. This practice gradually led, throughout the office, to 'a modern, organised system of writing minutes: the illegible scrawls which had frequently been unsigned and undated, became neater, more expansive and more clearly initialled and dated' (Pellew, 1982: 97). However, precisely because the whole sheet of paper now became available for comment and notes, and because file contents became much more accessible and more easily itemised, this led to a vast and almost uncontrollable increase in the amount of writing in India (E.H.H. Collen, 'Memorandum', 6 June 1899 – in EUR.F. 111, Curzon, 'Memorandum').

Another, equally revealing, instance of the paradoxes accompanying the deepening systematic quality of paperwork involved printing: on the face of it the development of printing rather than handwriting documents would seem straightforwardly a case of bureaucratic advance. In some respects, especially in Britain, increasingly cheap printing was a boon, but in India its relatively minute costs, apparent in the printing of even the obscure remarks of lower-level clerks, led to a profusion of documented material that again fed the monster of correspondence. Out of paradoxes and contradictions such as this was forged the qualified stability that these new worlds of paperwork brought to the governance of India and the empire. That this governance needs to be understood in terms that go beyond conventional understandings of power, politics and administration is illustrated by this particular instance and the agenda of analysis that it is part of, exemplified here in the particular but strategically very significant case of the file itself. This case serves to illustrate the importance of the material powers of bureaucracy in shaping not only the bureaucrat and the institution of bureaucracy but the nature of imperial governance itself and the imperial state.

Notes

* I would like to thank Gavin Rand for his invaluable research assistance in the writing of this chapter, and Antonia Moon, Archivist and Librarian of the Asia, Pacific and Africa Collections, British Library, for her help in navigating the enormous and daunting India Office Collections at the British Library, Collections still known colloquially as the 'India Office Library'.

1 See the summary of approaches to the state in Michael Mann *The Sources of Social Power, Volume 2*, chapter 3. The approach I take here has a certain amount in common with Mann's approach, in that both are concerned with particular forms of power. However, it will be apparent that Mann's notion of power is altogether different from that adopted here, as is my use of the concepts of materiality and the social. See Patrick Joyce (2010), 'What is the social in social history?', *Past and Present*, 206 (February).

2 See also 'Memorandum on the Home Government of India',1887, India Office Records/V/27/220/20.

3 Non-gazetted officials were not part of the official civil service establishment.

4 British Library, Mss.EUR.F.111.239 'Memorandum on the System of Noting in the Departments of the Government of India'. For the correspondence arising from the memorandum see also the collection of materials under the same classification number. In particular, Curzon, 'Notes on an Address System of Conducting Official Business'; hereafter Curzon, 'Memorandum'. See also Office Order number 1 of 1892, and Office Order number 20 of 1889, on previous rules on noting, referred to in Curzon's 'Memorandum', also Order number 5 of 1896. See also F111/158, letters of Secretary of State to Curzon, including letters from Sir Arthur Godley. Mss.EUR.F.102/17, Letter from Curzon to Sir Arthur Godley, 12 January 1898. See also for the many administrative and other exigencies of governing India as seen from the Indian side, the 41-page printed Minute, EUR.F111. 241A, A.P. Mcdonnell, October 1901, Taini Tal, marked 'Strictly Confidential'.

5 If we extend more generally these various understandings of what 'centres' and connectivity can amount to in stabilising the state, we might usefully embrace instances such as that described in the work of Timothy Mitchell on the governance of the British Empire, in particular the governance of colonial Egypt. This was in large part predicated on (or 'centred' by) the 'formatting' through material means of economic life in the shape of a bounded ('national') and autonomous, systemic and self-regulating, entity, in short 'the economy', now for the first time in the singular. The colonial state was in practice as much the result as a cause of the multiple forces at work in making a 'national economy'. Rather than the state configuring the economy, the state was configured around the economy. See Timothy Mitchell, *The Rule of Experts*.

From another point of view, one like the India Office nearer to the literal sense of centre, the work of Chandra Mukerji on the seventeenth- and eighteenth-century French state concerns the ways in which the power of the French state was performed in the French landscape, in terms of the state's 'territorialisation'. This was apparent in the fortifications at the periphery and the gardens at the centre of the new French state. Power was instantiated in the land of France itself, the gardens of Versailles and state fortifications articulating the territorialisation of the state around a new centre and new territorial boundaries to this centre. Territorialisation also took material form in the dispersal of state power into newly 'French' products and economic practices, encouraged and developed by the state, so that a new sort of more centred, as well as more conventionally politically centralised, France eventuated, in the form of 'France' as an economic actor in its own right. As her contribution to this volume shows this new state was halfway between the state as, on the one hand, the expression of the royal will and, on the other, of a new kind of material power and its technical executors. Chandra Mukerji, *Territorial Ambitions and the Gardens of Versailles* (1997) and *Impossible Engineering: Technology and Territoriality on the Canal du Midi* (2009).

6 In previous work I began to consider how the new administrative regime of the British state consequent on the changes at mid-century (themselves pioneered in East India Company days) ushered in the performance of transparency and 'publicity' by various means, particularly in the form of the examination for different grades of the civil service. See Patrick Joyce, *The Rule of Freedom*, chapter 3, and for an extended treatment Patrick Joyce, forthcoming, *The Soul of Leviathan*.

7 Ilana Feldman, *Governing Gaza* (2008) 'Reiterative authority', pp. 14–20, on the ways in which the authority of writing produces the authority of bureaucracy. I wish to thank Ilana Feldman of New York University for her helpful assistance.

8 Among a large range of materials on the subject, Donald Jackson, *The Story of Writing* chapters 9 and 11 are especially useful on these technological developments.

9 The online *Early Office Museum* is a cornucopia of information, although with a very strong US emphasis (from the late nineteenth century onwards the US took over from Britain and Germany as the leading world force in office technology). Joanna Yates, *Control through Communication* (1993).

10 Note by the Under Secretary of State 'India Office Procedure', 1910, India Office Records V/27/220/23. A striking contrast can be made between the detailed consideration given to paperwork procedure here, and the no less serious but extremely brief directions on procedure in the very earliest days of the India Office, in Sir Charles Wood (Permanent Under Secretary), 'Memorandum on the Business of the India Office', 1859, IOR/L./PO/MSC/5, and his 'Directions for the transaction of business in the India office', November 7, 1859.

11 For an example of a technical file a like this, see India Office Records, L.PWD.6.404, File 246/93, comprising a list of enclosures to Despatch No 2 Public Works 1893, 12 enclosures in total, on irrigation projects in different provinces and states. These comprise extensive 'technical' matter on costs, estimates, mapping, engineering design and so on.

12 See also India Office Records, 'India Office Procedure' (marked 'for official use only').

References

Agar, John (2003) The *Government Machine: a Revolutionary History of the Computer*, London: MIT Press.

Bayly, Christopher (1996) *Empire and Information: Intelligence Gathering and Social Communication in India, 1780–1870*, Cambridge: Cambridge University Press.

Becker, Peter and William Clark (eds) (2005) *Little Tools of Knowledge*, Ann Arbor and London: University of Michigan Press.

Blunt, Edward (1937) *The ICS: The Indian Civil Service*, London: Faber and Faber.

Chakrabarty, Dipesh (2007) *Provincialising Europe: Postcolonial Thought and European Difference*, Princeton and London: Princeton University Press.

Clanchy, Michael T. (1992) *From Memory to Written Record, 1066–1307*, London: Blackwell Wiley.

Early Office Museum, available at www.earlyofficemuseum.com, accessed on 23 October 2009.

Feldman, Ilana (2008) *Governing Gaza: Bureaucracy, Authority and the Work of Rule, 1917–1967*, London and Durham: Duke University Press.

Foucault, Michel (1991) *Discipline and Punish: The Birth of the Prison*, London: Penguin Books.

Jackson, Donald (1981) *The Story of Writing*, Monmouth: The Calligraphy Centre.

Joyce, Patrick (1991) 'Work' in F.M.L. Thomson (ed.) *The Social History of Great Britain 1750–1950*, vol. 3, Cambridge: Cambridge University Press.

—— (2003) *The Rule of Freedom: Liberalism and the Modern City*, London and New York: Verso.
—— (2008) 'Postal communication and the making of the British technostate', Centre for Research in Sociocultural Change Working Paper No. 84, available at www.cresc.ac.uk, accessed on 23 October 2009.
—— (Forthcoming) *The Soul of Leviathan: Political Technologies of the Imperial British State.*
Kaminsky, Arnold P. (1986) *The India Office, 1880–1910*, London: Mansell Publishing.
Kantorowicz, Ernst (1997) *The King's Two Bodies: A Study in Mediaeval Political Theology*, Princeton and London: Princeton University Press.
Latour, Bruno (1987) *Science in Action: How to Follow Scientists and Engineers through Society*, Cambridge and London: Harvard University Press.
—— (1999) *Pandora's Hope: Essays on the Reality of Science Studies*, Cambridge and London: Harvard University Press.
—— (2005) *Reassembling the Social: an Introduction to Actor-Network-Theory*, Oxford: Oxford University Press.
Mann, Michael (1993) *The Sources of Social Power, Volume 2: The Rise of Classes and Nation States, 1760–1914*, Cambridge: Cambridge University Press, chapter 3.
Messick, Brinkley (1993) *The Calligraphic State: Textual Domination and History in a Muslim Society*, Los Angeles and London: University of California Press.
Mitchell, Timothy (2002) *The Rule of Experts: Egypt, TechnoPolitics, Modernity*, Chicago and London: University of Chicago Press.
Moir, Martin (1988) *A General Guide to the India Office Records*, London: The British Library.
Mukerji, Chandra (1997) *Territorial Ambitions and the Gardens of Versailles*, Cambridge: Cambridge University Press.
—— (2009) *Impossible Engineering: Technology and Territoriality on the Canal du Midi*, Princeton and London: Princeton University Press.
Ogborn, Miles (2007) *Indian Ink: Script and Print in the Making of the English East India Company*, Chicago and London: University of Chicago Press.
Otter, Christopher (2008) *The Victorian Eye: A Political History of Light and Vision in Britain, 1800–1910*, Chicago and London: University of Chicago Press.
Pellew, Jill (1982) *The Home Office 1848–1914*, London: Heinemann Educational Books.
Pickering, Andrew (1995) *The Mangle of Practice: Time, Agency and Science*, Chicago and London: University of Chicago Press.
Potter, David C. (1986) *India's Political Administration*, Oxford: Oxford University Press.
Samuel, Raphael (1977) 'The Workshop of the World: Steam Power and Hand Technology in Mid-Victorian Britain', *History Workshop Journal*, 3: 6–72.
Vernon, James (2006) *Hunger: A Modern History*, Cambridge and London: Harvard University Press.
Yates, Joanna (1993) *Control through Communication: The Rise of System in American Management*, Baltimore and London: Johns Hopkins Press.

6 Abstraction, materiality and the 'science of the concrete' in engineering practice

Penny Harvey and Hannah Knox

News travels fast on the road. We heard about the accident when staying in the small Peruvian village of Chakachimpa.[1] Chakachimpa sits high in the Andes, within sight of the construction of the new Inter-oceanic highway, currently being built to connect Brazil to Asian grain markets across the Pacific Ocean. Some 30 or so people from Chakachimpa were working for the construction company, CONIRSA, bringing news each night which soon circulated between neighbours and kin. This was the first fatality of the construction project. The people we were living with were not sure exactly what had happened. At one remove the event circulated as 'gossip', 'word of mouth' in a world of not quite knowing – people knew that somebody had been killed violently, by heavy machinery, but the narrative ended there, in speculation as to what exactly had happened.

Road building is a dangerous business. The sheer weight and volume of mud, rocks and water that is mobilised and shifted, analysed and altered, manipulated and moved to turn crumbling tracks into an asphalted highway is a feat of human control over an unpredictable material world. The power of the material is palpable both in the construction process – the grinding roar of machinery, the earthworks that seem to scar the landscape – and in the vista of the completed highway – smooth black asphalt rolled out like liquorice over the rise and fall of changing ecological terrains. At the same time, the building of a highway is highly political, where for some the stakes are bigger than the loss of a human life. Huge amounts of money are ploughed into high profile road construction projects like the Inter-oceanic highway by the state and international banks and donors, in pursuit of social, economic and political rewards.

A construction project is a complex social field, where rumour and gossip, speculation and secrecy swirl around the calculations and mappings of engineering science, planning and management. We might describe this field in terms of a politics of knowledge, where diverse forms of expertise jostle for significance in contexts of contemporary capitalist infrastructural development, generating 'hierarchies of credibility' (White, 1993) through which the relative value of knowledges and knowledge practices are established. In the context of road construction, this politics of knowledge is embedded and extended through the material power of matter and things. As such, the co-implication of knowledge and materiality in a project like road building, draws our attention to state effects in new and challenging ways (Harvey, 2005). The exercise of state and corporate power through modern knowledge practices is now well documented (Foucault, 1977; Mitchell, 2002; Scott, 1998), providing an important antidote to an overly simplistic view of the state as a purely institutional agent of power. In this chapter we extend this view of the state to ask how problematic materialities work to challenge such knowledge practices, and what the implications of this challenge might be for our understanding of the relationship between knowledge, expertise and the shaping of particular state forms.

In what follows, we provide an ethnographic account of how mud, dust, rocks and 'land' come to comprise a material world, by looking at the separation of things and people, agents and objects, along the lines of their relatedness to or separation from nature as matter. We explore how materiality is in some contexts systematically set against the cultural achievements of human intentionality within the framework of modernist developmental political economy, but is also simultaneously revealed as inherently unstable, defying the purifications of nature/culture, human/non-human, reason/unreason on which iconic modern projects such as nation building, civil engineering and road construction appear to rely. Our aim is not simply to exemplify Latour's philosophical resolution to the problem of an enduringly incomplete modernity, but rather to explore through ethnography, how divergent materialities might coexist within an aspirational 'modern' world, and through the notion of material powers, to explore the processes through which apparently incompatible knowledges are differentiated and kept apart.

The accident

Driving down the road a few days after the accident, in the company of two engineers and their driver we saw two new crosses at the side of the road marking the site with the name of the deceased, the date of his death and flowers – one cross placed by his family, another by the company. In small actions such as the placing of a cross beside the road – an act all too frequent on Peruvian roads – events are embedded in particular places, and connections made between places and persons. The site becomes the place at which this man died, and raises questions as to how and why he died. We talked with their driver, while the engineers were out of the pick-up, asking him about what had happened. He said that the man had been working behind the bulldozer and had tripped, or somehow been distracted. The machine had driven straight over him and crushed him.

The driver said that there would be more fatalities, because the earth is alive, and demanding human lives. The earth grabs hold of people and they can't get away, that was why the young man had been crushed. We knew from conversations we'd had at a different point along the road that the company did in fact, as part of their community relations programme, make ritual payments to the earth before starting the works and asked our driver about this. 'No,' he said, 'the engineers don't believe, they are Brazilian'; suggesting, perhaps, that even if the company performed such rituals their lack of belief was in itself a failure to engage the vital force of the earth.

Nevertheless, the earth and its violent claims on human life still pose a problem for the company – in this case the immediate concern related to the belief that the souls of those who die violently do not rest, but rather assert their presence and tug at others to join them in death. Several workers were feeling the effects of this first accident. The bulldozer had mysteriously crossed in front of one of the night drivers almost causing another accident. The night watchman on that stretch of the works had fallen ill, his shifts disturbed by the presence of the dead man. After a few days the company arranged for a special mass to be held at the construction camp. They wanted to prevent the 'contagious' effects of the accident as more workers were falling ill, claiming that the dead man was troubling them. The mass, as with the ritual payments to the earth made at other stages of the project, recognised the need to engage with these beliefs, although their importance clearly related to calming the workforce rather than calming the Earth itself.

We wondered about the driver of the bulldozer, thinking how terrible it must be to have been caught up in this event – to have been the one to have driven over your work mate, however others might rationalise the event as caused by a voracious earth force. It turned out that this man had immediately lost his job, caught within a quite different rationale that acknowledged neither the earth, nor a vaguer sense of misfortune. Later that night, sitting in a dark, crowded classroom at the camp, listening to the induction talk for new employees from the head of safety we learned that from the company's perspective the cause of an accident can always be traced to some specific mistake.

The company, we were told, is totally committed to the safety of its employees – and it is a commitment which the employees are duty bound to respect, both in relation to their own safety and to the safety of others around them. There can never be an excuse for an accident. All accidents have causes, and all accidents are a waste of company time. Causes can always be identified, and will always come back to the incorrect action of a specific and identifiable person. The fatal accident – which was alluded to in the presentation, at times indirectly, at another moment with the shocking picture of the dead man lying on the road – had occurred through a mixture of lack of attention and overconfidence. The accident had broken the company target of zero accidents – but made this particular officer even more determined to ensure the ongoing importance and attainability of this target.

However, this logic caught the company in a deep contradiction. The same evangelical safety manager told the assembled workers that they were like 'birds of passage', they had a responsibility to fit into local people's ways of living, taking care not to interfere or damage their life ways. But those who came to work for the company, it turned out, were expected to radically reconfigure their notions of a responsible worker. The company was committed to teaching people to change their attitudes, to give security a high priority, and to help them in this task there were basic norms – instilled through daily meetings of work teams, and readings from the safety manuals. These meetings aimed to elicit active involvement in articulating the values and procedures through which the workers would transform a set of externally imposed rules into a personal decision (and commitment) to value one's own safety. The desired end result is that 'accidents' would be eliminated altogether. Needless to say these rules (which explicitly forbid play, alcohol, drugs, smoking, sleeping, reading, meetings, running or jumping!) are dramatically different from the basic sociality of agricultural working practices where joking, drinking, smoking, running, jumping and 'meeting' are constitutive of meaningful, communicative and effective collaboration.

We started with this example of the accident as it illustrates how the basic modern project of transforming the natural world through human agency (intention, capacity, skill, knowledge) produces a contested boundary between material and immaterial worlds. The 'foreign' engineers, the Brazilians referred to by the driver, are foreign not simply by dint of their nationality, for there are many professional Peruvians among the senior management of the company. 'Brazilians' in this context are those people from elsewhere, who do not actively assume a relationship with the land as a relationship between living beings – that carries responsibilities and onward consequences. Furthermore they are people whose self-understanding, knowledge and expertise is predicated upon this particular separation of the actor (the subject of action) from that which is acted upon.

'I believe in maths'

The driver's invocation of the non-human agency of the land reveals lines of difference that intersect the material production of the road. From the perspective of the engineers, local beliefs in the agency of the land are simply mistaken, 'cultural' understandings. One afternoon, we were chatting with a friend who runs a small hostel, and with one of the engineers who was staying there whilst waiting for the company camp to be completed. The friend had spent the best part of the day ruminating about all the ghosts that had appeared in and around her house over the years, listing her various encounters with them and sharing with us the vague sense of unease that their presence caused her. Turning to the engineer who had been listening to the conversation, she asked him, 'Do you believe in ghosts?' 'No', he replied emphatically, ' I believe in maths'.

The tension in understandings of how power becomes manifested through different kinds of agencies, invokes a long history of western thinking about comparative rationalities, about truth, reality and a modern commitment to scientific thinking. But as Latour (1993) has so eloquently taught us, the 'modern settlement' (that specific cultural attempt to distinguish humans from things, nature from society, facts from value, the West from the rest), is an intrinsically incomplete project. One of the questions which we follow up in the final section of this chapter concerns the character of this incomplete modernity, through a discussion of the ways in which even the most self-conscious and pragmatic agents of modern social transformation are drawn into spaces where 'maths' does not necessarily protect them from 'ghosts'. First of all, however, we allow ourselves some time to dwell on what kind of material powers are being invoked when mathematics is bracketed off from the spectral hauntings of alternative agentive powers.

Contemporary anthropological approaches to materiality have been interested in looking ethnographically and historically at the divisions people make or don't make between subjects and objects, between the inert and the animate, and at the social consequences of how people create or subvert such categories. For some, following in a broadly Marxist tradition, the presence of dangerous and unsettling beings such as ghosts and violent earth forces are understood as historically produced through the deeply unequal and destructive engagement of western imperial powers with non-western peoples. They argue that the efforts of capitalists to secure 'natural resources' for industrial production were in effect efforts to create material worlds that apparently floated free from ownership and/or human attachment, and thus facilitated extraction as a morally acceptable, even the only morally acceptable approach to such resources.

> Resource frontiers grew up where entrepreneurs and armies were able to disengage nature from local ecologies and livelihoods, 'freeing up' natural resources that bureaucrats and generals could offer as corporate raw materials. From a distance, these new resource frontiers appeared as the 'discovery' of global supplies in forests, tundras, coastal seas or mountain fastnesses. Up close, they replaced local systems of human access and livelihood and ecological dynamics of replacement and replenishment with the cultural apparatus of proliferation, out-of-control interstitial capitalist expansion, the frontier.
>
> (Tsing, 2005: 28)

In relation to such accounts the 'modern settlement' is shown to be not simply the cultural driver of modern political economy but to be a deeply compromised political agreement where the objectification of 'nature' and of human labour created the possibilities for ownership and profit and the safe, moral ground of reason from which to protect the interests of a powerful minority. The importance of some of the recent historical and anthropological accounts of these processes (Palmié, 2002; Taussig, 1987; de Boeck, 1996, 1998; Ferme, 2001; Tsing, 2005) has been to remind us of just what it is that people are trying to make sense of when they produce explanations that invoke violent non-human agents. Palmié (2002), for example, argues that Caribbean slave regimes, which legally made persons into things, are a prime example of what he terms 'a peculiarly modern tendency to conjure up quasi-objects, unstable mixtures between humans and things or between nature and society – and then attempt to think or legislate away their fundamental hybridity'. Slave owners knew that their slaves were humans, even as they worked to objectify and instrumentalise their labour. One sea captain threw sick and dying African slaves overboard so as to rationalise his investment and claim insurance money. Actions such as these produced the violent hauntings that derived from the recognition that slaves were only ambiguously 'things'.

The hauntings of dead slaves, or dead construction workers, express the constitutive violence of capitalism, where surplus is generated for some by the labour of others. In this respect such hauntings are neither irrational nor fictitious, but rather express a sense of deep moral concern from those who find themselves facing the darker effects of capital. In the Andean context the most famous of such explanations draws on Nash's powerful ethnography on the Bolivian tin mines (Nash, 1979) which described the violent sacrificial relationship between miners and the Tio, the spirit owner of the mine. This work was reinterpreted by Taussig as an instance of commodity fetishism (Taussig, 1980). Taussig argued that the dangers represented by the voracious devil figure, placated only temporarily with animal sacrifice and always ready to claim a miner's life, expressed people's deep understanding of the implications of market exchange, and the knowledge that in contrast with subsistence agriculture, what was taken from the land was not replaced – the extraction was thus violent and depleting and called forth a violent response.

However there is a further anthropological literature that while acknowledging the deep entanglement of western history with non-western social formations would not want to reduce the distinct understandings of materiality and agency of 'magical thinking' to a critique of, or resistance to, modern political economy. Taussig's analysis of the sacrificial cults in the Bolivian mines was premised on a sharp divide between agricultural and industrial production. Such divisions are not warranted ethnographically and he was criticised by Andeanists for his failure to account for the evidence of sacrificial cults to earth powers that existed prior to the arrival of the Spaniards in South America (Sallnow, 1987), or for the importance of the sacrificial rituals that are integral to subsistence agriculture and herding practices (Gose, 1986, 1994). As Kapferer explains so well in relation to Sri Lanka:

> Sorcery undergoes transformations in meaning in modern political and economic settings. It encodes many of the agonies of these transformations. But it is not a critique of capitalism or even a nascent resistance to it. Sorcery, at least in Sri Lanka, is deeply conservative and is intimately connected with the forces of domination and oppression, as it was in the past. Sorcery in Sri Lanka, incidentally, is not a modern practice. My evidence suggests that it stretches deep into Sri Lanka's ancient past.
>
> (Kapferer, 1988: 235)

Thus while the categorisation of such practices as 'magical' or 'non-rational' is clearly a response of modern thinkers to that which does not fit their particular culture of reason, and helps to explain the emotive force of such ideas in contemporary social life, the labelling process can also obscure the wider implications of such thinking. Viveiros de Castro (nd), following Lévi-Strauss' interest in the material philosophies of Amerindian peoples (discussed later), recently characterised 'magical thinking' as a category invented by 'western thinkers' to refer to situations where the universe is not divided into moral and physical spheres – where Latour's 'modern settlement' has not proposed the discontinuities between 'nature' and 'politics'. With this in mind we move in the following section to a discussion of Inka construction and the notion of Inka 'civil engineering' – to further the discussion of magical agency, to open the issue of materiality and power beyond that of the specific frames of modern western thinking, and to pave the way for the final section where we show how contemporary engineers struggle to keep the 'ghosts' out of the soil.

A structure: an engineer's response to Machu Picchu

As we were writing this chapter, we came across Wright and Zegarra's *Machu Picchu: A Civil Engineering Marvel* (2000). This book, written by an archaeologist and a hydraulics engineer sets out to demonstrate how Machu Picchu was built. They imagine their readers as fellow engineers likely to share their fascination with the technical details of this 'incredible' feat of pre-modern engineering. We found the account enthralling because of what it revealed about the impossibility of providing such a technical explanation in terms that in any way addressed the discontinuities in relation to understandings of form, matter, action and meaning which we were struggling to articulate in the process of writing this chapter.

Wright and Zegarra discuss the huge challenge posed by Andean ecology. They are deeply impressed by the evident capacity of the Inkas for systematic planning, particularly in relation to the hydraulic engineering, fundamental not only to the effective functioning of the site at the time it was built, but also to its survival over the subsequent centuries. It is clear to them that Machu Picchu was built to last and that it was built by people of considerable technical sophistication. They point out that the knowledges incorporated in this site include 'hydrology, hydraulics, agriculture, urban drainage, sanitation, soils and foundation technology, structural engineering, and a "store-house" of construction methods along with good survey control of elevations, distances, and alignment' (2000: 16)... and 'somehow the Inca understood the rudiments of hydrology along with the seasonal variations of water flow without the use of the piezometers, slide rules, or even a written language' (2000: 17). They write:

> Technical analysis of the Inca drainage works demonstrates that the drainage criteria used were reasonable and the implementation uncanny. It seems the Inca would have had the equivalent of an urban drainage manual similar to the ASCE Manual of Practice No. 77 (ASCE 1992) except that the Inca had no written language.
>
> (Wright and Zegarra, 2000: 36)

Indeed the wonder provoked by the site is directly linked to the incongruence between the sophistication of the technological achievement and the lack of modern technical knowledge, communicated to the reader by means of an insistence on measurements that were of course not used in the actual design and construction of the site.

> The Inca civil engineers did their work without the use of the wheel or iron. They had no draft animals for pulling huge rocks up inclined planes, yet they built Machu Picchu out of granite boulders, many weighing 10 to 15 metric tons (9–14 tons) and having lengths of 3 meters (9 feet). Try to imagine the site conditions with which the civil engineers were faced in about AD 1450. Two mountains had a ridge between them and sheer drop-offs on both sides to the river 500 m (1640 ft.) below. They faced rock fills and jagged rock out crops. Nearly 2,000 millimeters (79 inches) of rainfall per year, and no level fields for growing crops. It was also a remote area some 80 km (50 miles) from the capital, separated by steep passes and rugged mountain ranges. In 90 years the Inca civil engineers changed this challenging site to the archaeological jewel of the Andes, built so well that it endured for decades [*sic*].
>
> (Wright and Zegarra, 2000: 68)

Of course the notion of 'civil engineering' would have been totally meaningless in a sixteenth-century Inka world where modern separations between religious and political life would have been unthinkable. Mukerji's wonderful book on the Gardens of Versailles (Mukerji, 1997) points to the transition in the materiality of western state making in the move from empire to the territorial nation state in seventeenth-century Europe. She explains how in the case of France, an open, expansive sense of political domain and a spatial focus on the centre and its connections to more distant peripheries characterised the imperial sense of territory. Louis XIV's experimental engineering in the gardens of Versaille were significant because they marked a transition in the use of landmass as a political resource, with the focus now more clearly on creating borders and assuring their defence. There are clearly important points of comparison here. The Inkas certainly used landmass as a political resource and the structure of empire was quite explicitly focused on Cusco, the imperial capital, known to them as the naval of the universe, the centre of the four imperial provinces. Yet unlike their European contemporaries, Inka concepts of space and time were understood through the figure of the synecdoche (where the part stands for the whole or vice versa) – the spatial configuration of the imperial capital was the spatial configuration of the empire itself. The foundational social unit, the *ayllu* or kindred, similarly was understood to encompass the whole empire and a local descent group in the nesting structure of the Russian doll.

More distinctive still was the way in which the continuities between nature and politics were understood and imposed, where possible, to fit the imperial model. The fifteenth century was the era of imperial expansion for the Inka. A highly militarised and effective state organisation was presided over by the Inka and his royal sister, the Qoya. These divine beings (the male and female manifestations of an androgynous originary life force) headed the royal lineages to which conquered tribal groups were forcibly affiliated – by 'marriage' but also through the appropriation of their apical ancestors who were brought to Cusco, the imperial capital, and assimilated, in subordinate positions, into the Inka's own divine ancestry. These originary ancestors (the *huacas*) existed in human form (as mummified bodies of ancestors) and were simultaneously a manifestation of significant points in the wider sentient environment from where the ancestors first appeared in human form – a lake, a spring, a cave, often sites where the earth's surface fissured or appeared to open inwards, or stretch upwards to the sky. High mountains, water, the earth were all divine beings. The imperial city was connected to the wider empire through sacred site lines, marked again with rocks and other features of the landscape that symbolically ordered the imperial territory and those who lived within it. Young women sent as offerings to the Inka, and the conquered gods themselves, would walk these lines, literally enacting their connection to and encompassment by the imperial centre. The Inka also took soil from conquered groups which was 'incorporated' into the soil of empire in the central square of the imperial capital (Brush, 1977). The politics of connection were highly ambiguous. In some ways the *huacas* were prisoners, hostages and guarantors of compliance. However, their incorporation into the royal lineages was also a privilege and entailed a reciprocal guarantee of 'care' and responsibility on the part of the Inka to provide access to land and water.

In theory – the Inka had absolute power. Within the empire, social and physical reproduction were of a kind, both guaranteed by the Inka's control of the universe. The driving social relationship at the heart of this system was that of hierarchical reciprocity, in systems of interdependence where subject populations provided labour tributes in return for the possibilities of life itself. Their economy combined mining, textile production, herding and agriculture, but huge energy was also invested in the precise control of the wider sentient ecology. Offerings between orders of being were fundamentally sacrificial. Just as the subjugated populations offered their reproductive potential (in the form of animals, crops, and young women for sacrifice), so the Inka made huge ceremonial offerings to the wider environment at crucial moments of cosmic transition – for example at the summer and winter solstice, or on the death of an Inka ruler.

At some levels this Inka cosmology is clearly ideological and ethno-historians are increasingly publishing alternative Andean understandings of the world from this period, from the perspective of social groups who were never successfully incorporated into this model of the world. However, in relation to the construction of Machu Picchu these principles are highly significant and the brief synopsis of some of these core principles are sufficient for the points we want to make here.

There are two features of the Machu Picchu site which Wright and Zegarra discuss, but which they are unable to incorporate into their description of Inka technical skill – for they resist 'translation'. The first of these refers to a gold bracelet that was found deep down in the foundations of one of the walls. Unable to integrate the presence of this object with the hydraulic engineering under discussion, it is dismissed as 'an offering' clearly irrelevant to their discussion of the technical sophistication of the drainage systems. Interestingly, and not fortuitously the hydraulic cycle is at the heart of Andean principles of reciprocity and defines the universal circulation of vitality (Gose, 1994). The mountains produce rain, the rain activates the potential in the earth to grow food, to create human and animal life, fostered by continual offerings of sacred liquids (particularly maize beer) humans help in the hydration process, fostered ultimately by the bodies of the dead who travel within the earth to sacred mountains where their nourishment of the earth allows the further release of water. This cosmic cycle is imitated in smaller ways by the preservation of meat, and vegetable matter through dehydration (and traditionally the mummification of bodies at death). Dehydration is not death as finality, but rather death as a store of energy, awaiting rehydration for the release of live and animate force. In the context of these ideas and practices Allen's description of offerings as 'the pump of the system' is very significant (Allen, 1997). The technical description provided for the interest of the modern engineer erases the 'pump', for it is not 'technically' necessary. However, from an Inka perspective the bracelet, the only one to have been found on the site, would have been hugely significant in the cycles of reciprocity through which this site was connected to the cosmos. So too the second set of 'objects' which are incommensurate with the technical description, the mimetic granite carvings of the mountains that surround the site.

Again Allen's work on contemporary Andean materiality is very instructive. She draws attention to the principles of consubstantiality that have very deep roots in Andean understandings of materiality and power. In this ancient material philosophy the inseparability of mind and matter is assumed, as is the intrinsic interconnection of all beings, and the animacy (to some degree) of all material objects (Allen, 1997). Wright and Zegarra argue that these mimetic features were used to demonstrate the power of the Inka site to those beings with whom they were most intensely engaged – the surrounding mountain deities themselves. The point is not elaborated, but there are interesting resonances with the ways the Inka brought manifestations of other deities to the imperial capital in material form. Perhaps these carved shapes incorporated the mountains into the site itself. But Allen's work on miniatures suggests an even bolder communicative strategy on the part of the Inca rulers.

It is certainly possible that the Inka was attempting to harness the power of other gods to their site, through the imitative carvings of the granite in the shape of the surrounding mountains. But the integration of these miniature forms could also suggest a claim on the part of the Inka to be the very source of that power. Such a possibility would be commensurate with Inka use of miniatures in other spheres.

Miniatures were understood as condensed matter – storehouses of prosperity and well being, tended and ritually 'fed' with libations. Miniature ears of corn crafted in gold would be placed in their fields as prototypical instances of corn with the power to generate subsequent further versions of itself. Indeed Allen argues that the term Inqa is derived from the term for such prototypes, the Inka being the archetypal instance of a form that gives rise to the universal vitality embedded in his person.

From the perspective of Inka construction, then, the bracelet and the carved granite are at the heart of what would have made this site viable and effective, as an integral material-political-divine structure. They draw our attention to a moral universe of hierarchical reciprocity and the specific active, interactional techniques for changing the lived-in-world that Inka 'engineers' deployed. Finally they are illustrative of what Allen calls 'synecdochal thinking' and 'play with dimensionality', where parts (in this case miniatures) are taken as equivalents to wholes. In such a world, where connectivity is assumed, and actions are always understood to draw forth consequences, analogical reason provides an ontological basis for events that the more analytical abstractions of modern knowledge practices exclude as 'uncanny'; those events that according to 'rational' logic should not be taken as either relevant or real yet which nonetheless appear to exercise some kind of autonomous agency.

An uncanny example: the gold bracelet, dismissed as an 'offering' in Wright and Zegarra's account re-appears in their story. Before the bracelet was discovered, they had been trying to get permission from the Peruvian government to analyse the soils of the Machu Picchu site. The government had not allowed this investigation but had given limited funding to some Peruvian archaeologists to carry out this work. It was they who found the bracelet. The bracelet however changed the course of their investigation as the financial value and cultural significance of the gold object drew investors and state support back to the site and enabled the investigations to continue. Whilst excluded by Wright and Zegarra from explanatory accounts of the material processes of Inka construction, it seems that the bracelet found an alternative channel for the expression of its materiality, extending its power out from the domain of the analogical and reasserting itself anew in the analytical domain of accounting, management and finance.

Lévi-Strauss in his famous essay on the 'science of the concrete' (1981 [1962]) explored the utility of an intellectual distinction between analogical and analytical reason. For him magical thought differed from scientific thinking not in exhibiting deficiencies in its capacity to test and experiment, to question and discover, to actively seek knowledge and to apply that knowledge for practical ends. Rather, he preferred to think of

> two distinct modes of scientific thought. These are certainly not a function of different stages of development of the human mind but rather of two strategic levels at which nature is accessible to scientific enquiry: one roughly adapted to that of perception and the imagination: the other at a remove from it. It is as if the necessary connections which are the object of all science, Neolithic or modern, could be arrived at by two different routes, one very close to, and the other more remote from, sensible intuition.
>
> (Lévi-Strauss, 1981 [1962]: 15)

Lévi-Strauss' approach has its problems; after reading Bruno Latour, his reproduction of a fundamental distinction between nature and culture seems at best awkward and at worst untenable. However his work is useful for providing us with a language through which we might think about the relationship between the Inka construction and the engineering practice of contemporary road builders. For Lévi-Strauss, his two modes of scientific thought operated not through different levels of sophistication but through a different understanding of how knowledge emerges out of the relationship between the contingent and the necessary:

> Science as a whole is based on the distinction between the contingent and the necessary, this being also what distinguishes event and structure ... Mythical thought builds up structures by fitting together events, or rather the remains of events, while science, 'in operation' simply by virtue of coming into being, creates its means and results in the form of events, thanks to the structures which it is constantly elaborating and which are its hypotheses and theories.
>
> (Lévi-Strauss, 1981 [1962]): 21–22)

What is particularly interesting to us in the context of this chapter is that the two figures that Lévi-Strauss then deploys to exemplify these divergent sciences (and to contemporise the Neolithic/modern distinction) are the 'engineer' and the 'bricoleur'. For Lévi-Strauss, the engineer

> works by means of concepts, the bricoleur by means of signs ... One way in which signs can be opposed to concepts is that whereas concepts aim to be wholly transparent with respect to reality, signs allow and even require the interposing and incorporation of a certain amount of human culture into reality.
>
> (Lévi-Strauss, 1981 [1962]: 20)

This characterisation, whilst somewhat dichotomised, resonates with the evident necessity of engineering to rid their conceptual engagement with the material world of bracelets and ghosts. However this is not to say that for engineers their conceptual apparatus is fixed in advance of an interaction with the materialities that they encounter. Abstraction does not precede interaction, but is produced through particular kinds of engagement and experimentation that explain material powers in terms of their autonomy and separation from a social world. In this way engineers are highly sensitive to the constant move between the necessary and the contingent. At the same time, the sociality of the practices by which these material powers are revealed – laboratory work, surveying, application – mean that within the life of a construction project there is an equally firm assumption that such materiality is, in practice, never fully abstracted from its social entanglements, except perhaps momentarily in the laboratory environment.

In the final section of the chapter, we look at how these ideas play through the analytical practices of laboratory engineers on the construction sites. Here we find that while the analysis of 'soil' is the focus of laboratory work, there are considerable problems both in extricating the materials from their social bonds, and in re-introducing their structural analyses to the event time of the construction project. Our aim is to show how engineers, far from exemplifying Lévi-Strauss's ideal notion of modern science, are constantly drawn into a world where imaginative engagement with ambiguous material powers is required of them.

The laboratories – extruding the physical from moral entanglements

The first time we went to the labs we were struck by the difference in scale between the huge machines and open landscapes of the road, and the fine detail, precision and compactness of the objects within the lab. In its own way the lab produced the road in miniature. But this is not a world where the miniature holds the wider world within itself. Quite the contrary, here, in contrast to the analogical thinking of Inka miniatures, we are dealing with the analytical notion of the constituent element. In Inka engineering proportional difference produces condensed, intensified manifestations of a specific energy or life force. The samples in the laboratories are not wholes but parts. Thus while we can assume that Inka engineers proceed from plans to construction in relation to their knowledge of the wider universe (a universe that necessitated exchange offerings, and the installation of nodes of vitality within the structures themselves), modern engineering works from the detailed knowledge of the part, towards the completion of the wider structure (which will in itself not be commensurate with other, more encompassing entities, but rather be a step towards assembling the greater whole).

In relation to the aims of this chapter the labs are fascinating spaces, for within the road construction process, they are the sites of experimental transformation, and the locus for the deliberate construction of pure materiality through work on brute matter. It is in the labs that the 'mud' and 'dust' (those categories of problematic materiality that are most usually cited as the reason why proper asphalted roads are needed in the first place) are transformed into potential versions of the materials from which the new road will be built.

The processes are varied and complex – for our purposes here it is sufficient to know that samples are collected along the length of a proposed route – and re-collected each time route changes are proposed. Samples are also collected from the quarries and river-beds identified for the provision of stone and sand, and from the sites where waste materials will be deposited. The daily business is that of measurement – the soil samples are sorted, labelled, tested and measured, results recorded, compared, analysed, classified and charted. In many ways you could argue that the 'land' – the soils that come from specific places, from specific conditions of ownership and previous use – is gradually dematerialised in the lab via mathematical practice. And while the samples are worked on physically by the lab staff who carry out the tests, the samples are ultimately transformed into figures through which a particular understanding of their properties (plasticity, density, resilience, water retention, etc.) is calculated.

Periods of testing then begin as the samples, now understood as instances of particular properties or capacities are combined in diverse ways, re-tested, with new measures, until working models for construction are arrived at. The lab technicians are then responsible for continued measure of incoming materials to ensure that the formulas are not disrupted by any material unevenness across the incoming elements. Classification, measuring, modelling, testing and adjusting the materials is a constant process – which to those who work in the laboratories lies at the very heart of all construction projects.

It is important to point out however, that the lab work not only produces this abstracted materiality (the materials abstracted from their prior contexts of existence and reconfigured as an entirely non-human entity, the properties of those materials further abstracted in the analytical process) but that the abstraction is carried out with the explicit intention of subsequent human intervention. For once the specific quality of the available materials is understood the lab engineers begin to produce the formulas for producing better, more effective materials. The samples (and subsequently the massed materials) are thus acted on, 'cultured up' in Strathern's (1992) terms, to produce improved substance, until the lab team finally produces the formulas for the production of optimum materials for interaction with specific environments – which have also been analysed through the measurement of a range of things such as seismic quality, temperatures, weight and frequency of projected traffic, etc. It is in this sense, in this sequential combination of analysis and transformation, that the labs are the nearest we get within the construction project to the realisation of a division between human design (intentionality) and the brute materiality to which such intention is directed.

However this clear separation is more of a hiatus in the production process than an enduring social reality – despite the strength of the image of 'man's' domination of 'nature' in and around road construction sites. Indeed this division is only sustainable in so far as the construction materials are kept apart from wider physical and social environments from which they were drawn, or in which they will subsequently be placed.

The first step in the rehabilitation of the materials is in the move from the analytical labs of the construction camps to the roadside testing sites. Here the world has already become more uncertain. Revisions are constant because materials are unstable and things go wrong. The important thing here is that lab science is not an end in itself but a step in a wider instrumental process where the construction company seeks to produce effective materials for the construction of the road. Despite the claims by the lab engineers to be at the core of the construction process, the efficacy of their knowledge is only partially related to what they come to know about the material substances from which the road will be built. Engineers are, for example, aware that the stability of road construction is a collective achievement requiring a complex, diverse team of experts, and considerable dependence on both machines and human labour. The movements from abstract analysis to the specificities of volatile physical and social environments is constant. Rory Miller's account of the distinction between engineers and contractors in the history of railway construction is very apt for the contemporary road building process:

> Very early in the history of railway construction in Britain a clear distinction developed between engineers like the Stephensons and L.K. Brunel and

> contractors like Thomas Brassey. Contractors needed different qualities: in the words of Asa Briggs, financial acumen, knowledge of building, an ability to handle a heterogeneous labour force, some political capacity, and most of all experience. 'A contractor could fail,' Briggs (1963: 15) remarks, 'because he was deficient at the vital moment in only one of these skills. He could succeed only if he displayed them all'.
>
> (Miller, 1986)

From the perspective of the engineers all modern roads are a political compromise – both in relation to the routing and the cost – and these constructions, unlike the Inka construction at Machu Picchu are not seen as stable and enduring. Quite the contrary, the engineers 'know' that they are unstable, that they will deteriorate from the moment that they are first fixed in place. Such deterioration is inevitable and ultimately not under their control. The best they can do is assess the risks to the construction from the environment (particularly changes in temperature, precipitation and drainage, and subsidence) and from those who start to use it (the weight and frequency of traffic, and the standard of maintenance). The 'best' road is thus one that has a notion of cost/benefit at its core, not an 'ideal' material form. This situation puts a somewhat different slant on the laboratory work. Knowing that the 'best' road is not the 'ideal' road, the rational measures and procedures of the labs are in fact devised relative to the task which they are trying to achieve. Political decisions are taken about how long a road should last, about its quality and the engineers are required to work to these entirely social measures. You certainly don't need to tell an engineer that there is no abstract materiality as their daily work is about the 'translation' between design and practice in a complex material world, where the materiality is self-evidently social and unstable, yet their basic working methods proceed as if a stable material world pre-existed their activities, or could be brought into being.

Here we return to Castoriadis' concept of 'infrastructures of certainty' (Castoriadis, 1987), the things people do to enable them to proceed in an uncertain environment. Modern engineers mix science and politics. Inkas did too, with the difference that their politics was one of systematic incorporation of wider life forces, while the politics of modern construction rest more on the systematic differentiation of social and material powers, through the social enactment of technical (non-social) procedures. We conclude with a final example to illustrate this point.

Conclusion

While we were staying in one of the construction camps we spent some time with the lawyer in charge of land expropriation. She spent a great deal of time with the communities who live along the roadside, attempting to negotiate voluntary transfer of land from communities to the state, ensuring that the state pays the appropriate compensation, and dealing with the thorny issue of illegal 'possession' of what is technically state land along both sides of the existing road.

Although employed by the Ministry of Transport, she works in close cooperation with the company who are building the road, in particular with their Community Relations division. Within the company this division is primarily responsible for labour/employment issues – working with communities along the road to come to understandings about who can work for the company and under what conditions. Local people are not interested in these divisions of responsibility between the state and the company. The appearance of this road project in their communities signals two key issues: (1) the possibility of labour in the sure knowledge that there is not enough work for everyone and (2) the fact that some people are going to lose their farmland as alterations to the route of the existing road are effected. Many complex and interesting dynamics occur at the interface between the companies, the state and these local populations, but now we refer to one small incident. In an area not far from where the first fatality occurred, which was one of the first main fronts of construction work begun by the company, several of the communities became so angered and upset by the process that they blocked the road and halted production. There were labour issues: they felt that those most affected by the disruption of the road building process should be the first to benefit from the labour opportunities. This was an issue which the company managed to handle. But there was also a terrible sense of loss. They wanted the road, and indeed had actively campaigned for it to come their way but the sight of the bulldozers and diggers carving up their fields, and removing the soil was very distressing and they did not feel adequately compensated. This was an issue that the company could not address. It could not build the road without intervening in their land in this way. The lawyer told us that one of the communities had proposed to the company that if they could return the 'earth' to them, in some way this would keep alive a connection with their ancestors and history which they did not want severed. But the company could not meet this request. The reason was interesting. Obligated by the state to invest considerable resources not only in community relations but also in environmental protection the company could only 'return' the land if all the sites of 'reception' for this displaced land were adequately analysed along the length of the route. Such activity would be prohibitively time-consuming and expensive. It was not viable within the terms of the project.

Building upon the conceptual apparatus of a notion of material power which explains whilst at the same time undermining the purifications of modern knowledge, we have attempted in this chapter to draw together the multiple and often conflicting engagements of projects of nation building and civil engineering into a single space of analysis. The material powers exhibited in this short example take us from the tugging affective pull of a land lived-on and cultivated, to those physical transformations of matter whose potential effects on plants, landscapes and animals constitute the parameters of a process of environmental degradation. By turning our attention in this chapter from the politics of knowledge as a discursive or intellectual exercise, to a process that is always already materialised and materialising, we hope to have shown some of the ways in which the politics of engagement in processes of state building are manifest. This last example is particularly striking for the way in which it makes evident not only the political dimensions of different ways of knowing, but also the question of how the weight of moral responsibility might be offloaded through a rechanneling of material power. The problem of environmental impact in this case, allowed the land in its volume and complexity to rise up as a barrier to the community's requests, in a way that could not be surpassed by appeals to ancestral connections or 'community' relations. Yet the work to classify and separate land off as a substance whose autochthonous powers derive from its universal and inanimate properties, does not ultimately remove the ghosts from the soil. Rather it constitutes a refusal to engage the specific material relations through which 'ghosts', like gold bracelets, are credible forces to be reckoned with.

Note

1 Penny Harvey has been working in this area on and off since 1983. Our current ethnographic project builds on the long-terms relationships established over the past two decades.

References

Allen, Catherine (1997) 'When pebbles move mountains: iconicity and symbolism in Quechua ritual' in R. Howard-Malverde (ed.) *Creating Context in Andean Cultures*, Oxford: Oxford University Press.

Briggs, Asa (1963) 'Foreword' to Robert Keith Middlemass, *The Master Builders: Thomas Brassey, Sir John Aird, Lord Cowdray, and Sir John Norton-Griffiths*, London: Hutchinson.

Brush, Stephen B. (1977) *Mountain, Field and Family: The economy and human ecology of an Andean village*, Philadelphia: University of Pennsylvania Press.

Castoriadis, Cornelius (1987) *The Imaginary Institution of Society*, trans. Kathleen Blamey, Cambridge MA: MIT Press.

de Boeck, F. (1996) 'Postcolonialism, power and identity: local and global perspectives from Zaire' in R. Werbner and T. Ranger (eds) *Postcolonial Identities in Africa*, London: Zed Press, 75–106.

—— (1998) 'Beyond the grave: history, memory and death in postcolonial Congo/Zaire' in R. Werbner (ed.) *Memory and the Postcolony: African Anthropology and the Critique of Power*, London: Zed Books, 21–57.

Ferme, M. (2001) *The Underneath of Things: Violence, History and the Everyday in Sierra Leone*, Berkeley: University of California Press.

Foucault, M. (1977). *Discipline and Punish: The Birth of the Prison*, London: Allen Lane.

Gell, Alfred (1998) *Art and Agency: An Anthropological Theory*, Oxford: Oxford University Press.

Gose, Peter (1986) 'Sacrifice and the commodity form in the Andes', *Man* 21: 296–310.

Gose, Peter (1994) *Deathly Waters and Hungry Mountains: Agrarian Ritual and Class Formation in an Andean Town*, Toronto: University of Toronto Press.

Harvey, P. (2005). 'The materiality of state effects: an ethnography of a road in the Peruvian Andes' in C. Krohn-Hansen and K. Nustad (eds), *State Formation. Anthropological Explorations*, Cambridge: Pluto Press, 216–247.

Kapferer, B. (1988) *Legends of People, Myths of State: Violence, Intolerance, and Political Culture in Sri Lanka and Australia*, Washington and London: Smithsonian Institution Press.

Keane, Webb (2005) 'Signs are not the garb of meaning: on the social analysis of material things', in Miller (ed.) *Materiality*, Durham: Duke University Press, 182–205.

Latour, Bruno (1993) *We Have Never Been Modern*, London: Prentice Hall.

Lévi-Strauss, Claude (1981 [1962]) *The Savage Mind*, Chicago: University of Chicago Press.

Miller, Danny (ed.) (2005) *Materialities*, Durham: Duke University Press.

Miller, Rory (1986) 'Transferring techniques: railway building and management on the West Coast of South America' in R. Miller and H. Finch *Technology Transfer and Economic Development in Latin America*, 1850–1930, Liverpool: Institute of Latin American Studies, Working Paper 7.

Mitchell, Timothy (2002) *Rule of Experts: Egypt, Technopolitics, Modernity*, Berkeley: University of California Press.

Mukerji, Chandra (1997) *Territorial Ambitions and the Gardens of Versailles*, Cambridge: Cambridge University Press.

Nash, June (1979) *We Eat the Mines and the Mines Eat Us*, New York: Columbia University Press.

Palmié, Stephan (2002) *Wizards and Scientists: Explorations in Afro-Cuban Modernity and Tradition*, Durham: Duke University Press.

Pinney, Christopher (2005) 'Things happen: or, from which moment does that object come?' in D. Miller (ed.) *Materiality*, Durham: Duke University Press, 256–272.

Sallnow, Michael (1987) *Pilgrims of the Andes. Regional Cults in Cusco*, Washington DC: Smithsonian Institution Press.

Scott, J.C. (1998). *Seeing like a State: How Certain Schemes to Improve the Human Condition have Failed*. New Haven, Conn. and London: Yale University Press.

Strathern, Marilyn (1992) *After Nature: English Kinship in ihe Late Twentieth Century*, Cambridge: Cambridge University Press.

Taussig, Michael (1980) *The Devil and Commodity Fetishism in South America*, Chapel Hill: The University of North Carolina Press.

Taussig, Michael (1987) *Shamanism, Colonialism, and the Wild Man: A Study in Terror and Healing*, Chicago: University of Chicago Press.

Tsing, Anna Lowenthal (2005) *Friction: An Ethnography of Global Connection*, Princeton University Press.

Viveiros de Castro, Eduardo (unpublished m/s) 'The gift and the given: three nano-essays on kinship and magic'.

White, L. (1993) 'Cars out of Place', *Representations*, 43: 27–50.

Wright, K. and A. Zegarra (2000) *Machu Picchu: A Civil Engineering Marvel*, Reston, Virginia: ASCE press.

Part 3

Colonial materialities

7 Camerawork as technical practice in colonial India

Christopher Pinney

Techniques do not exist as such … but there is an *adjective*, technical, that we can use in many different situations.

(Bruno Latour, 1999: 190–191)

Let me start by engaging a paradox: the paradox of the reaffirmation of an old order that is frequently permitted by the conquest of a new territory, what (in another context) George Orwell described as "the loyalties and superstitions that the intellect had seemingly banished" which "come rushing back under the thinnest of disguises" (2008: 124). Consider for example the concept "visual culture". Many readers will have experienced the liberating potential which this quasi-anthropological demotic offered as a challenge to a civilizational art history still gripped by an exclusionary aesthetics. However, this promise of freedom bore within it what now seems like the return of the repressed. Michael Baxandall's "period eye" (1972) and Clifford Geertz's "Art as a cultural system" (1983) constituted the visual as a new territory for a familiar kind of anthropology in which culture, history, and locality continued to be the ruling concepts. It is this pattern of conquest and the ways in which we might escape it which will concern me in this chapter. My case study is photography – specifically in India – but the broader question I hope to illuminate is whether, as Latour put it, we must remain trapped within 'territories' (in this case India, and photography in India) rather than 'networks' (in this case a global 'camerawork' which can be illumined through the prism of practice in India).[1]

We will return very soon to the dichotomy that Latour offers us, but first if you will permit, a little scene setting. Let us rehearse the ecstatic moment of arrival when, in October 1839, William O'Shaughnessy reports to a meeting of the Asiatic Society in Calcutta on his experiments with the new *photogenic drawing* 'which was exciting so much attention' in Europe. This was a mere three months after Arago's announcement of Daguerre's photographic process in Paris. Daguerre's discovery also provoked three long articles on the subject in the *Bombay Times* in December of the same year (Desmond, 1985: 49), and by January 1840, the Calcutta firm of Thacker, Spink & Co. was advertising daguerreotype cameras for sale. By March 5, 1840 *The Calcutta Courier* was able to record what were almost certainly the first daguerreotypes produced in India, displayed at a "highly delighted" meeting at the Asiatic Society.

This early enthusiasm might serve as the launching pad for a familiar kind of account, driven by a translational and territorializing logic: photography imported into India or Japan or Peru, presumed in some sense to be French or English, is co-opted by a new set of local practices. This is certainly a view that I have previously argued myself[2] so it is worth marking the distance between the argument I am exploring here and that earlier position. A key exemplar of a process of "Indianization" would be the overpainting of the photographic surface (see Gutman, 1982; Allana and Kumar, 2008). Similar narratives have and could be developed in other locations. Following Shunnojo-Tsunetari's thwarted 1843 attempt and subsequent success in 1848 in importing a daguerreotype camera into Nagasaki, Eliphalet Brown takes a daguerreotype camera to Japan as part of Commodore Perry's 1854 Expedition, and in the same year the first Japanese daguerreotype manual appears ("Ensei Kikijutsu" – "Use of Novel Devices from the West") and it is then only a matter of time before photography appears incarnated in a territorialized guise. Thus Kinoshita Naoyuki in his extremely interesting account directs our attention to photography's co-option as "ihai," the wooden memorial tablets "on which were written the Buddhist names of the deceased" (Naoyuki, 2003: 18–19). Similarly, when approaching work by the fabulous Peruvian photographer Martin Chambi (or for that matter Figueroa Aznar) our desire is usually to localize: to find in their astonishing portraits and landscapes an embrace of a sophisticated Cusqueno indigenismo, a political romance of territory (Poole, 1997: 168–197).

These compelling localizing narratives all provide evidence of our desire to dissolve technical practice in the balm of heroic human activity. Photography in these accounts is simply, or chiefly, a void, waiting to be filled by pre-existing cultural and historical practice. These stories of photography are like those eighteenth-century object narratives (*The Story of My Pipe* or *Memoirs of an Armchair*, etc.) described by Roland Barthes which he suggested were in fact not the stories of the objects themselves, but of the hands between which those objects passed (Barthes, 1972; see also Pinney, 2002a). These stories of heroic culture and heroic man triumphing over the camera are articulated within a structured choice between what Latour describes as the notion of technology as "neutral tool" and its obverse, technology as "autonomous destiny" – a dichotomy that might be rephrased as a choice between "culture" versus "technological determinism" (Latour, 1999: 178–180).

My suggestion here, following Latour, is that we need a *different* kind of history of photography, one which allows us to escape from the choice of either a technological determinism, on the one hand, or (on the other) a belief in photography's *neutrality* in which what matters are remarkable individual practitioners, or photography's "Indian-ness" or "Peruvian-ness," all of which give color to an otherwise blank space.

Is "do cameras take photographs?" the wrong type of question?

Before we return to this dichotomy, and the possibility of transcending it, its broader historical frame can also be gestured to. The first matter about which I must be explicit is my reliance on Martin Heidegger, a figure whom Latour sees as simply deluded. I find in Heidegger's phenomenology, and in the historical narrative presumed in his "Age of the world picture", much that is hugely useful. Latour is undoubtedly correct in his claim that Heidegger problematically believed "what the modern Constitution says about itself," by which he means that for Heidegger, modernity's assumed rupture was a (baneful) matter of achieved fact, whereas for Latour it remains an unachieved and impossible fantasy. Heidegger's narrative is in certain respects parallel to that of Latour's except that for Heidegger there *is* definite rupture, no indeterminacy of the "we have never been". In part reflecting this difference in the evaluation of what we might describe as the *potency* of the modern, Heidegger and Latour deposit "enchantment" and "disenchantment" on different sides of the modern and pre-modern. For Heidegger, enchantment is something destroyed by the modern, for Latour the modern is a phenomenon that aspires, but resolutely fails, to destroy enchantment. Under the Modern Constitution (the binomialism of the human and non-human, culture and nature, self and other that characterizes the modern) enchantment is, in the Latourian paradigm, merely disguised. For Latour, Heidegger's limitation resides in his assumption that Being is *only* to be found "along the Black Forest Holzwege," and that science having "no other essence but that of technology" is part of the desert of disenchantment (Latour, 1993: 65). For Latour by contrast, "god is present"[3] as much in modern analogues as in those archaic forms extolled by Heidegger: "in Adidas shoes as well as in the old wooden clogs hollowed out by hand, in agribusiness as well as in timeworn landscapes." Heidegger, "hunkered down" in his forest is bound to feel a sense of "tragic loss" (Latour, 1993: 66).

But we should beware of throwing the Heideggerean baby out with the Latourian bathwater for Heidegger helps us frame a larger question that will assist us, namely, what we might term the "anthropologization" of agency which informs, and constrains, our thinking and language about the relation between humans and non-humans. "Anthropology" in the Heideggerean account is "that philosophical interpretation of man which explains and evaluates whatever is in its entirety, from the standpoint of man and in relation to man" (1977: 133). Evidence of this anthropologizing constraint might be seen in the terms under which agency manifests itself in influential approaches to the power of the material and visual, such as those advanced by W.J.T. Mitchell and Alfred Gell. For Mitchell the liberation of the object starts with the granting of a "face" to images: for Gell it starts with the exportation of "personhood" to images and objects (Pinney, 2005).

Both Heidegger and Latour can help us articulate a critique of this "democratization" of human qualities. Heidegger provides a fundamental point of entry into grasping the metahistorical conditions through which modernity transforms the world "into picture and man into *subiectum*" and the manner in which

> the more extensively and the more effectually the world stands at man's disposal as conquered, and the more objectively the object appears, all the more subjectively … does the *subiectum* rise up … and observation and teaching about the world change[s] into a doctrine of man, into anthropology.
> (Heidegger, 1977: 133)

Heidegger helps us understand the limitations of Mitchell's and Gell's approaches as part of that "doctrine of man," and as a further ingress into that doctrine which takes us away from where we really want to be.

Latour's questions about the ambivalence and un-accomplished-ness of this doctrine open up a practical methodology through which we can think about the manner in which (to return to the specific technical practice with which this chapter is concerned) the camera and its subjects remain un-decided. We will not get far if we attempt to give the camera a "face," or decide that the best way to proceed is through endowing the "non-human" with those qualities which we assume "humans" to have. A Latourian approach demands that we place both of these under erasure. Our task now is to refuse both the reductive alternative of "culture" or "technology," and those solutions which at the moment they appear to annul certain dichotomies in fact further, and more deeply, inscribe them.

We need to come up with a new kind of ratio, a new way of conceptualizing photography as *technical practice* itself in a state of continuous transformation (or as Barthes would say "declension"), which is imbricated with equally fluid subjects (both in front of, and behind, the camera) and to understand the ways in which this entangled practice has itself transformed that domain that many of us used to call "culture."

Entangled practice is one way of understanding Latour's argument about the relationship between guns and gunmen which can be seen to bear a starkly analogous relationship to camera and cameraman. The two propositions "guns kill people" and "guns don't kill people: people kill people" exemplify (in Latour's admittedly simplistic opposition) the useless choice between technology as "autonomous destiny" and its obverse, "neutral tool." In the first account the gun acts "by virtue of *material* components irreducible to the social qualities of the gunman," in the other the gun is a "neutral carrier of human will." The alternative, which folds human and non-humans "into each other," involves a translation between the essences of subjects and objects towards the "hybrid actor comprising … the gun and gunman": a collective actant (1999: 178–179).

Camerawork as process

This provides a useful model for thinking about the entangled practice that coheres around the translated forms of camera and cameraman – that "object-institution" (Latour, 1999: 192) – which in this chapter goes under the sign of "camerawork."

But this is only half the story for "entanglement" has to be temporalized: given a processual historicity. Photography is not something that magically drops into society pre-formed as a determinate "technology." It is, from the start (and remains until this day)[4] blurred and uncertain. Photography's potential had to be explored *experimentally* through engagement with equally blurred and uncertain subjects, and a blurred and uncertain history and temporality that reconstituted all of these terms.

Contemporary accounts show clearly how blurred and uncertain these positions were. The camera and its objects would emerge in a complex shared space (what elsewhere I've called a 'corpography' [Pinney, 2002b]), an experimental networked zone of technical practice. For instance the camera is experimented with as a prosthetic extension – a superbody – in colonial jurisprudence through the 1850s writings of the pathologist Norman Chevers concerning its utility in the investigation of rural murders (Chevers, 1870: 74). Photography in India (as in the US) was also from its inception intimately linked to telegraphy and attempts were made to integrate the photography of convicts with the network of telegraphy in the 1870s. In these early experiments photography's was explicitly and prophetically linked to the possibilities of prosthetic *tele-vision*.

So I hope to avoid any sense of photography's "autonomous destiny": I want to engage it as an experimental zone, with uncertain and unexpected outcomes. But equally I want to place under erasure that "culture" which the social sciences and humanities so often use as a template to foreclose interesting and difficult questions. In the case of photography among those questions are whether it was disruptive. Did it create new opportunities, prophesy new social formations, and focus anxieties about the new visibility of formerly secluded spaces and events? Along the way I hope also to show how the British in India would soon cease to be "highly delighted" by the potential that photography offered. Once again Roland Barthes seems to be on the mark when he notes the unwillingness of photographic historians to ask what photography *changed*: "Odd that no one has thought of the *disturbance* (to civilisation) which this new action causes" (1981: 12). Odd, in other words – he seems to suggest – how we don't want to think about how photography has transformed culture.

My argument may bear recapitulation. My concern is how we might explore photography as a technical practice that *disturbs* culture. This of course immediately sets this approach apart from accounts that would assimilate it as a neutral practice to those forces (heroic individuals and "cultural" practices) that determine it. Those approaches assume a congruence – a seamless fit – in which the question of *disturbance* would not arise. It is consequently, I trust, clear what I reject in this insistence on the *transformative* potential of photography. But it is equally important to make clear what this position does *not* embrace. The antinomies of the Modern Constitution may well predispose the reader to assume that an argument *against* culturalism is an argument *for* the technological. It is here that I need to make my argument as explicit as possible and to demonstrate my central desire to escape this choice. The *either/or* of the modern ineluctably re-inscribes its dichotomous constitution. Just as I reject *culturalism* I also reject its other (let us call it *technologism*). Instead of *photography as technology* I will explore here *camerawork as technical practice*, and in so doing move from pre-determination to fluidity, from fixity to process, from the knowable-in-advance to the partly-knowable-through-practice. A key part of this argument asserts the need not just for a history of *invention* (the default historicism of technologism) but a nuanced historicity of *process* and *practice*. It is this that now follows.

Camerawork as prophecy in mid-nineteenth-century India

In the spirit of what Walter Benjamin called "a delicate empiricism," let us establish some further basic markers of photography's arrival in India. In Bombay the inaugural meeting of the Photographic Society of Bombay was held in the rooms of the Geographical Society, in the Town Hall in October 1854. The records of the first meeting document 13 founder members of whom three were Indian (Venaik Gungathur Shastree, Ardaseer Cursetjee, and Dr Bhao [Bhau] Dajee, M.D). Within the first year of the Bombay Society's founding there were already upwards of one hundred members; by late 1855 it had attracted over 250 members and in the year after that further photographic societies were formed in Calcutta and Madras.

In 1855 in Bombay the Elphinstone Institution opened a Photography Class which attracted 40 pupils, including Indians such as Hurrychand Chintamon, winner of the government-sponsored prize (of Rs 50) at the end of that year and who went on to run a commercial studio competing with the dozens of other Indian-run concerns. Photographs made by Indians were also prominent in the annual displays of the Photographic Societies. For instance at a Meeting of the Bombay Society in January 1855, several photographs by Narain Dajee (the brother of Bhau Dajee) were exhibited.

What are probably the original displays are now in the Alkazi Collection of Photography and present a fascinating *tour d'horizon* of mid-nineteenth-century western India, seen through the eyes of a young doctor, a rising member of Bombay's emergent civil society. They exhibit a quality of all photography: the photographic event contingent on apparatus and object which are irreducible to the phantasmatic status of signifier and signified. As Barthes said, perhaps a corpus, but first, and foremost, a body.

Two of the most interesting of Dajee's images depict *A Native Travelling Bullock Cart* and *Gujarat Ryots, Bora Cultivators*. These reveal how photography at this moment is forced to abstract and freeze labor and movement in static tableaux. The camera is always an actor in the performances staged for it: the Bora cultivators have to be ushered from their field into an improvised studio area. Their hoes and axes – once in front of the camera – are transformed from functional tools into problematic accessories in an aesthetic project. In the pose of the bullock cart driver, we can see the effort that has been made to align his vehicle with the camera. Performances: but also traces in which we can see a wariness in the cultivators – their low status and vulnerability fixed in their uneasy gaze as they confront the camera – contrasting with the curious attentiveness of the bullock cart's higher status passenger.

These images were produced in a highly cosmopolitan context in which Indian practitioners would come to articulate what we might think of as a "photographic ideology" expressive of new ideas about evidence and the relation between individuation and what we would now call the "public sphere." But other structures of patronage also produced remarkable bodies of work. In Lucknow Ahmad Ali Khan, a designer/architect turned photographer in Wajid Ali Shah's court would produce a significant body of images in the early and mid-1850s (Gordon, 2006). Credited with having designed the Kaiserbagh – a key building in Lucknow with its mermaid court insignia – Ahmad Ali Khan then mastered photography, a medium in which both the Kaiserbagh and that mermaid insignia would resurface. Ahmad Ali Khan would also produce two albums (British Library Albums 269/1 and 269/2) dating from 1856–1857 which are now reunited in the British Library. The albums consist of faded salt prints of Lucknow residents, many of whom were to lose their lives in the 1857 Uprising in which Ahmad Ali Khan himself sided with the insurrection.

One of the images in the album referred to earlier, together with its caption, reveals with a peculiar clarity how the photograph as index, or chemical trace of an event, was unable to differentiate: it merely recorded whatever was placed in front of the camera. An image of the merchant L.E. Ruutz-Rees (subsequently celebrated for his *Personal Narrative of the Siege of Lucknow*, 1858) in Ahmad Ali Khan's "Lucknow Album" is captioned "Mr Rees in a Native Costume" (Figure 7.1), but what the photograph actually does, non-judgmentally, is record a body in clothes: it has nothing to say about the normativity or identity of that body or its adornment. I am reminded of Bernadette Bucher's observation that the visual (in general) is incapable of negating. She contrasts Theodor de Bry's late sixteenth-century copperplate engravings of Brazilian Tupinamba "cannibals" which can only present their nude bodies in a state of non-judgmental positivity, with Montaigne's observation – in his essay "On Cannibals" – "Look they have breeches" (Bucher, 1981: 35). Her point is that language is capable of discriminating, of asserting difference, in a way that the visual cannot. The image of Ruutz Rees bears this out and reveals the way in which the syntagmatic quality of language can assert identity and difference ("Mr Rees" versus "Native Costume") in ways that the paradigmatic photographic image – fated simply to record whatever is placed in front of it – cannot.

Two other images by Ahmad Ali Khan might help us make use of Jacques Attali's notion of form and prophecy. He argued that music, in certain circumstances, acts in advance of social reality – its code is "quicker" than that of society as a whole; its prophecy operating on a semiological frontier (Attali, 1985). Photographic self-presentation also seems – I would like to suggest – to often act as prophecy, as a tactic of enquiry and imagination. This is a quality again perceptively engaged by Roland Barthes: "once I feel myself observed by the lens, everything changes: I constitute myself in the process of 'posing', I instantaneously make another body for myself, I transform myself in advance into an image" (1981: 10).

Consider for instance the striking images photographed by Ahmad Ali Khan of Begums in the Avadh Court in Lucknow, circa 1855 (Figure 7.2). The physician

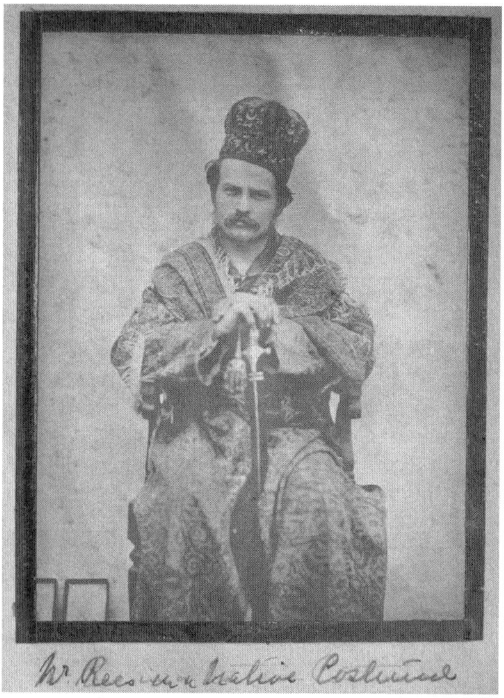

Figure 7.1 A body in Indian clothes: the camera records, the caption normalises. Salted paper print by Ahmad Ali Khan c. 1856–7. Courtesy of British Library (BL. Photo 269/2[89]).

Joseph Fayrer recorded a visit, at around the same time, to treat one of the Begums who "dangerously ill."[5] Fayrer was taken to the sick room where the chief eunuch and various female attendants were present: "A cashmere shawl was stretched across the room, behind which the Begum was seated." Fayrer immediately requested that the *parda* be removed. The screen was removed to reveal the Begum "seated upon a silver charpoy, enveloped in shawls." Fayrer repeated that "without seeing her nothing could be done, she giving faint and muffled replies from the depths of the shawls." Fayrer was eventually able to hold her wrist and by the third visit "was allowed to see her face and her tongue and to ascertain something of the nature of her case" (Fayrer, 1900: 105–106). Ahmad Ali Khan's photographs record a much greater readiness to unveil, and suggest that the space in front of the camera became for many a zone for the presentation of selves that could not be so easily presented elsewhere. The presence of several of these images in an album – in the Alkazi Photographic Collection – seemingly compiled by a European (one of them is captioned *One of the King of Oudh's* [i.e. Avadh] *Ladies*)[6] indicates that they were not circulating only within the seclusion of the Avadh court. If Fayrer's account can be said to record the everyday court practices

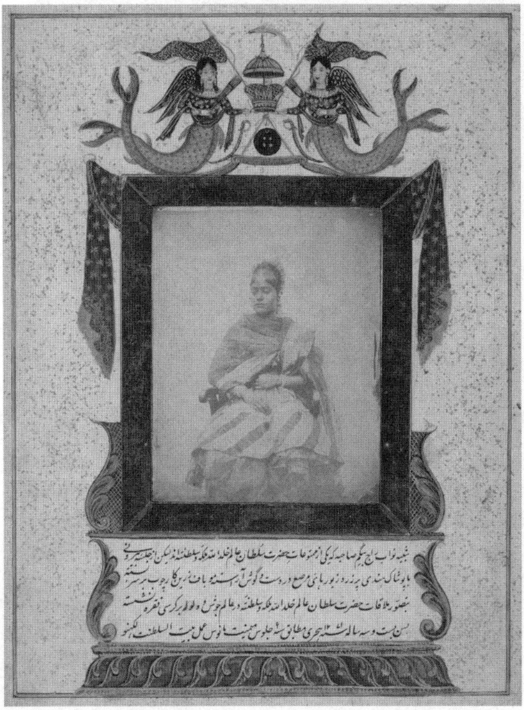

Figure 7.2 Nawab Raj Begum Sahiba. Salted paper print c. 1855 by Ahmad Ali Khan with watercolour surround. Courtesy of British Library.

of visibility and seclusion, Ahmad Ali Khan's photographs seem to record that peculiar space of prophetic experimentation – of disturbance and transformation – that the camera engenders.

Twenty years later another photographer – Abbas Ali – was active in Lucknow (Gordon, 2006: 86ff). He produced a series of works – the 1874 *Lucknow Album*, a portfolio of *The Beauties of Lucknow*, and in 1880 (on behalf of the local Government) a mass-produced photographic vanity book aimed at the post-insurrection social order. *The Beauties of Lucknow* was a nostalgic eulogy for Wajid Ali Shah's Lucknow court, illustrated with 24 photographic portraits, an attempt to address an Indian male audience, eager for the scent of a "Lucknow immemorable for the Oriental magnificence of the entertainments" (cited by Gordon, 2006: 90).

At about the same time, a Jaipur Photographer – possibly Maharaja Sawai Ram Singh II – was photographing "courtesans of the Jaipur Court."[7] One of the images A *Nautch* [dancing] *Girl at Her Toilet* grants the viewer access into an intimate space which would not normally be available to the male viewer. The image has similarities to Kalighat paintings,[8] and slightly later chromolithographs, produced in Calcutta in which the woman's self-regard in a mirror serves almost as an alibi for the viewer's visual interest, but in the Jaipur image the prosthesis of the camera introjects us into an actual space, inhabited by real and thrilling bodies. In the absence of a mirror legitimating our desire to join in with this "looking" – Abbas Ali grants the viewer the alibi of a lost cultural splendor, of the "Oriental magnificence" of the Awadhi court, through the vector of these "dancing girls." Eschewing the paraphernalia of classical columns, books, and flower vases which so often clutter images of this period, Abbas Ali invites us to repose in the utopian luxury of bundled silk saris and jaunty poses on a *chez lounge*.

These moves from the concealed to the un-concealed, from the visible to the visible, from seclusion to the public, all transect with a powerful narrative about the transition to the modern. They alert us to camerawork's role in these transformations – as an agent rather than a passive recorder. They echo Walter Benjamin's observation that "It is a different nature which speaks to the camera than the eye," and suggest that part of photography's "optical unconscious" lay in its prophetic potentiality to probe formerly occluded and private spaces (Benjamin, 1999: 510). From a certain Habermasian perspective this prophetic conjuring of new *public* possibilities may manifest as a disturbance that is wholly positive. The history of India during this period quickly reveals, however, a profound perception of the negativity attendant on photography's disturbance and prophecy.

The colonial dromosphere and the aesthetics of the same

Six years later, in 1880, Abbas Ali was involved in another project, a sustained attempt to use photography by the colonial administration to flatter its subjects. *An Illustrated Historical Album of the Rajas and Taaluqdars of Oudh* was published in 1880 in a joint English and Urdu edition by North-Western Provinces and Oudh (Avadh) Government Press. A compact volume crammed with more than 300 *carte-de-visite* size albumen prints of local landholders, the intended audience for the *Rajas and Taaluqdars* album was those very landlords who were depicted in the album (Figure 7.3).

This book was an explicit celebration and recognition of those landlords who had demonstrated political loyalty during the Insurrection of 1857 and an attempt to integrate those who had been given land as a reward for their loyalty into a pre-existing social order. The normalizing space of the photographic portrait was the chief instrument of this integration: regardless of the size of landholding, each individual was pasted four to a page.

The *Rajas and Taaluqdars* text provided accounts of the loyalty of the two-thirds of the t*aaluqdars* who retained their properties and of the one-third of the new landholders who had been rewarded with land confiscated from those who had supported the insurrection. Thirty-seven out of the 344 *cartes-de-visite* images give the name of the sitter, but instead of a face present a medallion on which is written *pardanashin*, that is, maintaining the veil. This was a courtesy extended to all females, both Muslim and Hindu, with the result that

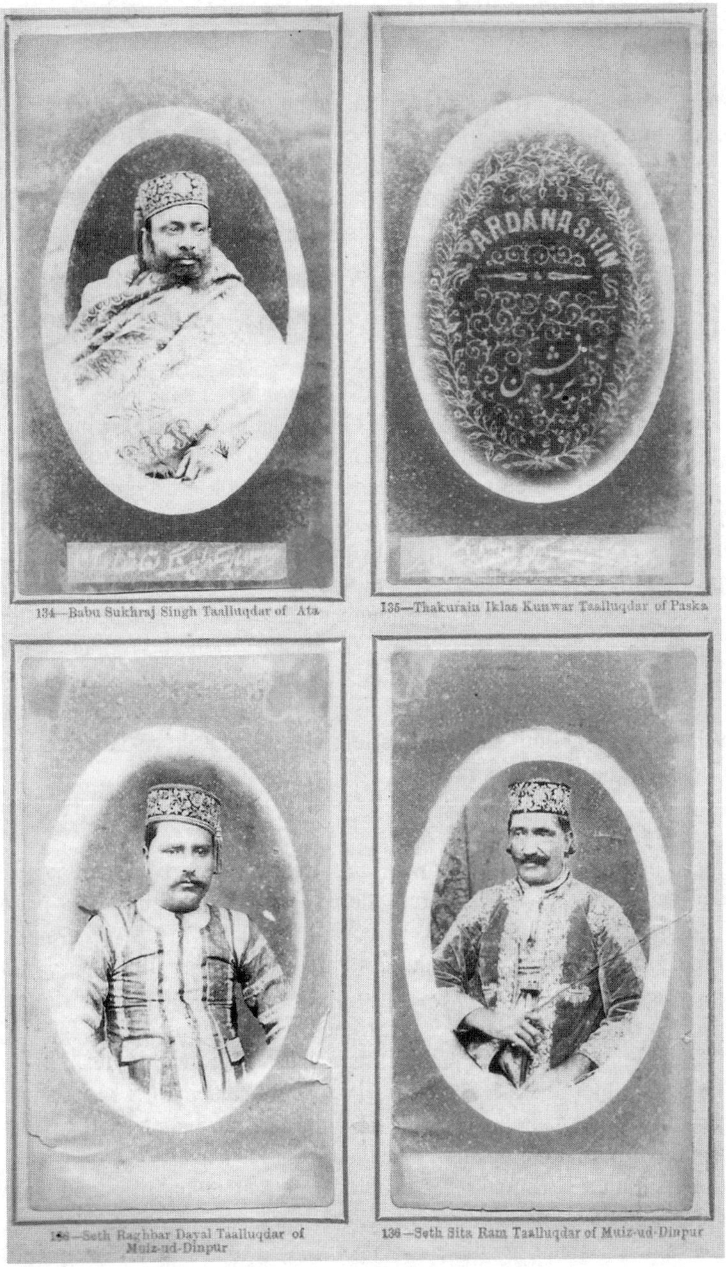

Figure 7.3 One page from An Illustrated Historical Album of the Rajas and Taaluqdars of Oudh, 1880. Four tipped-in albumen prints by Abbas Ali.

the only faces one sees in the volume are male. No doubt Abbas Ali – who had earlier produced *Beauties of Lucknow* let us remember – understood an elite rural sensibility of seclusion. But it is possible that George Couper – who devised the work – made this concession to the heterogeneity of the scopic regime of the landlords they represented, because he had learnt something from an earlier objection to the *summa bonum* of nineteenth-century Indian colonial photography, *The People of India* (Forbes Watson and Kaye, 1868–75). Couper had in 1861 been an enthusiastic proponent of the photographic survey that ultimately led to *The People of India*, published in 8 volumes between 1868 and 1875.

Consider the objection that was voiced by Syed Ahmed Khan, the most significant Indian Muslim of his time,[9] in a letter of 1869 from London to the Aligarh Scientific Society:

> In the India Office is a book in which all the races of India are depicted … giving the manners and customs of each race … The young Englishmen … desirous of knowing something of the land to which they are going … look over this work. What can they think, after perusing this book and looking at its pictures of the power or honour of the natives of India? One day Hamid, Mahmud (Syed's two sons), and I went to the India Office, and Mahmud commenced looking at the work. A young Englishman … came up and after a short time asked Mahmud if he was a Hindustani? Mahmud replied in the affirmative but blushed as he did so, and hastened to explain that he was not one of the aborigines, but that his ancestors were formerly of another country. Reflect therefore, that until Hindustanis remove this blot they shall never be held in honour by any civilised race.
>
> (Graham, 1885: 188–189)

How might we best understand this powerful reaction? Was it perhaps because Syed Ahmed objected to the letterpress description accompanying a plate captioned "Moghuls, Mussulmans, of Royal family of Delhi"? "They were for the most part" the caption notes "vicious and dissolute, idle and ignorant; too proud to seek employment, and too discontented to abstain from plots and intrigues, as futile as they were foolish." Well Syed Ahmed would almost have certainly agreed with that judgment for he had himself famously written vituperously in his influential 1858 pamphlet *The Causes of the India Revolt* (a copy of which he had sent to Governor-General Canning) that "Such an imbecile was the ex-King that if one had assured him that the angels of Heaven were his slaves, he would have welcomed the assurance" (Ahmed Khan, 2000: 4). Perhaps what offended Syed Ahmed was the prejudicial descriptions of Aligarh landowners, some of whom, as David Lelyveld has noted, would have been known to his father (Lelyveld, 1978: 6). However there are good grounds for thinking that Syed Ahmed's reaction was a response not simply to the ideological slant of this or that caption, but rather to the systematic normalizing and rendering visible of diverse communities within a unitary framework (Figure 7.4).

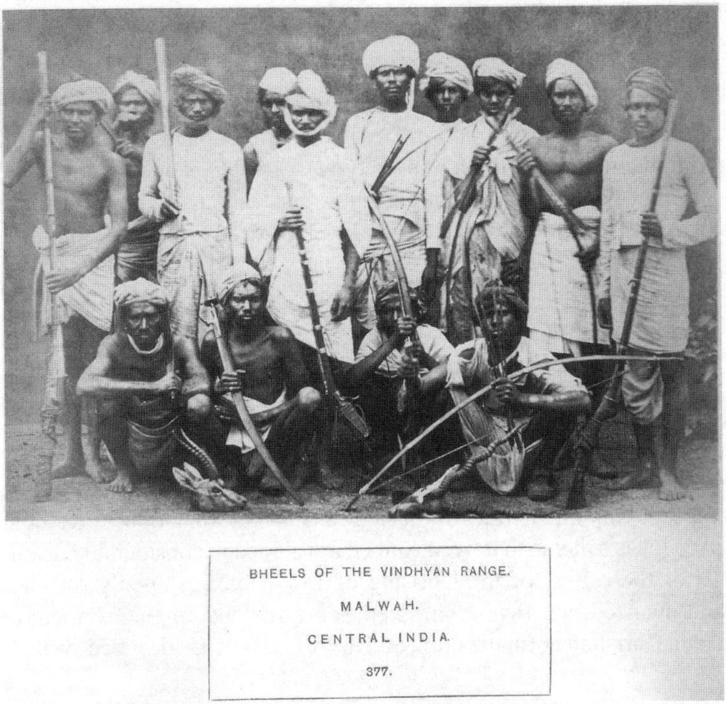

Figure 7.4 'Malwa Bheels'. Photograph by James Waterhouse 1862, as it appeared in The People of India 1868–1875. Tipped-in albumen print.

Recall Mahmud's blush when asked if he was a Hindustani. Perhaps we should imagine Mahmud looking at Waterhouse's illustration of the Malwa Bheels (a group of *adivasi* or "tribal" people from central India), and understand Mahmud interpreting his English interlocutor's question as an invitation to identify himself with "aborigines" rather than as a foreign noble. Mahmud's grandfather – as Francis Robinson has noted – was descended from Husaini Syeds who migrated from Herat at the time of Akbar. As Syed Ahmed had earlier written in his 1858 *The Causes of the Indian Revolt* "The Muhammadans are not the aborigines of this country. They came in the train of former conquerors and gradually domesticated themselves in India" (2000: 35).

Syed Ahmed had described *The People of India* as "a book in which all the races of India are depicted both in picture and letterpress, giving the manners and customs of each race," locating quite precisely what Walter Benjamin termed the "sense of sameness in the world" that photography uniquely engendered. In his 1931 "Little History of Photography," Benjamin wrote:

> The peeling away of the object's shell, the destruction of the aura, is the signature of a perception whose sense for the sameness of things has grown

> to the point where even the singular, the unique, is divested of its uniqueness – by means of reproduction.
>
> (Benjamin, 1999: 519)

We can see this sense of the sameness of things in John Tressider's remarkable 1857–1863 album of Agra and Cawnpore. Tressider photographed many different Europeans and Indians from all strata of society with great care and on one page he presents a mixture of individuals and couples, and one group, some Indian, some English. At the top left of this page, side-by-side are two images, captioned (on the left) *Lala Jootee Persad* (*The Richest man in NW India*) and to the right of this a smaller blurred shot of a figure shot against the same background captioned: *The Poorest man in NW India* (*an insane fakeer or religious mendicant*). Here photography makes possible a new kind of fundamental juxtaposition – individuals who outside the studio might not inhabit the same terrain are here brought within a common epistemological space 'divested of [their] uniqueness – by means of its reproduction' (Benjamin, 1999: 519). While for Benjamin this sameness offered revolutionary potential, for Syed Ahmed Khan *The People of India* was perceptually threatening, for it suggested a representational levelling and uniformity. This is a theme that Syed Ahmed developed in considerable detail in his analysis of the causes of the Uprising of 1857. Syed Ahmed's account is complex and nuanced, but two strong themes are Indians' anxieties about a technological and Christian normalization; and the reversal of an idealized system of vision.

It was the systematicity of the emergent bureaucracy, its *ineluctability*, and the prospect of *sameness* which in Syed Ahmed's words led Indians to feel that "The ground seemed at last to have given way beneath their feet." In 1893 in a letter written at Shelidah, Rabindranath Tagore would express a similar rejection of this law of the same and his distrust of what we might call the "colonial *dromosphere*" when he wrote that "Curiously enough, my greatest fear is that I should be reborn in Europe! Like the roads there, one's mind has to be stone-metalled for heavy traffic – geometrically laid out, and kept clear and regulated" (1921: 106). The dromosphere is a term which cultural critic Paul Virilio (1997) devised to name the heightened *race-like* quality of late modernity's temporality, but it is also a term that resonates with a peculiar clarity in nineteenth-century India. A year later Tagore would write of his repugnance of Calcutta which "is as ponderously proper as a Government Office. Each of its days comes forth like a coin from a mint, clear cut and glittering, Ah! Those dreary, deadly days, so preciously equal in weight" (Tagore, 1921: 121). Roland Barthes' description of cameras as "clocks for seeing," (1981: 15) helps us conjoin Tagore's horror of colonial modernity's temporal homogeneity with Syed Ahmed's apprehension of photography's optical homogeneity.

For Syed Ahmed, *The People of India*, by virtue of its reliance on photography's normalization, its sense of sameness in the world, was equally deadly: it threatened the destruction of the heterogeneity, hierarchy, and aura, which constituted his learned and value-laden life world. But something else also clearly bothered him.

In the past when things were good, Kings had made themselves visible to their people. From time immemorial the people of India had relished Durbars – the opportunity to see rulers as objects of public visibility: "This feeling of gladness at the sight of the sovereign is a feeling instinctively felt by every one. Man feels the power of the ruler when thus brought face to face with him," Syed Ahmed wrote. But the ruler had faded from visibility … the days when those munificent, visible rulers were deemed "Shadowed of God" seemed long gone (2000: 45–46). He recognized that the new colonial public life was a "way of seeing," but one that horrified him.

This invisibilization of power, a force traditionally magnified in Indian polities, went hand in hand with the increased and enforced visibilization of India's subjects. Syed Ahmed reports anxiety about the compulsory education of unveiled females:

> Man[y] believed it to be the wish of the Government, that girls should attend, and be taught at these schools, and leave off the habit of sitting veiled. Anything more obnoxious than this to feelings of the Hindustanees cannot be conceived.
>
> (Ahmed Khan, 2000: 20)

A similar sense of a moral world turned upside down is apparent in Tagore's thought that 'We [Bengalis] shall grow ashamed of going about without socks, and cease to feel shame at the sight of their [English] balldresses'(1921: 46). The 1880 *Rajas and Taaluqdars of Oudh* had learned the offence that unveiling could cause, and substituted all females in its scheme with the *pardanashin* medallion, although in all other respects the law of the same was retained.

Syed Ahmed's anxiety provides a pathway through which we might think about practices – such as overpainting – which appear to operate in a world free of the "asthetics of the same" and which might be taken as a sign of the triumph of "culture" over an "autonomous technology." But it makes more sense to understand this as a complex experimental negotiation around the technical practice of photography: selective over-painting of figures within images reinserts that very heterogeneity that the camera has banished. Let us consider two images from the Alkazi Collection in Delhi (Figure 7.5).

They form an intriguing pair and can help lead us towards a clarification of the logic of photography and the logic of painting. One of the images shows three men from Rajasthan and the other from the 1920s to the 1940s shows six Swetambara Jain monks with three attendants. Some of the figures are overpainted and some of them are not. In the case of the three Rajasthani men the two – we assume higher status – Shaivaite figures on the right are heavily overpainted, while their Vaishnava attendant on the left is not. Photography deposits the three figures equivalently, unable to impose a hierarchy between them. The painter however wields his brush selectively, demonstrating through the time and precious substances invested in the figures on the right their differential value (Figure 7.6).

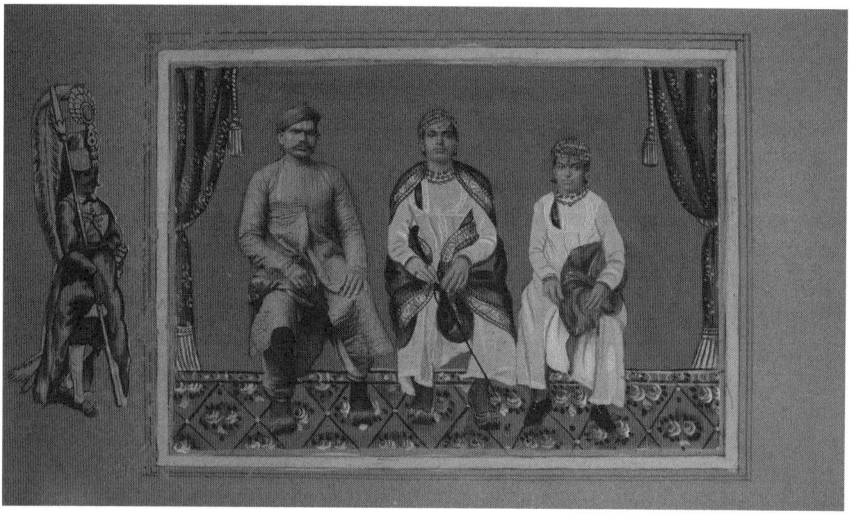

Figure 7.5 The presence of paint signifies higher status. Overpainted albumen print, western India, late nineteenth century. Courtesy of Alkazi Collection of Photography.

The ratio is inverted in the image of Jain monks whose status claims proceed from their renunciation of the life of the householder. The camera again was unable to register difference between these various figures and certainly not able to understand the claim made through the absence of ornament. Only the painter can impose these gradings, signalling through the opulence of the attendants how much the monks have left behind.

Here we see perfectly what photography does – what it is that photography insists upon – and how painting is able to countermand it. What Syed Ahmed called the "blot" – photography's systematic inability to discriminate, and the potential it has to write new histories in its radically different prophetic epistemological space – is here over-scripted by a different hierarchizing language of signification. My suggestion has been that for many Indians, paint – as a supplement to photography – was attractive because it bore similar promise: the promise of an added value and discrimination. Photography's radical and dangerous egalitarianism could be tempered – in a way that might have pleased Syed Ahmed – by the archaic and hierarchical potentiality of paint.

But in the longer term photography did engineer many of the transformations that Syed Ahmed glimpsed and feared. For instance, both Sujith Kumar Parayil (2007) and Malavika Karlekar (2005: 125ff.), in different ways, have made important claims about the way in which photography transformed women's relationship to public space, and helped create new modes of domesticity. Here the space of the photographic studio enforced a new focus on marriage as conjugality – the relationship between husband and wife, rather than the alliance between lineages.

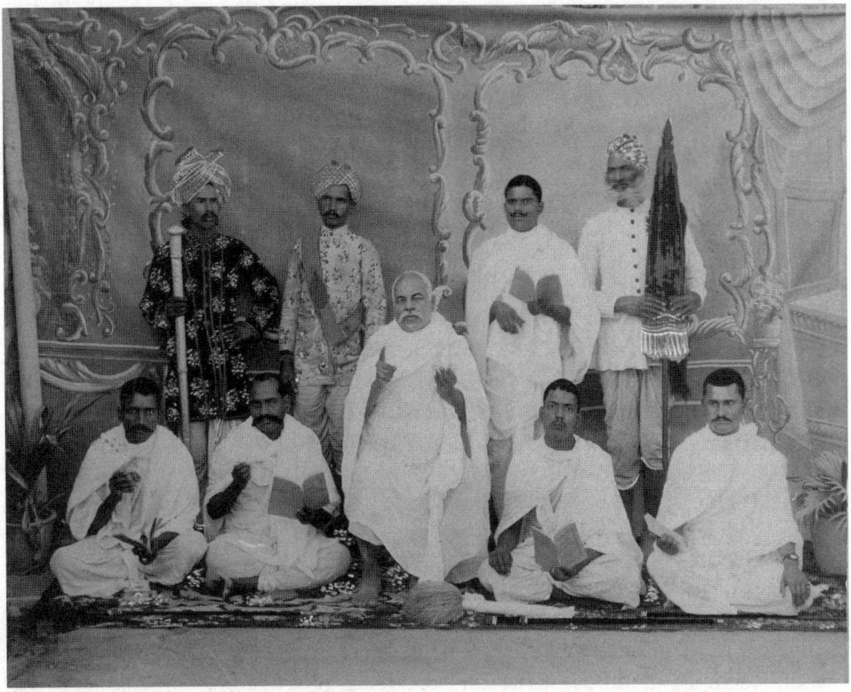

Figure 7.6 The presence of paint signifies lower status. These Svetambara Jain monks' attendants bear marks of their continuing attachment to the world. Overpainted albumen print, western India, late nineteenth century. Courtesy of Alkazi Collection of Photography.

The standard unit of photographic record becomes (in large part simply because of the space that the camera was most easily capable of recording) a man and a woman together, not two large *gotra* (or sub-caste) collectivities. This new technology, brought to bear on what might reasonably be seen as the fundamental mechanism of Indian society, restructured it (at least at the ideological level) as a conjugal relationship. Conjugality, especially in various Indian reformist movements, was defined and enacted in front of the camera ("prophesized" Attali would say) before being exported to more everyday spaces. Individuation and conjugalization – precipitated by the *space* which the early technical practice of photography normalized – was also linked to its economies of scale in the epoch of the *carte-de-visite* and cabinet card. This was the point where "once a critical mass of data is reached: quantity becomes quality" (Coetzee, 2007: 81).

Sujith Parayi (personal communication) also convincingly argues that photography (not as "representation but as "event") also articulated new modes of the public, and the physical act of photographing women outside their homes (precipitated by the need for light and new *mise-en-scène*) was not simply a representation of new modes of spatiality but the simultaneous physical enactment of that new world. Photographs become "image acts" (Bakewell, 1998) which, like J.L. Austin's "speech acts", are "performatives": in the act of enunciation they do not simply describe the world: they change it (Austin, 1975: 6).

These contrasts between photography as the documenter of what has already been achieved socially, and as a space of experimentation where new identities can be conjured, are made possible by photography's inability to normalize: it records both the existent and the subjunctive equally well and this is why such powerfully different expectations can be brought to bear on the same technical practice. It can only ever record the event: it can never make a judgment about the relationship between the bodies in that "event" and the normativity of a "corpus".

From cure to poison: camerawork and the transformation of habitus

Photography, re-conceptualized as "camerawork", is – as I hope is by now very clear – not reducible to a "neutral tool". While it is most certainly inflected by pre-existing practices and expectations, the manner in which the camera is used and its consequences are never simply reducible to that cultural and social infrastructure. Within the complex "object-institution" of camerawork a *disturbance* is continually at play. What is more, this *disturbance* is never static for the technics at the heart of this technical practice are forever changing, becoming (at the risk of a radical simplification in our analysis) ever smaller and cheaper.

Photography's arrival in India would transform not only the domestic sphere: it would also impact dramatically on public politics, and to understand how we must grasp the manner in which camerawork as an ever-changing technical practice became increasingly mobile, how its declensional form transmuted but, as Barthes would write about the central object in Bataille's "Story of the Eye," "its sound remained the same". In the mid-nineteenth-century photographs could only be produced by complex apparatus which required significant logistical support. Towards the end of the nineteenth century, the supple nature of photographic technology entailed a progressive miniaturization of equipment and the mobility of the photographer. Photography's central technological claim – its chemical connection to reality – was thus continually re-inscribed through a fabulously protean material base. From the announcement of photography in 1839 until (very roughly) the beginning of the twentieth century, photography was perceived – by agents of the colonial state – as a cure. As the twentieth century progressed, however, photography was increasingly viewed as a curse, or a poison. Deployed by agents other than the colonial state it revealed its dangerous ability to store evidence of a problematic kind.

The early photographic enthusiast Joseph Mullens, when demanding in 1856 that his fellow photographers leave their verandahs and explore "all the minute varieties of Oriental life" had also reassured them that it "is open to us to explore these peculiarities to the last degree while enjoying a perfectly European security" (1857: 33). At the back of the issue of the *Journal of the Photographic Society of Bengal* carrying the text of Mullens' talk, there was an advertisement for "Newland's Photographic and Daguerrian Depot" which gestured to the decay of that security for James William Newland would be murdered in Meerut in May 1857, "taken from the dâk carriage and mutilated with great barbarity" as one contemporary account put it.

Newland's fate alerts us to the implosion of a colonial habitus as (in Pierre Bourdieu's words) "structuring determinations" that inculcate a normalized worldview "through convergent experiences which give a social environment its *physiognomy*" (1977: 86).[10] This colonial *habitus* allows us to understand how highly specific repertoires of photographic subjects were "naturalized" and how certain pathways and standpoints appeared "obvious." Newland suffered the dismantling of this *habitus* by those whom it oppressed. But many other photographers during this period found themselves absorbed in what Bourdieu further describes as the "homogeneity" of *habitus* which "causes practices and works to be immediately intelligible and foreseeable, and hence taken for granted" (Bourdieu, 1977: 80). This taken-for-granted quality, and the technomaterial "guarantee" of the physiognomy of this colonial environment, can be seen in the *habitus* of important photographic practitioners such as Samuel Bourne in which we can see the seemingly effortless and unavoidable reproduction of highly particularized colonial interests.

Samuel Bourne (in India 1863–1870) – perhaps the pre-eminent figure in any aesthetic history of photography in colonial India – presented his photography as omniscient, but his detailed accounts of his travels continually connect his photographic transcendence with a material world of coolies and official permission to use government staging-bungalows. Bourne published a celebrated series of reports in the *British Journal of Photography* between 1863 and 1870. In general, his narrative presents an unattractive picture of a photographic imperialist intent on achieving high altitude viewpoints from which he could look down onto a picturesquely ordered India. But this Google Earth-like omniscience is the transcendent top-dressing on a complex web of negotiations with customs officers, government officials, and labour agents – *chowdrees* and *lumbadars* – to which his text endlessly refers. These reflect the fact that all of his photographs are as he says of his famous image of the Manirung Pass (the highest altitude photograph of its day) "a memento of the circumstances under which it was taken" (Bourne, 2004: 85).

Bourne's written narrative perpetually re-inscribes the logistics – the network – which his indexical encounters with the scenes in front of his cameras entailed. Railways from Calcutta to Benares and then Allahabad to Agra, the "clattering dak" (or mail coach) (Bourne, 2004: 3) and most of all the endless marches with huge teams of coolies – "retinue[s] of thirty coolies carrying cameras, chemicals, tents, bedding, provisions etc." (Bourne, 2004: 15). Bourne makes us continually aware of the techno-material complexity of mobile photography at this time: "everything has to be carried on the backs of coolies: it is therefore necessary that the packages should be as far as possible small and light, so as to form only one man's load." Behind the remarkable beauty and technical perfection of Bourne's images we continually feel this trudge, the movement of feet, the straining of packages held by leather straps, of large boxes of negatives suspended on poles and carried by several coolies, none of whom, he writes, like being "puckeroed"[11] in these expeditions (Bourne, 2004: 31).

But as photographic technology became increasingly miniaturized and increasingly mobile, especially in the early twentieth century, the *habitus* by which it was constituted and which it also instantiated, changed. It was no longer dependent on the kinds of official support or financial investment which were so central to photographers such as Bourne. If nineteenth-century Indian photography's paradigmatic location was the Himalayan foothills, in the twentieth century, photography's preferred location became the street. One of the key moments of transition was Curzon's decision that the 1903 Delhi Durbar should be covered by as many photographers and journalists as possible. Curzon had announced his hope, in a speech in September 1902, that "a good many eyes in a good many parts of the globe will be directed upon Delhi" (cited in Wheeler, 1904: 247) and encouraged the international press and freelance photographers to document the event. A mobile photographic technology was more easily able to document the increasingly chaotic public spaces in which colonial hegemony appeared increasingly fragile. It is with two examples of this – both occurring within a few years of each other in Amritsar – that I will conclude my discussion of the disturbance which photography brought to India.

The Jallianwallabagh (Amritsar) massacre of April 13, 1919 was to kickstart a resurgence in anti-colonial struggle. Soon after this a committed young photographer, Narayan Vinayak Virkar, arrived to photograph the evidence of this atrocity. Virkar's images document the bullet-pocked wall against which so many hundreds of villagers died and which is now covered in anti-Dyer graffiti. Bullet holes are ringed with white chalk and various crouching figures point to these. In 1922 Amritsar was once again a flash point. In this year however, cameras were there to record events as they unfolded. One of the cameras belonged to an American cinematographer named A.L. Varges.[12] An official report described how Varges had photographed an Akali protest procession en-route for the Guru-ka-Bagh. Four waves of protestors attempted to access a disputed piece of land and were beaten back by *lathi*-wielding police, all of this being filmed and photographed by Varges. "Eventually 23 of the Akalis were taken off on stretchers, the remaining two, who were more obstinate, were treated more roughly by the Police … meanwhile the cinematograph operator and other photographers and Press representatives were all busy," an official report noted.[13] The Governor in Council proclaimed that he did "not feel happy about the activities of the cinema operator and the possible ill-effect of these films in fostering anti-British feeling in the United States" and then instructed the Home Department to ascertain whether there was any way of stopping Varges from shooting more film, of identifying his whereabouts, and making clear to him the necessity of "exercis[ing] caution that none are exhibited which are likely to cause misunderstanding."[14]

In Varges' images – these scratched, panicked slices of reality – we see evidence of photography's indiscriminate capture which (as the German media theorist Friedrich Kittler noted) "shifted the boundaries that distinguished … random visual data from meaningful picture sequences, unconscious and unintentional inscriptions from their conscious and intentional counterparts."[15] Official response to Varges initiated a notion of the "embedded" photojournalist whose resonance in the early twenty-first century will be obvious. The Guru-ka-Bagh episode precipitated an official discussion about whether un-sanctioned filming of public places could be controlled. In December 1922 the Secretary of State for India concluded that section 144 of the Criminal Procedures Code could be used to "prevent the photography or filming of objectionable subjects" and asked for further clarification of this possibility by the Legislative Department. They replied that section 144 probably did not apply but even if it did "it would be quite useless" (National Archives of India, Home Political 1922, 949.2). In practice a film would be taken long before an order preventing it had been received.

It was clear that at that moment a profound anxiety was at large, an anxiety that marked the deep and destabilizing realization that the control of photography as a technical practice had now slipped from the hand of the state. Photography's "penetrating certainty," which earlier colonial figures had extolled, had been desirable to the extent that it was a certainty that the state could own. Colonial surveillance and proscription, like photography itself, was now caught in a vortex of its own making. Perhaps nothing sums up – and prefigures – this paradox better than the official anxiety about Sher Ali, a convict who had murdered Lord Mayo during a visit to the Andamans in 1872. This was the same Mayo – Richard Southwell Bourke – who, three years earlier, had awarded the Viceroy's medal to Samuel Bourne in the Bengal Photographic Society annual exhibition. Sher Ali was first photographed as an object lesson in colonial punishment but his love of the camera and sense of himself as a celebrity started to unhinge a colonial system of discipline structured around visibility. Clare Anderson notes W.W. Hunter's description of how Sher Ali was 'childishly vain of being photographed as the murderer of a Viceroy' and Hunter's subsequent refusal to publish details of his identity. Anderson also notes how although there are three images of Sher Ali in the British Library, in only one of these is he named: in the other two he is an anonymous murderer and assassin (Anderson, 2004: 161).[16]

I started this chapter with a critique of the reduction of photography as "neutral tool" through the over-determination of an archaic anthropological "culture." At this point we might add that the Foucaldian version of this thesis (popularized in photographic theory by John Tagg [1988])[17] deserves equal critique: in its account technical practice is a transparent screen through which a proxy "culture" shines. The (Taggian) vision of photography as an epiphenomenal reflection of discourse and power could hardly be less appropriate to the history I have telegraphed in this chapter. The logic (or perhaps better "propensity") that I have been describing here is not the logic of the state: it is the complex outcome of a mobile technical practice operating in an experimental zone. Here we see another aspect of photography's "disturbance."

Conclusion: propensities and declensions

A poison extracted from a cure: when photography first arrived in India it was greeted by many as a magical cure for a set of already existing representational problems. It seemed to provide perfect chemical traces of the world: the largest spaces could be recorded, the tiniest spaces probed, past events appeared as though they might be recoverable (even the retinas of murder victims, it was thought, might reveal the identity of their attackers). The camera seemed to be a truly magical prosthesis and its possibilities seemed limitless.

One of the most enthusiastic proselytisers on behalf of the wondrous new technology had been Joseph Mullens. In his celebrated lecture *On the Applications of Photography in India* delivered to the Photographic Society of Bengal in October 1856, he had noted that:

> There are some applications of Photography, less peculiar but equally professional and of great importance to the Government. *The scene and circumstances of a riot, the damage inflicted by rioters*; the mode in which a robbery was committed; the scene of a murder and all its attendant circumstances … *A very active Photographer, in whom the ruling passion was very strong, might be able to sketch a riot during its actual progress, and by successive pictures to show who was most active, to identify the ringleaders, and show the murderous hand in the very act of inflicting a fatal blow. The purpose of justice would in this manner be served to the most material degree.*
>
> (Mullens, 1857: 34, emphasis added)

Mullens assumed that the photographic event would serve the interest of the British colonial presence. We have seen how that same quality did come to serve the purpose of justice (and ultimately of an emergent democracy), but not in the way Mullens anticipated.

This transformation reflected not a distortion of photography or the fragmentation of diverse and incompatible photographies, but a set of potentialities and propensities latent in photography itself. A technology dependent on a colonial *habitus* found itself reproducing that *habitus*' "structuring determinations." As this protean technical practice found itself freely roaming the streets it located new subjects through which to construct new publics. A "declensional" photography proved itself capable of generating several directly opposed outcomes. From cure to poison, and all the while the same.

This volatility – this movement across a range of very different outcomes – is usually the alibi for the triumph of the cultural or of the social. Conversely, if "technology" is relevant, then we expect it to be determining, and determining in a simple way ("guns kill people" or conversely they don't kill people). Both cultural and technological explanations would be, in Latour's term, "territorial." The Latourian move from technology to "technical practice" permits our escape from these stale dichotomies. Just as with reference to guns we might want to ask what "kind" of gun, and concern ourselves with what we might term "ballistic amplification,"[18] so camerawork facilitates the focus on a protean technical practice in which the hybrid of camera and cameraperson are subject to a continuous revision of possibility. At one historical moment technics demand the recruitment of 30 coolies, at a later moment the technics allow the photograph-producing-device to be slipped in a pocket. These transformations are what we might (following Friedrich Kittler) call "technomaterial," but to stress the sole agentive role of technicity would be to fall into the bifurcated trap against which Latour so eloquently warns us. Neither "culture" nor "technology" but instead the hybrid zone of technical practice, the experimental, and materially embedded space of the "collective actant" of the camera and the operator, where the human and non-human are folded into one another, and where devising and revising are forever in process.

Notes

1 Latour's precise wording is must "anthropology [be] forever condemned to be reduced to territories, unable to follow networks?" (Latour, 1999: 116).
2 It informs the early part of Pinney (1997).
3 Latour here refers to Heidegger's comments on Heraclitus' proclivity for crawling into a baker's oven, exclaiming "here, too, the gods are present" (Latour, 1993: 65).
4 Who in 1839 would have imagined X-ray photography? The possibilities of "back-scatter X-rays" and millimeter wave scans (recent surveillance technologies) are still unknown in the twenty-first century.
5 Which may have left its literary deposition in Salman Rushdie's description of Dr Aadam Aziz's examination of Naseem Ghani in *Midnight's Children*.
6 Alkazi Collection of Photography, Warner Album 2001.18.0001.
7 There are 5 images in this series in the Alkazi Collection of Photography in London (ACP. 94.48.0006).
8 Mass produced paintings notable for the swiftness and fluidity of their execution, produced and sold in the vicinity of the Kalighat temple in Calcutta from the mid-nineteenth century onwards, and often addressing changing social mores and gender issues.
9 Described by Francis Robinson as "the greatest Indian Muslim of the nineteenth century" Syed Ahmed Khan (1818–1888) was raised in proximity to the Mughal Court. In 1838 he started work in the judicial branch of the East India Company. From 1878–1882 he sat on the Viceroy's Legislative Council and founded the Muhammadan Anglo-Oriental Educational College at Aligarh in 1877 and the Muhammadan Educational Conference in 1886 (Robinson, 2000: vii–viii).
10 Bourdieu elaborates a generic *habitus* as a feature of all social practice. The colonial prefix used here embodies my own attempt to use it in a more localized fashion.
11 Hobson and Jobson note that "*puckerow* belongs essentially to the dialect of the European soldier, and in that becomes itself a verb 'to *puckerow*', i.e. to lay hold of (generally of a recalcitrant natives)" (Yule and Burnell, 1886: 735).
12 Varges worked for International News, a Hearst organization and specialized in filming colonial wars and political struggle: he had previously made films in Macedonia, Mesopotamia (Home Pol. 1922, 949: 25) and would subsequently film the Italian incursion in Abyssinia (1935) and the Spanish Civil War (see anon. 1938).
13 National Archives of India, Home Political 1922. 949: 2.
14 Handwritten note 18/9/22 in previous file.

15 I draw here on Kittler's translators' words (Winthrop-Young and Wutz,1999: xxvi).
16 These being Photo 125/2(46) 'The Murderer of Lord Mayo'; Photo 127/(96) 'Sher Ali (assassin of Lord Mayo); Photo 127/(99) 'Assassin of Lord Mayo.'
17 A closer reading of the Foucauldian *dispositis* might absolve Foucault himself from some of the blunders of his followers.
18 See Sven Lindquist (1996) for the impact of the Maxim gun on colonial conflicts and Graves-Brown (2007) on the Avtomat Kalashnikova and the social organization of warfare.

Bibliography

Ahmed Khan, Syed (2000) *The Causes of the Indian Revolt … written in Urdoo, in the Year 1858, and Translated into English by His Two European Friends* (Benares, Medical Hall Press, 1873), reprint. Karachi: Oxford University Press.

Allana, Rahaab and Pramod Kumar (2008) *Painted Photographs. Coloured Portraiture in India*, Ahmedabad: Mapin Publishing Ltd.

Ali, Abbas (1874) *The Beauties of Lucknow Consisting of Twenty-Four Selected Photographed Portraits, Cabinet Size, of the most Celebrated and Popular Living Histrionic Singers, Dancing Girls, and Actresses of the Oudh Court and of Lucknow*, Calcutta: Calcutta Central Press Company Ltd.

Anderson, Clare (2004) *Legible Bodies: Race, Criminality and Colonialism in South Asia*, Oxford: Berg.

Attali, Jacques (1985) *Noise: The Political Economy of Music*, Minneapolis: University of Minnesota Press.

Austin, J. L. (1975) *How to Do Things With Words*, 2nd edition, Harvard: Harvard University Press.

Bakewell, Lisa (1998) 'Image acts', *American Anthropologist*, 100 (1) March, 22–32.

Barthes, Roland (1972) 'The metaphor of the eye', in *Critical Essays* trans. Richard Howard, Evanston: Northwestern University Press, 239–248.

—— (1981) *Camera Lucida: Reflections on Photography*, trans. Richard Howard, New York: Hill & Wang.

Baxandall, Michael (1972) *Painting and Experience in 15th Century Italy*, Oxford: Oxford University Press.

Benjamin, Walter (1999) 'A little history of photography' in *Walter Benjamin: Selected Writings* vol. 1, part 2, 1931–1934, trans. Rodney Livingstone et al., ed. Michael W. Jennings et al., Cambridge, MA., Belknap Press.

Bourdieu, Pierre (1977) *Outline of a Theory of Practice* trans. Richard Nice, Cambridge: Cambridge University Press.

Bourne, Samuel (2004) *Photographic Journeys in the Himalayas* (reprints of *British Journal of Photography* letters 1863–1870), ed. Hugh Ashley Rayner, Bath: Pagoda Tree Press.

Bucher, Bernadette (1981) *Icon and Conquest: A Structural Analysis of the Illustrations of de Bry's Great Voyages.* Chicago: University of Chicago Press.

Chevers, Norman (1870) *Manual of Medical Jurisprudence including an Outline of a History of Crime against the Person in India* 2nd edition, Calcutta: Thacker, Spink and Co.

Coetzee, J.M. (2007) *Diary of a Bad Year*, New York: Penguin Books.

Desmond, Ray (1985) 'Photography in Victorian India', *Journal of the Royal Society of Arts*, 134, December.

Falconer, John (2002) ' "A pure labour of love". A publishing history of *The People of India*' in Eleanor M. Hight and Gary Sampson (eds) *Colonialist Photography: Imag(in)ing Race and Place*, London: Routledge, 51–81.

Fayrer, Joseph (1900) *Recollections of My Life*, Edinburgh: William Blackwood.

Forbes Watson, J. and J.W. Kaye (eds) (1868–1875) *The People of India: A Series of Photographic Illustrations with Descriptive Letterpress, of the Races and Tribes of Hindustan*, London: India Museum, 8 volumes.

Geertz, Clifford (1983) 'Art as a cultural system' in *Local Knowledge: Further Essays in Interpretative Anthropology*, New York: Basic Books.

Gordon, Sophie (2006) 'A city of mourning: the representation of Lucknow, India in nineteenth-century photography', *History of Photography*, 30 (1) Spring, 80–91.

Graham, G.F.I. (1885) *The Life and Work of Syed Ahmed Khan*, Edinburgh: Blackwood and Sons.

Graves-Brown, Paul (2007) 'Avtomat Kalashnikova', *Journal of Material Culture*, November 12: 285–307.

Gutman, Judith Mara (1982) *Through Indian Eyes: 19th and early 20th Century Photography from India*, New York: Oxford University Press & International Center of Photography.

Heidegger, Martin (1977). 'The age of the world picture' in *The Question Concerning Technology and Other Essays*, New York: Harper Torchbooks.

Karlekar, Malavika (2005) *Re-Visioning the Past: Early Photography in Bengal 1875–1915*, Delhi: Oxford University Press.

Latour, Bruno (1993) *We Have Never Been Modern*, trans. Catherine Porter, London: Prentice Hall.

—— (1999) *Pandora's Hope: Essays on the Reality of Science Studies*, Harvard University Press.

Lelyveld, David (1978) *Aligarh's First Generation: Muslim Solidarity in British India*, Princeton University Press.

Lindquist, Sven (1996) *Exterminate the Brutes*, Cambridge: Granta.

Mullens, Joseph (1857) 'On the Applications of Photography in India', *Journal of the Photographic Society of Bengal*, 2 (1) January.

Naoyuki, Kinoshita (2003) 'The early years of Japanese Photography', in Anne Wilkes Tucker et al. (eds) *The History of Japanese Photography*, New Haven: Yale University Press & Houston: Museum of Fine Arts.

Orwell, George (2008) 'Inside the whale' in George Packer (comp.) *All Art is Propaganda: Critical Essays*, Orlando: Harcourt Inc.

Parayil, Sujith Kumar (2007) 'Photography in 20th Century Kerala', PhD thesis submitted to Manipal University.

Pinney, Christopher (1997) *Camera Indica: The Social Life of Indian Photographs*, London: Reaktion/Chicago: University of Chicago Press.

—— (2002a) 'Creole Europe: The reflection of a reflection', *Journal of New Zealand Literature*, 20: 125–161.

—— (2002b) 'Automonster' in P. Wollen and J. Kerr (eds), *Autopia* London: Reaktion, 227–232.

—— (2005) 'Things happen: or from which moment does that object come?' in Daniel Miller (ed.) *Materiality*, Durham: Duke University Press, 256–272.

Poole, Deborah (1997) *Vision, Race and Modernity: A Visual Economy of the Andean Image World*, Princeton: Princeton University Press.

Robinson, Francis (2000) 'Introduction' in Syed Ahmed Khan *The Causes of the Indian Revolt*, Karachi: Oxford University Press.

Tagore, Rabindranath (1921) *Glimpses of Bengal: Selected from the Letters of Sir Rabindranath Tagore 1885 to 1895*, London: Macmillan.

Varges, Ariel (1938) 'Ace newsreeler gives light on how he films News of the World', *American Cinematographer*, July, 275–276.

Virilio, Paul (1997) *Open Sky*, trans. Julie Rose, London: Verso.

Wheeler, Stephen (1904) *History of the Delhi Coronation Durbar Held on the First of January 1903 to Celebrate the Coronation of His Majesty King Edward VII Emperor of India*, London: John Murray.

Winthrop-Young, G. and M. Wutz (1999) 'Introduction' to Friedrich A. Kittler *Gramophone, Film, Typewriter*, Stanford: Stanford University Press.

Yule, Henry and A.C. Burnell (1886) *Hobson-Jobson: The Anglo Indian Dictionary*, London: John Murray.

8 Exploring the senses and exploiting the land

Railroads, bodies and measurement in nineteenth-century French colonies

Nélia Dias

That colonisation and communication are intertwined is now widely accepted. The construction of infrastructure, or what used to be known as public works, including railroads, roads and telegraphs, has been one of the main material instruments of colonisation. A part of my concern in this chapter is to contribute to our understanding of this connection by demonstrating that the creation and development of communication networks was a constitutive part of the colonisation process in French West Africa throughout the second half of the nineteenth century. For the governments of the Third Republic the construction of railroads served as a means for implementing a new politics of colonisation based on the exploitation of both land and human resources. As several historians of French colonialism have pointed out, the policy of continued conquest gave way throughout the 1890s 'to a constructive phase of the *mise en valeur* of territories already acquired', thus implying 'a more systematic management of French overseas resources' (Conklin, 1997: 41). And these resources included, above all, the bodies of the colonised. How did these two concerns – the development of material infrastructures and the management of bodies – interact with one another? Answering this question is my second concern. I do so by exploring the respects in which the notion of milieu connected the management of both territory and bodies in programmes of colonial administration.

The argument is developed in three stages. I look first at how the development of a communication network including railroads and telegraphs made possible and facilitated the development of colonial governance in French West Africa. The implementation of a politics of public works in the colonies was deemed to foster trade, to create new consumers and to overcome political unrest. Thanks to the railroad and the telegraph, information could be transmitted quickly and troops dispatched more rapidly, thus allowing the French government to control territories and to prevent protest. The construction of infrastructure in the colonies was not a mere technological operation but a constituent part of a vast political project aiming to impose discipline at a distance. I then go on to examine the conceptual ties between the regulation of the colonised body and the administration of territory by way of infrastructure. I show how the notions of *circulation* and *milieu* provided a theoretical frame for conceptualising both the colonised body and the land. Just as the circulatory system was vital for the functioning of the body and its regulation, so the communication system was also central to the regulation of society and to its survival. The circulation of blood, goods and people required a specific setting, the milieu, through which these elements could flow and become adjusted to one another within that milieu. The assumption of equilibrium between the milieu and the diverse internal elements of a society presupposed the possibility of acting on the milieu. Aware of the determinant action of the milieu, French administrators, anthropologists and politicians highlighted the importance of human intervention in relation to both the land (through a politics of public works) and colonised bodies (by means of the nervous system) for the well-being of the colonised society as a whole. Insofar as bodies and land were both envisioned as sites of management, the exploration of colonised bodies was conceptually interrelated with the exploitation of the land. In view of this interrelation, it is not surprising that colonised people's resistance was directed both at the communication system and at the recruitment of labour for public works. These are the issues I discuss in the third part of the chapter. Although French colonial administration attempted, by means of the railroad and the telegraph, to centralise, transmit and command information as well as orders at a distance, colonised people were nevertheless reluctant to submit to these forms of control and discipline. The forms this resistance took (from the physical destruction of telegraph lines to escape from labour recruitment for public works) entailed a rejection of the ways in which the administration of both territory and bodies was conceptualised and enacted.

Colonial governance required knowledge and practices, which served as a basis for political characterisation and as a framework for specific political interventions. Studies of the human body's resistance and its sensitivity to pain differentiated according to ethnicity had an obvious utility in the management of colonial labour. Likewise, technologies, particularly telegraph lines, played a central role in the exercise of colonial power. However, rather than considering these forms of knowledge and the development of infrastructure as two distinct entities, I aim to articulate the production of knowledge about the body and the development of public works as intertwined elements of the material processes of colonial administration. I do so by showing that a common theoretical and material framework underlies both the conception of the nervous system and the politics of public works.

Circulation and milieu

It was no coincidence that the first railroad, the Dakar-Saint-Louis line, was opened in Senegal where, thanks to the politics of Léon Faidherbe (1818–1889), the development of infrastructure was a central component of colonial governmentality. An engineer officer by training, Faidherbe, who ruled Senegal from 1854 to 1861 and from 1863 to 1865, was well aware of the need to establish a railroad as a means of pursuing France's inland expansion. Faidherbe's 'project of penetration' aimed to avoid the use of force by having recourse to 'peaceful means', that is, setting trading stations alongside the railway line, thus opening up Senegal to commercial exploitation (Faidherbe, 1889: 387). The assumption that trade could be a substitute for war was also pleaded by Jean-Louis de Lanessan (1843–1919), deputy and Governor-General of Indochina during the 1890s. Referring to the Dakar-Saint-Louis railroad, de Lanessan noted that 'the construction of routes of communication is the most indispensable and useful means of colonisation' (1886: 121)[1]. Consequently, in his book devoted to the economic, political and geographical analysis of French colonies, Lanessan paid particular attention to the development of roads and railroads and to the navigability of rivers. If infrastructure could pave the way for trade, it was nevertheless indispensable to 'create' the desire or the 'need' for goods among colonised people. As he remarked perceptively, it was France's task to teach Africans how to work and to 'stimulate the development of needs' (1886: xx). By stressing the close relationships between trade and the 'creation' of needs and wants, Lanessan was merely reiterating a statement developed by Paul Leroy-Beaulieu, professor of political economy at the Collège de France and one of the main theoreticians of French colonisation. In his famous book, *De la colonisation chez les peuples modernes*, which went through three editions between 1874 and 1886, Leroy-Beaulieu praised the Dakar-Saint-Louis line for increasing imports and exports to and from Senegal, and outlined how France's economic power depended on infrastructure investments.

It was, Gary Wilder suggests, in the aftermath of the French economic crisis of 1876 and 1877 that 'colonies were treated primarily as economically dependent reservoirs of productive resources (natural as well as human) useful for French industries and consumer markets to combat metropolitan under-consumption' (Wilder, 2005: 83). To create potential consumers in the colonies and to bring African peoples into the realm of capitalism entailed imbuing their minds with European conceptions of time and work, thus recasting labour in terms of an abstract quantity (time). It was necessary, as Faidherbe has pointed out, to teach natives to work according to presumed rational principles (that is, in a steady and regular way), so that they could sell their products more frequently and obtain what they needed, namely, weapons, salt, horses and liquors, through regular forms of exchange (Faidherbe, 1889: 7–8). Along with the imposition of a discipline of time and of a regulated work time, colonial power introduced the notion of labour force, indispensable for the market economy. As Anson Rabinbach (1990) has remarked, questions concerning the body's resistance, physical strength and labour power became matters of concern for the nineteenth-century science of work focused on the European worker's body. The politics of public works in the colonies similarly presupposed precise knowledge of African bodies, particularly in what concerned their ability to work and sensitivity to pain.

For Laurent Bérenger-Féraud (1832–1900), a well-known publicist, the main purpose of the Senegal colony was to increase French national wealth by means of commercial exchanges. Consequently, colonial labour was recruited to maintain and repair the existing routes, to allow direct communication between the sites of production and the colonial trading posts, and to thus facilitate 'the circulation of men and goods' (1879: 405). A similar argument, the 'circulation and exchange of goods', was supported by Leroy-Beaulieu in his advocacy of a politics of public works in the colonies (1886 [1874]: 486). It is no accident that the term *circulation* was in widespread use at this time conveying three different yet related dimensions: the circulation of goods, information and blood. As Wolfgang Schivelbusch has pointed out 'the nineteenth century's preoccupation with the conquest and mastery of space and time had found its most general expression in the concept of circulation, which was central to the scientistic social notions of the epoch' (Schivelbusch, 1986: 194). Far from being a mere rhetorical device, the term circulation implied an analogy between the routes of communication, namely the railroad, and the body's circulatory system; in addition, it implied a specific conception of society as a regulatory system that paralleled the organic system of the body. In other words, circulation was related to the regulation of the individual body as well as to the administration of territory and the governance of the social.

The creation of transversal railroads linking the West African Coast to the East was deemed to bring 'moral and material development to the colonies'. This function was reflected in their conception as 'arteries' (*Les Chemins de fer* ..., 1906, vol. xii, t.1: 77). Like arteries, railroads were supposed to carry goods away from their sites of production to the sites of exchange; the former contributed to the regulation of the circulatory system, the latter to the regulation of the commercial system in particular, and of the society in general. Circulation in the commercial sphere implied necessarily a free-market as Arthur Bordier (1841–1910), a physician and professor of medical geography at the Ecole d'Anthropologie de Paris, had outlined in his book, *La Colonisation scientifique et les colonies français*: 'we should,' he writes, 'develop trade, exchange, and roads; we should allow everywhere the circulation of life and make, thanks to competition, individuals' lives pleasant' (1884a: xvi). An apologist of free-market competition, Bordier was also one of the main theoreticians of the notion of milieu and a strong supporter of scientific colonisation. These apparently diverse interests were nevertheless linked by a common denominator, the notion of circulation.

As a fervent apologist of organicism, Bordier set forth parallels between the structure and functions of organisms and societies. In his book, *La vie des sociétés*, Bordier claimed that societies, like 'healthy organisms', should 'function freely and without constraints' (1887: xiii), as if they were vast, automatic self-regulatory systems. The diverse internal elements that composed societies were deemed to serve them in the task of adapting to the *milieu*.[2] 'Science teaches us,' Bordier argued, 'that the organism should adapt to the milieu, and that it is necessary to facilitate the free circulation and the free evolution of anatomical elements, in other words the free functioning of the physiological laws' (1884b: xiii). By combining adaptation to the milieu with the belief that all human beings were in competition, Bordier was not merely restating Herbert Spencer's principles, he was also attempting to translate them into an efficient political practice in the colonies.

Milieu played a role in the social sphere analogous to that played by the *milieu intérieur* in relation to individual bodies. Conceptualised by the French physician Claude Bernard, the *milieu intérieur* (comprising the circulatory system and the fluids that flowed through it) regulated the diverse functions of the body by conserving a constant internal temperature and securing the organism's adaptation to the external milieu and its development. Although the notion of milieu was widely diffused in nineteenth-century social thought, specifically in the debates opposing advocates of heredity to partisans of environmentalism, Bordier's use of the notion of milieu deserves particular attention. He distinguished three dimensions of milieu: the external milieu (the soil, the flora and the fauna), the *milieu intérieur* (varying according to individuals, races and sexes), and the moral milieu (the ensemble of social and cultural institutions) (Bordier, 1884a: 108; 1884b: 30). Since it was science's task to determine the best milieu for individuals as well as for societies, Bordier urged that colonisation should be conducted according to scientific principles. *Scientific colonisation* entailed the modification of the colonial milieu by acting on the territory (through a politics of public works) as well as on individuals (by means of work and laws) for 'the well-being of the colony' (Bordier, 1884a). Far from being a homogeneous process, scientific colonisation required a constant adjustment to the specificities of the *milieu intérieur*, the external milieu and the moral milieu of each colony.

As a field of human intervention, milieu required circulation, through which the regulation of society could be achieved. In his acute remarks on the notion of milieu, Michel Foucault emphasised the close links between milieu and circulation; it is through milieu that circulation is made possible. Conceived as an ensemble of natural (rivers, tides and hills) and artificial phenomena (agglomerations of individuals and houses), milieu is 'the medium of an action and the element in which it is circulated' (Foucault, 2004: 22). In other words, it is milieu that accounts for 'the action at a distance of one body on another'[3] and thus makes possible 'the phenomenon of circulation of causes and effects' (Foucault, 2004: 23).[4] Moreover, milieu doesn't operate at the level of the individuals, but at the level of the population whose health, resources and regularities are the objects of particular techniques of governance that Foucault called 'governmentality'. Thus, it is the space of circulation itself (including the material network as well the regulations, the constraints and the limits assigned to the circulation of goods and people) that becomes the privileged object of government (Foucault, 2004: 333). What better solution for colonial governance to impose a disciplinary regime than a network of cables spreading over the land?

Railroads, telegraphs and posts

In the aftermath of the 1870–1871 Franco-Prussian war a vast railroad scheme, the Freycinet Plan (named after Charles de Freycinet, minister of public works), was developed throughout France. France's military defeat in the 1870s was partly ascribed to the superiority of the German communication system (Casson, 1998: ix) and therefore to its centralised administration. By contrast with the previous French railroad system based on a 'common centre from which the main lines were to radiate in all directions', the new system relied on lateral or transversal lines linking up and connecting the main lines (Casson, 1998: 171). This expansion of a railroad network throughout France was intended to facilitate progress and civilisation in rural regions. Pierre Larousse, in his famous dictionary, devoted more than 30 pages to the railroads, depicting them as 'energetic agents of centralisation' and as purveyors of the 'unity of the collective life' facilitating both 'communication between the administrator and the administered' and the 'circulation of ideas' (Larousse, 1867: 1147). This rhetoric of a new type of society functioning without intermediaries and allowing the free circulation of people, goods and ideas would later be transposed to the tropics. Just as French rural provinces were, thanks to the railways, connected to Paris, so French colonies could also be connected to the metropole through the network of lines spreading over the land. As Gary Wilder remarked 'the French state's project to integrate the nation, assimilate the provinces and constitute republican citizens was entwined with its overseas project to integrate the empire, assimilate its colonies, and constitute colonial subjects' (2005: 25).

Along with the creation of a railroad network expanding throughout France, the Freycinet Plan included the construction of three railroads in West Africa: a line linking the ports of Dakar and Saint-Louis, a section connecting Thiès with Medina (near Kayes), and a line from Kayes to Bamako. It was no accident that these railroads were called 'lines of penetration'; starting at Senegal, they would eventually extend transversally into Sudan, thus opening up the regions between the upper Senegal and the Niger to French commerce. Later on, other lines departing from the Ivory Coast, Guinea and Dahomey would be connected with this transversal line. The railroads were supposed to function as a vast web strengthened by posts at intervals and complemented by storehouses and railway stations at central points. Since most of the rivers were not navigable during part of the year, the railroad network was aimed at setting up a communication system allowing the circulation of goods and troops.

The project of a railway from Dakar to Saint-Louis planned by Léon Faidherbe as early as the 1860s was put into practice during the 1880s. This line was primarily conceived to facilitate the conquest of the Cayor's province (a Wolof state located between Dakar and Saint-Louis) and to dismantle the monopoly on peanut production controlled by Muslim states (*Les Chemins de fer* ..., 1906, vol. xii, t. 1: 5; Hargreaves, 1967). To a certain extent, the Dakar-Saint-Louis line served as one of the main agents of economic submission allowing the French government to overcome or at least to 'control' a difficult political situation. In the wake of the economic benefit provided by this line, which helped to stimulate peanut production, reduce the costs of transporting goods and increase the movement of passengers and goods (*Les Chemins de fer* ..., 1906, vol. xii, t.1: 12), the French government took it for granted that the other lines of penetration would follow this path. But the slow and costly progress of the other railways, recurrent epidemics, the rainy seasons that made work difficult and the shortage of labourers contributed either to the abandonment of some of these projects or to tremendous delays. The task of developing a unified programme of public works and thus establishing the administrative unification of the French West African colonies fell to Ernest Roume, the Governor-General of French West Africa from 1902 to 1904.[5]

France progressively established protectorates all over Senegal in parallel with the building of telegraph lines, military posts and railroads. Shortly after a convention signed in 1879, France recognised Cayor as part of the Damel's property and in return the Damel, Lat Dior (1842–1886), was forced to accept French rights on a planned new commercial route as well as on the construction of a railroad.[6] Setting up posts and railroads was undoubtedly a strategic way for French colonial administration to extend land possession and to control it. The several treaties signed between the Governor of Senegal and the local chiefs sought to give legitimacy to the illegal appropriations that accompanied the development of these infrastructures. In 1883 French authorities expropriated the Damel's land by taking possession of the spaces around the posts (1 kilometre), and the railway station (100 metres), and alongside the railroad (50 metres). Another treaty, also dated from 1883, obligated the King of Baol (Senegambia basin) to facilitate the construction of the railroad and allowed France to build 'fortified posts to protect the railroad' and the telegraph line (Anon, 1885: 419).

While Senegal functioned as a sort of laboratory for the French politics of public works, it was in Sudan that a concerted plan based upon the simultaneous development of railroads, posts and telegraph lines was put into practice. During his military campaigns at Sudan between 1886 and 1888, Joseph-Simon Galliéni (1849–1916),[7] the commander of the French forces, was aware that the development of railroads depended on the telegraph and that communication networks played a key role in military conquest. Galliéni's military strategy comprised three distinct yet related steps: to penetrate, to occupy and to pacify. Such a strategy required a communication network supplying labourers and troops with building materials, arms, provisions and military information. It entailed a specific method of railroad construction, entitled the 'telescopic' method: 12 different construction sites involving diverse labourers (fitters, plate layers, railway engineers) working at the same time on multiple tasks (fixing the rail, clearing the road of trees and bush, maintaining the track, measuring the ground, surveying the work and constructing small railway stations). As a result, the distance between the beginning or the head of the construction site and the extremity of the rail remained always constant, that is, it did not exceed 25 to 35 kilometres (*Les Chemins de fer* …, 1906, vol. xiii, t.2: 17–33). The benefits of the telescopic method, tested on the Kayes-Bafoulabé line, were economic, military (supplying troops with provisions and arms) and political (conquering new territories). In his apologetic account, *Deux campagnes au Soudan français* (1891), Galliéni described his daily tasks at French Sudan and how he had to deal simultaneously with health issues (opening cemeteries), public works (extending the Kayes-Bafoulabé line and building a telegraph line) and military operations (subduing populations); these three spheres were conceived as constitutive parts of the 'pacification project'.

The creation of a network of routes of communication was undoubtedly central to the exercise of colonial power: it made it possible to fix the population in knowable and controllable spaces around the military posts, to transmit information from one military unit to another, to control the territory and to 'deploy a police surveillance' without having recourse to a considerable number of troops, an advantage stressed by Bérenger-Féraud (1879: 406). By facilitating the rapid deployment of troops in case of 'troubles', the communication network made unnecessary the continuous presence of troops at the posts; as Bordier has sharply noted, thanks to the Kayes-Bafoulabé line, troops could be stationed either at Dakar or at Saint-Louis (1884: 290). During the Sudan campaign, the 'telegraphic brigade' (as it was called) arrived at the Niger coasts at almost the same time as the army. Thus, thanks to the 150 kilometres of telegraphic lines 'whose wires rested on isolateurs that were attached to the trees in the forest', Galliéni could immediately transmit to France the results of his military operation (Galliéni, 1891: 389). To a certain extent, the length of telegraph wires was a good indicator of the military control of a territory; whereas there were 279 telegraphic bureaux and 10,000 kilometres of telegraph wires in Algeria during 1889, there were 32 telegraphic bureaux and 4,700 kilometres of telegraph wires in Senegal during the same year.[8] In 1907 more than half of the 16,542 kilometres of telegraphic wires covering French West Coast Africa were located in Senegal's territory (*Les Postes et Télégraphes*, 1907, vol. ix: 92).

Apart from being intertwined elements of a communication system, telegraphs and railroads were constitutive parts of the colonisation process. According to James Carey, cable and telegraph 'turned colonialism into imperialism: a system in which the centre of an empire could dictate rather than merely respond to the margin' (Carey, 1989: 212). Thanks to the communication network, the metropole could not only centralise information and knowledge but also transmit orders to the colonies, thus imposing a disciplinary regime at a distance. Moreover, 'the development of the railroad, steam power, the telegraph and cable' contributed to the emergence of 'a coherent empire' based on 'a coherent system of communication' (Carey, 1989: 212). The centre could 'act at a distance' by means of the telegraph and the railroad on the movement of things and persons. Along with reducing the physical distance between the metropole and the colonies, the telegraph reinforced the division between the centre of decision making and the points to which action needed to be applied. As Lanessan, a colonial official, aptly put it: 'Through the wire, the central administration thinks, predicts, and commands the governors' policies' (1895: v).

The communication network, especially the telegraph, enabled French colonial power to administer distant territories; it also made possible the instantaneous transmission of information. The telegraph was, as Iwan Rhys Morus put it, 'a technology that worked by breaking down time' allowing 'its operators to know the system at any given moment' (2000: 473). I now go on to consider how this way of conceptualising the administration of territory as a coherent and integrative system was carried over into and, in its turn, was informed by the conceptualisation and administration of bodies.

Muscles, sensitivity and pain

'The best policy will be that which best utilises the conquered people while making them suffer the least'[9] (Harmand, 1910: 152). This pronouncement of Jules Harmand, a fervent advocate of French colonisation, highlights one of the main aims of the colonies: to provide for the compulsory recruitment of the workforce that was indispensable for public works projects. The passage also discloses the harsh treatment afflicted on colonised bodies, submitted to forced labour and conceived as mere tools (*outils*), as the workforce was called, that could be easily replaced after use.[10] According to the conceptions of the human body prevailing at the time, the body was a machine, just as the machine was a surrogate for the body. The colonised body was thus assessed rather like railway pieces, as so many parts that could be easily replaced depending on their tolerances and affordances. This was most evident in the application of the physiological discourse of fatigue to the management of colonial labour. As L. Conan, the chief of the Medical Service of the Sudan's railroad, put it 'the *nègre* could endure all sorts of fatigue if he knows that he will find enough food at the camp' (Conan in *Les Chemins de fer* …, 1906, vol. xii, t. 1: 183). Another contemporary author reporting on human porterage in Guinea, stressed that porters carrying 28 kilos did not seem to suffer from physical fatigue, as they were used to working like animals.[11] These remarks on the presumed absence of fatigue on the part of African bodies paralleled similar concerns about European workers' bodies. The emergence of a physiological approach to labour focused on the laws of muscles and nerves, with the measurement of fatigue aiming, as Rabinbach argues, to 'reveal the most beneficial methods of organizing the expenditure of energy – both muscular and "nervous" – so that the resources of both the individual and society might be properly deployed' (1990: 25). Similarly, a precise knowledge of the capacity for endurance, susceptibility to fatigue and sensitivity to pain of the colonised would contribute to the colonies' rational development of their *mise en valeur*.

The resistance of the colonised body, and of its various component parts, to hard work and pain was a recurrent topic in the writings and policies of colonial administrators. Apart from his administrative skills, Faidherbe was a keen student of ethnography and linguistics, an interest that led him to the vice presidency of the Société d'Anthropologie de Paris in 1873. In his extensive account of the Senegal colony and the states contiguous to it, Faidherbe asserted that 'the populations of these states are all prone to war and turbulence' and were consequently 'enemies to be afraid of' (1859: 98). However, he then went on to detail the moral characteristics, physical traits, levels of intelligence, and the muscular and nervous systems deemed to be inherent to the three ethnic groups in Senegal. His purpose in doing so was to provide useful and strategic information about which groups were willing to collaborate with the colonial power and those opposed to it. Faidherbe's account can be read as a sort of catalogue of the vices and virtues innate to each ethnic group: the Peuls had 'svelte forms, a quite developed intelligence and docile customs' (1859: 26); the Malinke-Soninke were 'warriors by temperament' and possessed 'a well-developed muscular system'; and the Wolof-Serer were 'the most beautiful', 'calm', 'inconstant', 'brave', but 'with a nervous system that was not quite fully developed' (1859: 28). Faidherbe's reasoning traced a set of correspondences between psychological traits, the nervous system and the muscular system, and was grounded on the assumption that Africans were prone to inconstancy and had less control of their emotions. In sum, their nervous system was not as well regulated as that of Europeans.

Bérenger-Féraud also paid particular attention to the physical characteristics of Senegambia's people, especially their muscular strength: Mandingue people had 'a well-developed muscular system', although 'their lower limbs were feeble' and they lacked 'strong thighs' (1879: 202); Bambara possessed 'large shoulders', 'muscled arms', 'a remarkable force', and 'well-developed lower limbs' with prominent thighs; and the Serer had 'athletic force'. The focus of Faidherbe and of Bérenger-Féraud on the muscular system, and particularly on the lower legs and thighs, was related to the needs of military recruitment and workforce management. It was important for the colonial administration to have precise knowledge of which ethnic groups were stronger, better nourished, best suited for work or for the army, particularly for the famous Senegalese rifles, *tirailleurs sénégalais*, an army unit created by Faidherbe in 1857. However, these descriptions of the physical attributes of colonised bodies were not based on measurements and on measuring instruments,[12] such as the dynamometer (an instrument for measuring physical force), but rather on superficial observations whose warrant derived from familiar culturally-endorsed preconceptions. The muscular system thereby served as an index of strength and thus of the human body's capacity for work, while the nervous system indexed physical sensibility, and particularly susceptibility to pain.

These preconceptions derived from earlier traditions for the measurement and analysis of the organs of sense among non-Western peoples which, during the second half of the nineteenth century, had been one of the main objects of inquiry pursued by French anthropologists (Dias, 2004). Since sensibility was presumed to vary inversely with intelligence, non-Western peoples were deemed to be superior to Europeans in the acuity of the senses in general and their tactile sensibility in particular. How could this greater sensory acuity of non-Western peoples be explained, particularly when viewed alongside the indifference to pain that was also attributed to them? Was it an innate capacity or the result of experience and particular ways of life? The *Questionnaire de sociologie et d'ethnographie* formulated by the Société d'Anthropologie de Paris in 1883 devoted a section entitled 'General and particular sensibility' to these questions concerning the senses and their measurement. Travellers were asked to ascertain which parts of the body registered the sharpest tactile sensibility and were advised to use the esthesiometer to measure the degree of distinctness of sensations in different parts of the body (Hamy *et al.*, 1883: 581–582). This methodological guide urged travellers to provide information regarding pain thresholds in two specific situations: injuries resulting from wounds and those produced by surgery. The question of tactile sensibility among non-Western peoples was closely linked to the issue of susceptibility to pain. While their ocular, olfactory and auditory capacities were generally thought to be keener than those of Europeans, 'primitives' were deemed to have a high threshold for pain, a premise that paved the way for all sorts of physical abuses ranging from harsh physical punishment to heavy work.

Referring to David Livingstone's remarks about black people's capacity to endure surgery without expressing pain, Bordier asserted that indifference to pain, far from being a sign of courage, was mainly proof of a lack of peripheral sensitivity. As one of the means of communication with the external world, peripheral sensitivity was, according to Bordier, related to the generation of ideas. Thus, the presumed intellectual inferiority of the 'black race' was closely linked with an obtuse peripheral sensitivity. As a result, the greater capacity of black races for enduring pain could be explained by the specific particularities of the nervous system (Bordier, 1884b: 460). The transmission of information from the brain to the body's extremities was not instantaneous, leading to a loss of information or to a delay in its transmission, and thus to a failure of the nervous system's functioning. As a result, the brain could not 'oversee and control the various functions of the bodily organs' leading to a lack of regulation as 'a key function of the nervous system' (Morus, 2000: 472). The assumption that Africans' bodies functioned without instantaneous connections between the brain and the body's extremities accounted for their emotional character. Africans were said to be innately impulsive, intuitive and governed by instincts like animals; Galliéni did not hesitate to assert that the *tirailleurs sénégalais* developed an appetite for military action after having smelt gunpowder (1891: 76).

How could a body lacking proper internal regulation be rationally exploited? To what extent did the administration of the territory serve as a model for administrating colonised bodies? Like the network of railways and telegraph lines spreading over African land, the populations of French West Africa were shunted from one French colony to another to help conquer new territories and to construct infrastructure. If the communication network entailed a huge movement and circulation of population, information and goods, the politics of public works also required the circulation of population. The recruitment of men for public works followed the model of enrolment in the colonial army; as William B. Cohen noted 'colonial soldiers from one colony could be used to subjugate for France another country' (1983: 31). During the construction of the Ivory Coast railroad in 1903 there were 750 workers from the West Coast and 375 from Dahomey, according to François Clozel, governor of the Ivory Coast colony (1906: 326; Weiskel, 1980: 160). Dahomey's colony provided men for digging the trenches, a task in which they were supposed to excel compared to other African workers. More than 2,000 workers, mostly from Senegal and Guinea, were employed in this line's construction by the end of 1905. This huge recruitment of forced labour for public works was made possible by the key role played by local administrators, *commandants de cercle* (Clozel, 1906: 331). Although the construction of the railways in the colonies was in the hands of private contractors, namely the Société des Batignolles, the French government, acting through the Ministère de la Marine et des Colonies,[13] was responsible for the line's maintenance and control (*Les Chemins de fer* …, 1906, vol. xii, t. 1: 9). In cases of conflict between the concessionary construction companies and the labourers, the French governor could intervene (*Les Chemins de fer* …, 1906, vol. xii, t. 1: 50).

It is, however, in the reasons that were given for recruiting labour from different parts of West Africa or elsewhere that the logics connecting, on the one hand, the anatomo-politics relating to the physiologies of the colonised and, on the other, the requirements of different kinds of infrastructure are clearest. The building of the Dakar-Saint-Louis line lasted several years due in part to the difficulties in recruiting a workforce. Although Senegalese people were judged to be docile, as Faidherbe noted, they were also believed to be unable to dig ditches due to their presumed idleness, indolence and their inability to handle digging tools (Faidherbe, 1889: 4).[14] Chinese and Moroccan workers were therefore recruited for these tasks even though this was more costly (while it cost 4.57 francs a day to have a Chinese worker, it was estimated that a Moroccan worker cost 3.33 francs and a Senegalese 1.30 francs [Peyron, 1884: 10]) even though their poorer acclimatisation to Senegal contributed to the delay of the line's construction. The construction of the Kayes-Bamako line was also delayed due to the failure to recruit the right kinds of workers. In 1885 the total length of track laid didn't exceed 40 kilometres due to 'personnel fatigue followed by mortality' as Faidherbe euphemistically noted (1889: 7). Several factors such as physical exhaustion due to hard work, poor nutrition and diseases, especially yellow fever, contributed to labour shortage and to high mortality rates among workers. In 1881 'around thirty deaths' occurred among 81 workers (Lanessan, 1886: 159). In addition, the number of workers suffering from diseases increased considerably during November 1883: from 88 on 6 November to 111 on 14 November and to 137 on 18 November (Lanessan, 1886: 161). The total number of dead and of those suffering from diseases was certainly higher than reported by official sources. Thus, it was only because of the 'indigenous *corvées* conceded by local chiefs' and 'the 500 to 600 indigenous *corvées*' provided by the chiefs of the villages that Galliéni could expand the railroad from Kayes to Bafoulabé covering an extension of 128 kilometres (Galliéni, 1891: 149; see also Faidherbe, 1889: 8). It is worth noting the ways in which Africans were reduced to a mere approximate number ('500 to 600' or 'around') and the institutionalised racism that denigrated them by expressions such as 'pauvre diables' (Galliéni, 1891: 376). As for the other railways lines, more than 6000 workers were employed by the Conakry-Niger line in November 1900; the following month, the number of workers was reduced to 2,500 and in February 1901, to 1,000, a drastic reduction due to hard work, poor nutrition and diseases such as malaria, diarrhoea and beriberi. Changes in the nutritional regime and the addition of meat to the dairy rations helped to eradicate beriberi by 1902 (Pinard and Boyé, 1904: 512) but, as Georges François pointed out, 'labourers didn't want to stay at the construction sites' (*Les Chemins de fer* …, 1906, vol. xiv, t. 3: 15).

The French government's espousal of scientific ideals and its belief in creating a new milieu as a means of adapting individuals to new environmental circumstances played a key role in organising the anatomo-material aspects of colonisation. As several authors have pointed out, acclimatization became one of the key scientific issues in the nineteenth century,[15] and one that had profound implications for labour management. 'In France and its colonies,' Michael Osborne argues, 'where the term came to signify a rationally forced adaptation to new environments, acclimatization connoted biological changes at physiological and sometimes structural levels' (2001: 137). The faith in the milieu as a site of intervention helped to explain why France pursued its politics of public works in West Africa in spite of all sorts of obstacles and at considerable human cost. The assumption that the individuals who best adapt to their changing environment will be the ones most likely to dominate resources functioned as a rhetorical tool for such apologists of free-market competition as Bordier. In a certain sense, scientific colonisation was a sort of extension of medical geography, a topic professed by Bordier at the Ecole d'Anthropologie de Paris during the 1880s. Whereas in France social hygienists and reformers were discussing the importance of improving social milieu for the well being of the workers (Rabinbach, 1990: 206–207), in the colonies the main issue was to improve the external milieu and the *milieu intérieur*. In both cases, the emphasis placed on milieu implied that 'society was a delicately balanced organism whose interdependent functions required state intervention' (Rabinbach, 1990: 206).

The dislocation of entire populations from villages that became deserts to work in public work projects affected their ways of life, contributing to the disruption of local production and to the dismantlement of indigenous cultural practices. Moreover, the increased number of the dead due to infrastructure construction left entire villages without a male population. More than 20,000 workers perished of disease and hard work during the construction of the Congo-Océan line in the 1920s (Sautter, 1967); in their reports, published in the late 1920s, André Gide and Albert Londres fiercely denounced the sacrifice of human lives in the name of technological progress and civilisation. Paradoxically, the railroad, which was identified during the early 1840s with Saint-Simonian's ideals, namely, with fraternity and the circulation of ideas, became progressively equated with human exploitation and death.

The colonised were aware of the role of technologies in the exercise of power over their bodies; thus their continuous and persistent resistance, on one hand, to the construction of the telegraph and the railroad and, on the other hand, to being enlisted as labour power in public works programmes. As Albert Londres noted, colonised people attempted by all means to escape being recruited to the 'machine', or to the railroad (1929: 316–317). In other words, colonised people's resistance was directed simultaneously at the administration of territory and at the colonial regime for the management of bodies.

Resistance to wires and to rules

As a symbol of French domination, the telegraph line was frequently damaged, destroyed, and burnt by the indigenous populations of French West Africa. It is not by accident that almost all the treaties signed between French colonial administrations and local chiefs contained a specific clause regarding the protection of and 'respect' for the telegraph line. In a certain sense, the telegraph line was a sort of 'sacred object' surrounded by protections and prohibitions; populations who violated these prescriptions could be subject to punishments that were meant to dissuade others from following their example.

The resistance to the telegraph parallels its very construction. The building of the Dakar-Saint-Louis line[16] generated, from the very start, a fierce opposition from the Cayor's authorities[17] leading to the line's destruction in 1866. In 1871, a treaty between the Governor of Senegal and Lat Dior obligated the latter 'to protect the telegraph line going from Saint-Louis to Gorée against all sorts of violence' (Anon., 1885: 411). In 1883 a treaty mandated Futa chiefs to 'facilitate' the building of a telegraph line between Saldé and Bakel and allowed them to punish the villages where the line was damaged.[18] Ironically the treaty specified that Futa inhabitants had the choice to work on the line's construction and would receive a salary of 1.50 francs per day and a ration (Anon., 1885: 436). One of the treaty's clauses stipulated that the 'local chiefs swear to protect and respect our telegraph'. It is noteworthy that, at the same time that local chiefs were forced to swear an oath of loyalty to the French government, Saldé's inhabitants refused to transport the materials for the line's construction (*Les Postes* …, 1907: 147). French authorities used both local influence and force to persuade Futa chiefs to install the telegraph line along the territory; as Faidherbe remarked 'once the telegraph line was set up, indigenous people took up the wires and burnt the telegraph poles' (1889: 398). Futa's resistance lasted till 1885 and ended with an agreement according to which Futa's chiefs were forced to protect the construction of the line and to maintain it in exchange for financial compensation. In Western Sudan, Samory, a Muslim reformer well known for his constant and systematic opposition to French occupation (Conklin, 1997: 35), rejected the telegraph line that was to be built between Kita and Bamako; as Galliéni noted 'Some looters, loyal to Samory, took possession of a certain amount of wire netting' (1891: 61). These examples show the limitation of the extent to which French authorities were able to impose the telegraph line on the colonised, with resistance to it lasting well into the late nineteenth century.

The railroad's construction also provoked protest from local populations who were coerced into working on it. A convention signed by France and Lat Dior in September 1879 regarding the Dakar-Saint-Louis line regulated such labour issues as wage levels, and the minimum age for work (Anon., 1885: 416–417). Lat Dior was obligated to provide men, according to the administration's needs, for clearing the road of trees and bush at a salary of 1.25 francs per day or 0.73 francs if rice was provided for them. The minimum age for work was fixed at 12 years old. Although the convention didn't explicitly mention the number of hours constituting the length of the working day it was assumed that this was marked out by the natives' capacities of endurance. How else are we to explain the specific clause added to the convention in 1883 stating that 'Cayor's people will only work within the limits of their strength' (Anon., 1885: 416). Having been forcibly recruited to work in the public works project, Cayor's population resisted by destroying the line, as was reported by Faidherbe: 'Lat Dior's emissaries spread the rumour that they had cut the railway's line' (1889: 442) as well as by Bois (1886: 66) and Lanessan (1886: 143). Following the Damel's death in 1886, French authorities, fearing eventual attacks on the Dakar-Saint-Louis line, put into practice a tactical plan: a small mobile armed train preceded by one hour both the trains from Saint-Louis and from Dakar, thus providing security for travellers and protecting the line against destruction (Diouf, 1990: 280).

The telegraph and the railroad were undoubtedly the preferred targets against which the colonised manifested their anger and directed their revolt against colonial power. They were aware that the supposed civilising benefits associated with the communication network were merely rhetorical so far as they were concerned, and that the heavy taxes France required to build railroads and telegraph lines would only serve colonial interests. In addition, they were conscious that the network of cables spreading over their land was a means of imposing authority at a distance. Beyond the rejection of the telegraph and the railroad in their physical materiality, it was the refusal of the mechanisms underlying the communication network that was also at stake here. As Iwan Rhys Morus has astutely noted, the telegraph was both an instrument of surveillance 'by its capacity to deliver instantaneous knowledge of the state of the system' and an instrument of discipline 'in the way in which it could be exploited for pre-emptive action' (2000: 462). Resistance to the wires was a means by which colonised people expressed their resistance to the rules transmitted by the wires, as if, to quote Morus, the issue was that of 'ruling the waves/waving the rules' (2000: 458).

Although there is a vast literature on the parallels between the communication system and the organic system in nineteenth-century Europe,[19] little attention has been paid to the specific case of the colonies. The parallels between nerves and wires that were widely diffused in nineteenth-century scientific writings concerned the transmission of information as well as the ways in which that information was processed (Otis, 2002: 106). Like the communication system, the nervous system also transmits information through the brain, which receives, centralises, commands and transmits signals to the peripheries. The assumption that the nervous system could be regulated by itself was a distinctive aspect of nineteenth-century medical thought. In the *Dictionnaire de Pédagogie et d'Instruction primaire* (1887) the nervous system is depicted as 'a marvellous complicated machine' which, thanks to the centralisation of information, is able to distil order and harmony in the living being. As a result, just as a 'properly ordered brain maintained discipline over the rest', so the telegraph could also fulfil the same tasks and be 'the nervous system of the body politic' (Morus, 2000: 458). Thus, regulation of the individual body through the nervous system and the regulation of the body politic by means of the telegraph were two related dimensions of the metaphoric aspects of the vocabularies of late nineteenth-century administration (Morus, 2000: 473). But as we have noted earlier, the low degree of conductivity between the brain and the peripheral extremities of the nervous system that was imputed to the colonised accounted for their presumed lack of corporeal self control and regulation. Driven purely by their sensory-motor faculties, the bodies of the colonised were construed as so many mechanical parts, like mere soldiers waiting for a rational and cerebral order from a commanding centre to coordinate their activities. Mathias Duval, a well-known French anthropologist whose work was partly dedicated to the sense organs, exemplified the comparison between the nervous and communication systems by means of an analogy with the battlefield. The troops represented the peripheral sensible zone, the general situated at the centre was in charge of 'receiving information (the impressions) and transmitting orders for action' (1883: 20). Although fruitful, this comparison between the nervous system and the telegraph concealed a key point: the difference in velocity between the nerve impulse and the electric stimulus. Quoting Herman von Helmholtz's researches[20] on the measurement of the speed of nerve transmission or 'reaction time' (as it was called), Duval argued that the nerves functioned far more slowly than copper wires, and thus that the nervous system was not akin to the telegraphic one (1883: 20). This does not, though, detract from the face that resistance to the communication technology was directed against the rationale underlying the notion of a system itself, that is, the regulation of the interrelations between its component parts for which, as we have seen, the nervous system was a model.

Conclusion

By focusing on infrastructure, my purpose in this chapter has been to bring to the foreground the technologies, people and administrative practices that typified colonial rule in France's West African colonies. Far from being mere technological machines, the telegraph as well as the railroads served as 'technosocial solutions to political questions' (Joyce, 2003). It is not surprising that the first signs of social 'disorders' in French West Africa erupted during the construction of the railroads and telegraphs, as if technologies were good tools for measuring social and political 'temperature'. Paradoxically the civilising mission that France aimed to bring to its colonies by the construction of railroads and of railways stations in remote regions and the connectivity of the telegraph was doomed to failure owing to its disregard for the power of human agency.

There has also been a broader theoretical purpose to my discussion. Scientific colonisation required, as Bordier had put it, exact knowledge of the elements that compose societies and how organisms should adapt to the milieu. In contrast to France, where 'labour power was a scarce resource' (Rabinbach, 1990: 217), the workforce in the colonies was not only in abundance but also, it was believed as a convenient colonial fantasy, less prone to physical exhaustion. Thus, state intervention would concentrate not on the social milieu, as was the case in the metropole, but on the external milieu and the *milieu intérieur* of the colonies. 'Transforming individuals' and 'managing their milieu', far from being two distinctive tasks pertaining to different loci of power with, as Gary Wilder argues, legislators being responsible for the former and administrators for the latter (2005: 48), are thus perhaps better envisioned as aspects of a combined process of administrating both territory and bodies.

Acknowledgements

I would like to express my gratitude to Tony Bennett who has carefully revised my draft and provided helpful comments.

Notes

1 On Lanessan's colonial politics see Rabinow (1989) chapter 5.
2 On the notion of milieu, see Canguilhem (1965: 129–154).
3 The milieu, 'is what is necessary to account for action at a distance of one body on another', Foucault (2004: 22). Foucault refers to Canguilhem's discussion of the notion of milieu as it was used in the place accorded ether in Newton's mechanics.
4 It is worth noting that in *The Rules of the Sociological Method* (1895), Emile Durkheim tried to make the internal social milieu the explanation of social facts.
5 On Roume's policy see Conklin (1997) chapters 1 and 2.
6 Anon., (1885: 414–415).
7 On Galliéni's career and politics in Indochina see Rabinow (1989: 142–150).
8 'La Télégraphie électrique', *La Nature* (1889: 295).
9 'Dans la domination, la meilleure politique sera celle qui utilisera le mieux le peuple conquis d'une part en le faisant le moins souffrir, de l'autre en lui procurant le plus d'avantages' (Harmand, 1910: 152).
10 '... l'expérience des pays où l'on exploitait le nègre, qu'on en tirait ce qu'on pouvait, quitte à changer de nègre quand l'outil était usé', Bordier, 1884b: 57.
11 'C'est un travail de bête de somme', *Les Postes* ... (1907: 270).
12 On the measurement of fatigue and physical strength in nineteenth-century Europe see Rabinbach (1990) chapter 5.
13 The Colonial Ministry was created in 1894.
14 As A. Rabinbach noted one of the aims of the science of fatigue was to determine which tool was appropriate for which organism in order to make possible a rational selection of persons for the diverse professions (1990: 133).
15 On the botanical, biological, and medical concept of acclimatization during the nineteenth century and its links with imperialism, see Michael Osborne 2001.
16 This line was explicitly constructed to put Damel's acts under surveillance: 'the telegraph line had given the chef-lieu the means to closely monitor the movements and deeds of Damel and his warriors', *Les Postes et Télégraphes* ... (1907: 134).
17 On Cayor's resistance to French occupation see Diouf (1990), chapter 19.
18 'Traité avec le Fouta central, 14 août 1883', Anon., p. 435.
19 See Carey (1989), Morus (2000), Otis (2001, 2002) and Schivelbusch (1986).
20 'The nerve-fibres have often been compared with telegraph wires traversing a country, and the comparison is well suited to illustrate this striking and important peculiarity of their mode of action. In the network of telegraphs we find everywhere the same copper or iron wires carrying the same kind of movement, a stream of electricity, but producing the most different results in the various stations according to the auxiliary apparatus with which they are connected', Helmholtz (1995 [1868]: 150).

References

Adas, Michael (1989) *Machines as the Measure of Men: Science, Technology and Ideologies of Western Dominance*, Ithaca: Cornell University Press.

Anon (1885) *Annales sénégalaises de 1854 à 1885, suivies des traités passés avec les indigènes*, Paris: Maisonneuve et C. Leclerc.

Bérenger-Féraud, Laurent (1879) *Les peuplades de la Sénégambie: histoire, ethnographie, moeurs et coutumes*, Paris: Ernest Leroux.
Bois, Alexis (1886) *Sénégal et Soudan: travaux publics et chemins de fer*, Paris: Challamel.
Bordier, Arthur (1884a) *La Colonisation scientifique et les colonies françaises*, Paris: Charles Reinwald.
—— (1884b) *La Géographie médicale*, Paris: Charles Reinwald.
—— (1887) *La vie des sociétés*, Paris: Charles Reinwald.
Canguilhem, Georges (1965) *La connaissance de la vie*, Paris: Vrin.
Carey, James W. (1989) *Communication as Culture: Essays on Media and Society*, London and New York: Routledge.
Casson, Mark (ed.) (1998 [1915]) *The Railway Revolution, t. II – The Rise of Rail Power in War and Conquest 1833–1914*, London: Routledge/Thoemmes Press.
Clozel, François-Joseph (1906) *Dix ans à la Côte d'Ivoire*, Paris: A. Challamel.
Cohen, William B. (1983) 'Malaria and French imperialism', *Journal of African History*, 24, 23–36.
Conklin, Alice L. (1997) *A Mission to Civilize: The Republican Idea of Empire in France and West Africa, 1895–1930*, Stanford: Stanford University Press.
Dias, Nélia (2004) *La Mesure des Sens: Les Anthropologues et le corps humain au XIXe siècle*, Paris: Aubier.
Diouf, Mamadou (1990) *Le Kajoor au XIXe siècle: Pouvoir ceddo et conquête coloniale*, Paris: Editions Karthala.
Duval, Mathias (1883) *Leçons sur la physiologie du système nerveux (sensibilité), proféssées à la Faculté de médecine de Paris. Cours auxiliaire de Physiologie*, Paris: O. Doin.
Faidherbe, Léon (1859) *Notice sur la colonie du Sénegal et sur les pays qui sont en relation avec elle*, Paris: A. Bertrand.
—— (1889) *Le Sénegal: La France dans l'Afrique Occidentale*, Paris: Hachette.
Foucault, Michel (2004) *Sécurité, Territoire, Population. Cours au Collège de France.1977–1978*, Paris: Hautes Etudes-Gallimard, Seuil.
Galliéni, Joseph Simon (1891) *Deux campagnes au Soudan français 1886–1888*, Paris: Hachette.
Gide, André (1981) *Voyage au Congo suivi de Le Retour au Tchad (1927–1928)*, Paris: Gallimard.
Hamy, Ernest-Théodore, Abel Hovelacque, Julien Vinson and Charles Letourneau (1883) 'Questionnaire de sociologie et d'ethnographie', *Bulletins de la Société d'Anthropologie de Paris*, 578–597.
Hargreaves, John D. (1967) *West Africa: The Former French States*, Englewood Cliffs: Prentice Hall.
Harmand, Jules (1910) *Domination et Colonisation*, Paris: Flammarion.
Helmholtz, Hermann von (1995 [1868]) 'The recent progress of the theory of vision', *Science and Culture. Popular and Philosophical Essays* edited by David Cahan, Chicago: University of Chicago Press, 127–203.
Joyce, Patrick (2003) *The Rule of Freedom: Liberalism and the Modern City*, London: Verso.
'La Télégraphie électrique' (1889), *La Nature. Revue des Sciences et de leurs applications aux arts et à l'industrie* vol. ii, Paris: G. Masson, p. 295.
Lanessan, Jean-Louis de (1886) *L'Expansion coloniale de la France: étude économique, politique et géographique sur les établissements français d'outre-mer*, Paris: Félix Alcan.
—— (1895) *La colonisation française en Indochine*, Paris: Félix Alcan.

Larousse, Pierre (1867) 'Chemins de Fer', *Grand Dictionnaire Universel du XIXe siècle*, Paris, vol. 3, 1130–1164.

Leroy-Beaulieu, Paul (1886 [1874]); 3rd edn 1886 *De la Colonisation chez les peuples modernes*, Paris: Guillaumin.

Les Chemins de fer en Afrique occidentale. Gouvernement général de l'Afrique occidentale française (1906). Notices publiées par le gouvernement général à l'occasion de l'Exposition coloniale de Marseille, vol. xii–xiv, t. 1–3, Corbeil, Imprimerie de E. Crété.

Les Postes et télégraphes en Afrique occidentale. Gouvernement général de l'Afrique occidentale française (1907) Notices publiées par le gouvernement général à l'occasion de l'Exposition coloniale de Marseille, vol. ix, Corbeil, Imprimerie de E. Crété.

Londres, Albert (1929) *Terre d'Ebène* (*La Traite des noirs*), Paris: Albin Michel.

Morus, Iwan Rhys (2000) "The nervous system of Britain": space, time and the electric telegraph in the Victorian Age', *British Journal for the History of Science*, 33, 455–475.

Osborne, Michael (2001) 'Acclimatizing the world: A history of the paradigmatic colonial science', *Osiris*, 15, 135–151.

Otis, Laura (2001) *Networking: Communicating with Bodies and Machines in the Nineteenth Century*, Ann Arbor: The University of Michigan Press.

Otis, Laura (2002) 'The metaphoric circuit: organic and technological communication in the nineteenth-century', *Journal of the History of Ideas*, 63 (1), 105–128.

Peyron, Alexandre (1884) *Rapport adressé au Président de la République française sur les opérations concernant les ports, le chemin de fer et les autres services du Haut Sénegal pendant les exercices 1881–1882*, Paris: Imprimerie du Journal officiel.

Pinard E. and Boyé (1904) 'Guinée française. Maladies observées chez les indigènes', *Annales d'Hygiène et de Médecine coloniales*, volume VII (October/December) 475–520.

Rabinbach, Anson (1990) *The Human Motor: Energy, Fatigue, and The Origins of Modernity*, New York: Basic Books.

Rabinow, Paul (1989) *French Modern: Norms and Forms of the Social Environment*, Chicago: University of Chicago Press.

Sautter, Gilles (1967) 'Notes sur la constitution du chemin de fer Congo-Océan (1921–34)', *Cahiers d'Etudes africaines*, vol. 7, 219–299.

Schivelbusch, Wolfgang (1986) *The Railway Journey: The Industrialization of Time and Space in the 19th Century*, Berkeley and Los Angeles: The University of California Press.

Weiskel, Timothy C. (1980) *French Colonial Rule and the Baule Peoples: Resistance and Collaboration, 1889–1911*, Oxford: Clarendon Press.

Wilder, Gary (2005) *The French Imperial Nation-State: Negritude & Colonial Humanism Between the Two World Wars*, Chicago: University of Chicago Press.

9 Making and mobilising worlds

Assembling and governing the other

Tony Bennett

Were the dream-times an invention of Western anthropology or an autochthonous aspect of Aboriginal cosmology? Patrick Wolfe, in arguing the former, attributes the primary responsibility for its fabrication to Baldwin Spencer and Frank Gillen.[1] The term was first used by Gillen in the memoir he contributed to the report of the 1894 Horn Expedition into Central Australia. Discussing Arunta[2] accounts of the origins of fire, Gillen reported that it was believed to have been acquired by ancestors 'in the distant past (*ūlchurringa*), which really means in the dream-times' (Gillen, cit. Wolfe, 1991: 200). In his introduction to the report of the Horn Expedition, which he edited, Spencer, transforming Gillen's spelling into *alcheringa*, also widened the term's reference by describing it as a more general system of morality. Used again in their 1904 book *The Northern Tribes of Central Australia*, the concept was subsequently extended beyond the Arunta to encompass other tribes and, in a further step, to function as a pan-Australian marker of a generalised Aboriginal culture. Wolfe interprets this extension of the term as being ideologically motivated rather than resting on ethnographic evidence. He traces the history of the associations which, in the natural history of the Comte de Buffon, had connected the inability to distinguish dreams from reality to animality and which subsequently, in Darwin's work, were interpreted as a marker of the distinction between primitive and civilised humans. His contention, in the light of this, is that the anthropological invention of 'the Dreaming complex' was, when viewed in association with evolutionary conceptions of time, 'the culmination of a historical discourse which subordinated dreaming savages to the level of animal nature' (Wolfe, 1991: 206).

Wolfe attributes particular significance to the differences between Spencer's position and that of the Lutheran missionary Carl Strehlow who, in the same year as the Horn expedition, had been appointed to supervise the Hermannsburg Mission in Central Australia. Questioning Gillen's translation and his orthography, Strehlow disputed the contention that the word *Altjira* referred to a distant past. 'The native,' as he put it, 'knows nothing of "dreamtime" as a designation of a certain period of their history' (Strehlow, cit. Hill, 2002: 141). Interpreting it, rather, as a reference to a god, he attributed a religious significance to it which provided the basis on which a programme of salvation evangelism could be built. By construing the *alcheringa* as purely a moral code, and by insisting on the evolutionary inscription of the dream-times as primitive, Spencer denied the dream-times the religious potential that Strehlow's salvation evangelism needed in order to find something within Aboriginal culture that it might latch on to. It was better, in Spencer's view, to leave the dream-times intact especially since, from an evolutionary perspective, attempts at the spiritual-cum-cultural uplifting of the Aborigine were doomed to failure as the inexorable laws of racial competition meant that extinction was the unavoidable destiny of the Aboriginal race. When passing the Hermannsburg Mission a few months prior to Strehlow's appointment there, Spencer had recommended that it should be closed or run by the government. He viewed the missionary endeavour as not only hopeless in attempting to teach the Arunta abstract ideas they were '*utterly incapable of grasping*' (Spencer cit. Hill, 2002: 58) but potentially dangerous since it undermined their faith in the precepts handed down by their elders and thus threatened to undo colonial forms of rule that worked through the reinforcement of customary morality.

The point at issue between Spencer and Strehlow was thus clearly by no means a purely ethnographic one. Their different interpretations of the dream-times were bound up with, and functioned as operative parts of, different strategies of colonial rule which worked through the organisation of different 'transactional realties' mediating the relations between white and Aboriginal populations in ways that would allow the latter to be acted on in differently: absorbed into a Christian civilisational programme in the case of Strehlow, or, at this stage in his career, having had their passage into extinction soothed via a benign colonial administration in the case of Spencer.[3]

I borrow the concept of 'transactional realities' from Foucault who uses it to refer to a series of historical realities – civil society, sexuality and madness are among the examples he cites – which 'although they have not always existed are nonetheless real, are born precisely from the interplay of relations of power and everything which constantly eludes them, at the interface, so to speak, of governors and governed' (Foucault, 2008: 297). Foucault's concern is with the roles played by such transactional realities as parts of 'liberal governmentality' (2008: 296). However, the same principles apply – to generalise the issue from the specific example of the dream-times – to the role that different versions of Aboriginal culture and its constitutive elements have played in organising the complex 'transactional realities' across which the agency and counter-agency of both colonised and coloniser have been enacted in the development of, and resistance to, the varied forms of 'indigenous governmentality' that have accompanied the twentieth-century project of Australian state formation.[4]

It is from this perspective, then, that I want to consider the role played by Spencer's photographic and museum practices in producing and circulating Aboriginal culture as parts of new socio-material arrangements for the management of Aboriginal bodies in the context of the 'Aboriginal domain' (Rowse, 1992) that increasingly mediated the relations between white and black Australia in the early twentieth century. I shall seek some accommodation between the concerns of governmentality theory and assemblage theory in doing so, outlining the respects in which this key period in the 'museumification' of Aboriginal culture constituted, in Deleuze and Guattari's terms, a form of colonial capture which inscribed Aborigines in a new scientific-governmental assemblage (Deleuze and Guattari, 1988: 435; see also Patton, 2000: 122–131).

From field to museum and back again

Shortly after returning from the Horn expedition Spencer was appointed to the Board of Trustees of the Public Library, Museums and National Gallery of Victoria, and, in 1899, was appointed to the directorship of the Museum. Thereafter, the various expeditions he conducted into Central Australia, building on the partnership he had established with Gillen, were conducted with a view to bringing back items of Aboriginal material culture, and film and sound recordings, to add to the National Museum of Victoria's collections, and to writing scientific books and articles, and delivering more popular public lectures, based on their field notes, films, photographs, and the artefacts assembled in the Museum's collections. When later introducing his display of the ethnological collection at the National Museum of Victoria, first arranged in 1901, Spencer stressed the Museum's role in mediating the relations between his and Gillen's fieldwork and the texts through which the results of that fieldwork were more broadly disseminated.

> Every specimen figured in *The Native Tribes of Central Australia, The Northern Tribes of Central Australia, Across Australia*, and *The Native Tribes of the Northern Territory* is in the Museum collection, together with the whole of the material, including negatives and phonographic records secured by Mr Gillen and myself during the progress of our work.
>
> (Spencer, 1922: 8)

His actions in this regarded are usefully viewed through the prism of Bruno Latour's reminder that the chief problem facing fieldwork expeditions is how to render the worlds they explore mobile so that those who take part in them might take something back with them that they will, in turn, be able to mobilise within the world that sent them and to which they return. It's worth quoting the relevant passage in full:

> If you wish to go out of *your* way and come back heavily equipped so as to force others to go out of *their* ways, the main problem to solve is that of *mobilisation*. You have to go and come back *with* the 'things' if your moves are not to be wasted. But the 'things' have to be able to withstand the return trip without withering away. Further requirements: the 'things' you gathered and displaced have to be presentable all at once to those you want to convince and who did not go there. In sum, you have to invent objects which have the properties of being *mobile* but also *immutable, presentable, readable* and *combinable* with one another.
>
> (Latour, 1990: 26)

And in *Pandora's Hope*, Latour notes how, in many of the sciences, the relations between expeditions and museums played a key role in the processes of mobilising worlds through which 'nonhumans are progressively loaded into discourse', citing the galleries of the Muséum national d'Histoire naturelle and the collections of the Musée de l'Homme as places in which 'all the objects of the world are thus mobilised and assembled' (Latour, 1999: 99–101). Or if, in another Latourian formulation, one wants to 'muster on the spot the largest number of well aligned and faithful allies' (Latour, 1990: 23) then, for leaders of scientific expeditions, a museum is a very good place in which to put the 'silent witnesses' they bring back with them.

The relations between Spencer's expeditions and the collections he assembled at the National Museum of Victoria are of a fourfold significance from this point of view. First, they formed part of a key moment in the development of the fieldwork phase in anthropology that significantly reorganised the relations between a range of agents compared to those that had characterised the earlier phase of 'armchair' anthropology. While the latter was also dependent on distant worlds being made mobile and assembled in European museums, those collections were typically assembled via networks of commercial or amateur collectors either plying their wares or acting on instructions. Museums in colonial contexts typically acted as intermediaries for the transit of objects from local sites of collection to metropolitan institutions for interpretation and synthesis by anthropologists who had stayed at home knowing that the world would come to them. Spencer's work ranks in significance with the other major expeditions of roughly the same period through which anthropologists working in European or American museums mounted scientific expeditions in order to go away and collect the world for themselves so that they might return with a more systematic set of immutable mobiles.[5] This also led, as Morphy puts it, to 'the combining of theorist and ethnographer in the same person' (Morphy, 1996b: 138) with the consequence that the processes through which other cultures were collected, made mobile, gathered and assembled, exhibited, and translated into inscriptions were more closely integrated. Collecting worlds and mobilising them in distant settings were activities undertaken by the same agents.

Second, the Horn expedition, Philip Jones argues, was the first scientific expedition within Australia that (i) was charged to accord significant attention to the collection of Aboriginal artefacts, (ii) actually did so, (iii) returned those collections to an Australian museum (the South Australian Museum) where the work of scientific interpretation – previously done overseas – was done by a curator, Edward Stirling, who had also been the leader of the expedition team, and (iv) which resulted in that museum providing the first institutional setting for the public exhibition of those artefacts (Jones, 1996). As well as continuing this tradition, Spencer played a key role in staunching the flow of Aboriginal objects to Europe and America by supporting the introduction of export licensing requirements, and he contributed considerably to their local accumulation when he donated his own collections to the National Museum of Victoria in 1916 (Lydon, 2005: 17) whose ethnographic holdings increased from 1,200 to over

36,000 during his period as director (Mulvaney and Calaby, 1985: 252). Spencer was thus able to install the immutable mobiles he accumulated at the National Museum of Victoria in two sets of relations at once. The *in situ* presence of the collections in his museum gave him a large number of 'well aligned and faithful allies' that he could 'muster on the spot' in the context of specifically national political and administrative fields. So far as the international scientific community was concerned, his collections also provided the material basis and warrant for the inscriptions through which, in journal articles and books and the copies of original artefacts he continued to send to European museums, the various kinds of data that he and Gillen had accumulated were recombined in accounts of Aboriginal culture that had a considerable influence on the development of European anthropology as the main source data for Durkheim's account of the elementary forms of religious life, sociology.[6] This had significant consequences for Spencer's position and unrivalled authority in the Australian scientific field.

Third, as the first Australian expedition to involve the use of film and sound recording, Spencer and Gillen's first encounter with the Arunta of Central Australia contributed to a significant shift in the organisation of ethnographic authority. According to Wolfe (1999), the phase of Victorian anthropology represented by Edward Tylor's work had been primarily concerned with constructing and defending anthropology's claims to disciplinary specialism and authority against those of the materially-based discipline of archaeology and the text-based language disciplines, particularly philology. It had done so by proposing that anthropology was able to produce a distinctive knowledge of the prehistoric past by reading its traces as these had survived not in texts or objects but in ritual forms of behaviour carried into the present through the habitual mechanism of repetition. With the increasing use of film, photography and sound recording to capture traces of presently existing cultures, however, ethnographic authority became less concerned with defining its specificity in relation to the claims of historical or language disciplines and focused instead on countering rival claims to have gone there, into the field, and to have observed, recorded and collected. It was the colonial administrator, the journalist and the tourist – not the archaeologist or philologist – whose rival productions of the Other had to be disqualified, with the prolonged fieldwork of the anthropologist often proving critical here – as it did with Spencer and Gillen's film and photographs of Arunta corroboree – in validating the authority of the ethnographer as having so penetrated the culture of the Other as to have gained admission to secret events (Cantrill and Cantrill, 1982).

Fourth and finally, and by way of connecting back to my starting point, if all of these conditions made it possible for Spencer to become an actor on the national stage, it is because they made it possible for him to make and to mobilise a specific production of Aboriginal culture. By bringing things together from diverse locations, combining these in new ways, simplifying and condensing them by subjecting them to further processes of inscription, Spencer produced something that had not existed before: Aboriginal culture not as a set of autochthonous realities that preceded his inquiries but as a new pan-tribal and pan-national surface of connection between white and black Australia, a surface that organised new sets of governmental and administrative interfaces through which the former might act on the latter. His activities are, of course, by no means unique in this regard. The diverse forms in which photographs, recordings, tools, weapons, sacred objects, films, and art works referenced as 'Aboriginal' have been assembled, recombined and rearranged in relation to each other in different productions of Aboriginal culture have, both before Spencer and since, had significant implications for both different modes of governmental action on Aboriginal communities and Aboriginal counteractions to these.[7] As Philip Jones notes, however, it was not until the first two decades of the twentieth century that Australian museums installed permanent exhibitions of Aboriginal culture, seeing in this a form of symbolic capture and display of the Other that was closely connected to the process of national state formation following the Federation of Australia in 1901 (Jones, 2007: 228, 327–328). Spencer's role was a particularly significant one in this respect, providing a key point of connection between the anthropology/museum nexus and the development of what Tim Rowse has called 'the Aboriginal domain': that is, the domain of indigenous institutions, practices, customs, languages, etc., which, by organising a zone of interaction, provided the means through which different Aboriginal communities were absorbed into the colonial state (Rowse, 1992). Rowse identifies the introduction of rationing in 1894 – the year of the Horn expedition – as a key moment in the development of this domain. While by no means replacing the sheer exertion of colonial power and racial violence that had characterised frontier relations in the 1870s and 1880s, with episodic massacres continuing into the 1920s (Rowse, 1998), the introduction of rationing to compensate for indigenous food supplies displaced by cattle grazing constituted a significant shift in balance toward the regulation of food supplies as the primary means of control over a dispossessed population (Rowse, 1996).[8]

Spencer's role in the Horn expedition involved his participation in this rationing system and, as Rowse records, he was uncomfortable with aspects of it as a form of giving which, lacking transparency and reciprocity, secured control through an obscured gift relationship (food given in exchange for compliance). Rationing was, however, the basis for the development of a new mode of government that regularised (unequal) exchanges across the colonial frontier and, in place of racial violence, substituted an administrative infrastructure for managing these exchanges. Spencer was to become directly involved in this for a short period when he was responsible for the administration of Aboriginal affairs in the Northern Territory, and he contributed to its development more generally through the various advisory roles he was called on to play.

In discussing the relations between scientific fields and the contexts, such as museums and laboratories, in which specimens from such fields are brought together and subjected to new forms of combination with one another (Latour, 1999), Latour emphasises how this results in the production of new grids of intelligibility which, when circulated back to the field, make possible new forms of action on the varied entities or agents that make up the field in question. Applying this perspective to Baldwin's work will help to clarify how his museum, scientific and administrative practices interacted with each other in ways that helped to shape a new, distinctively racial logic for the Aboriginal domain. Through the varied roles he played – anthropological fieldworker, photographer and film-maker, collector, lecturer, curator, writer, and scientific administrator – Spencer played a key role in what Latour calls the 'circulation of reference' from sites of collection to centres of calculation and back again in the form of grids for administrative action on the colonial social. By producing the race as such as the transactional reality through which the government of Aborigines was to proceed, these different aspects of Baldwin's work functioned as the moving parts of a new machinery of administration which brought about a new socio-material ordering of the management of Aboriginal bodies in both space and time.

Racial essentialism and governing strategies

Spencer's photographic practice was quite varied, including humanistic portraits of individual Aborigines that suggested a degree of intimacy and mutual respect between photographer and subject, as well as photographs informed by the conventions of the noble savage (Batty, Allen and Morton, 2005). I focus here, however, on the photographs that he selected to accompany the paper he presented to the British Association for the Advancement of Science at its 84th meeting in Melbourne (Spencer, 1914). I have chosen this text for a number of reasons. First, in terms of the type of photographs selected, the elements it assembles are similar to those in Spencer and Gillen's *Native Tribes of Central Australia* (1899) on which it draws, as they are also of the principles informing Spencer's arrangement of Aboriginal materials at the National Museum of Victoria.[9] Second, however, going beyond his and Gillen's fieldwork in Central Australia, he draws on the photographs and publications of other anthropologists – A.W. Howitt, W.E. Roth, John Mathew and Daisy Bates – for other parts of Australia, to present an account which, by bringing together different tribal practices, produces a new reality which underlies and, ultimately, discounts apparent differences between them. That unity is grounded in a shared bloodline which accounts for the Aborigines' status as – allowing for possible exceptions – 'the most backward race extant' revealing 'the conditions under which the early ancestors of the present human races existed' (Spencer, 1914: 33). Third, as a text that was presented to, and circulated widely within, the national and international scientific communities,[10] Spencer's address played an important role in circulating the conception of a common racially defined Aboriginality produced by abstraction from a variety of field sites through scientific and administrative circles and eventually back onto the inhabitants of those sites, subjecting them to an administrative grid which subordinated their specific differences to a common racial logic.

There are three main types of photographs assembled in the text. First, there are photographs of various ceremonies, rituals and medical practices from different tribes – the Urbunna's Tritichinna ceremony of snake totem and the Arunta ceremony of witchetty group totem, for example – presented, side-by-side, as evidence of a shared level of cultural development. Second, there are various photographs of churingas, objects of magic, weapons, tools, utensils and shields, again from different tribes from different parts of Australia, testifying to a shared level of material culture, associating the Aborigine with a stone age set of tools at the primitive level of the hunter-gatherer. Third, but as the first set of photographs, providing a racialised context for the interpretation of the photographs of ceremonies and objects that follow, there is a series of head-and-shoulder anthropometric portraits of naked Aboriginal, men, women and children from different tribes whose distribution in different parts of Australia is shown in an accompanying map. While noting considerable differences in bodily appearance (height, breadth of nose, slope of forehead) and in bodily practices (presence or absence of beards, practices of scarification), Spencer argues that the colour of all these men, women and children is uniform ('the native is dark brown chocolate, not black') and rooted in a shared bloodline (he rules out, in this text, the possibility of 'the mixture of two races differing in colour' [34]).[11]

It is important to note, as Morphy (1996b) does generally of Spencer's anthropological practice, that Spencer by no means minimises the variety of practices between different tribes. To the contrary, this is a constant refrain throughout his text: 'there are very considerable variations in regard to totemic customs and beliefs in different tribes' (Spencer, 1914: 43); 'there are endless varieties of clubs and spears' (78); 'Clothing and ornament vary very much in different tribes' (79). However, the terms in which he explains these variations retrieves them to a racialised production of the Aborigine. This variation is accounted for as a result of the dispersal of the tribes from shared ancestors, who observed common customs and forms of social regulation, to different parts of the continent where those shared ancestral traditions were adapted to different climatic and physical conditions of existence. However, such variation registers no departure from the constraints of a common bloodline connected to a shared stage of evolution or, more accurately, of arrested development. Spencer accounts for this arrested development in terms of the combined lack of natural and racial competition: unlike Europeans whose wits had been sharpened by savage natural competitors (lions, tigers, etc.), the Aborigine, Spencer argued, had had nothing more fearsome to compete with than giant diprotodons and kangaroos 'who were quite as anxious to get away from him as he was to capture and eat them'; and he had 'never had to contend with any higher race' (Spencer, 1914: 33). The only differentiation Spencer allows is a temporal/racial one separating the Australian Aborigine from the Tasmanian who, in spite of a larger skull size, Spencer describes as at a lower stage of development and, therefore, as certain to have been exterminated by the Australian Aborigines had the two races come into contact.

This commitment to a necessary racial unity is evident in a later paper in which Spencer puzzles over linguistic evidence suggesting a range of blood and shade divisions among Aboriginal tribes. Spencer pours cold water on this thesis by reporting his own comparisons of standard colour tints with 'the actual colour of the skin of very many natives in various tribes' (Spencer, 1921: 4). He states that he could find no variation of colour within any tribe except for, in some case, minor ones between men and women which, however, he discounts as the probable effect of men's use of darker pigments in bodily decoration. More distinctively, Spencer seeks to disqualify the linguistic evidence of colour variation by applying the colour tests that had been developed by W.H.R. Rivers in the context of the late nineteenth-century debates over the colour blue. The impetus for these debates derived from William Gladstone's contention that the philological evidence suggested that the ancient Greeks had not developed the capacity to distinguish blue within the colour spectrum. This led to the development of tests to assess whether contemporary 'primitives', as the survivors of the past in the present, also lacked this capacity (see Dias, 2004: 90–108). This tradition, in which the capacity to separate blue off from other colours serves as a sensory index of civilisation, is mobilised by Spencer to discredit the theory that the range of variation of blood and shade registered in Aboriginal languages might be the legacy of real distinctions of blood and shade. Reporting the results of his own applications of Rivers's colour tests, he claims that Aborigines were only able to distinguish between black, white, red and yellow, had difficulties in distinguishing black, brown and grey from each other, and were – in their natural state[12] – unable to distinguish blue. Spencer's conclusion is that the variations of shade registered in language use must be disconnected from the supposition that they reflected the perception of real colour differences as supposing 'a fine colour sense that at least our Aboriginal does not possess' (Spencer, 1921: 4) and, in accordance with evolutionary accounts of the development of colour perception, could not have possessed in the past either. In this way, an enduring racial continuity rooted in a common bloodline is ensured in which the only difference in colour that is allowed is that between children and adults. 'Every child at birth is copper-coloured,' Spencer tells us in a formulation which restates his position in his 1914 address, 'but in the course of a few days the skin darkens and assumes the chocolate brown of the adult' (Spencer, 1921: 50; see also Spencer, 1914: 36). While granting Aborigines the ability to distinguish variations of shade within this blood category, variation can neither range more widely nor be perceived because of an essentialist racialisation that chains Aboriginal blood and eye together in a tight double-bind.

To place this racial production of the Aborigine in a proper historical perspective, it is necessary to understand the role it played in deleting – or at least weakening the force of – the earlier transactional realities that had organised the interfaces between coloniser and colonised. The key role that Spencer accorded the tribe as a major unit of analysis is important here comprising, as Kevin Blackburn (2002) notes, a significant departure from earlier traditions in Australian anthropology. These were typically concerned with identifying the existence of different nations at the supra-tribal level: not, though, nations as sovereign political entities but, in the words of A.W. Howitt, as agglomerations of tribal groups which 'represent a social aggregate, namely a community bound together, despite a diversity of class systems, by ceremonies of initiation, which, although they vary slightly in different localities, are yet substantially the same and common to all' (Howitt, cit. Blackburn, 2002).[13] It was in accordance with this biblical conception of the nation as a cultural group of common descent that Howitt and other contemporaries sought, well into the 1880s and 1890s, to map the relations between different Aboriginal nations as ones between different cultures which, Howitt argued, differed in their languages, practices and identities as much as the Scots from the Welsh.

The significance of the tribe as a unit of analysis that was favoured internationally in the late-nineteenth, early-twentieth-century development of fieldwork with, Blackburn notes, Spencer as its leading Australian exponent, was threefold. First, it formed part of a new hierarchical distinction between societies that were nations and those that were tribally organised that was mapped on to a racially organised distinction between the civilised and the uncivilised.[14] Second, in place of the wider self-identifications that Aborigines had often testified to in earlier studies, and which, in the context of the land claims that have followed in the wake of the Mabo and Wik judgements, they have since reclaimed, it substituted the tribe as a unit of colonial ordering that served to nullify cultural differences operating at a meta-tribal level, denying them any political or administrative significance. Third, it substituted a racial conception of Aboriginality as the common factor which cohered the customs and practices of different tribes into a single whole, thereby producing the race as such, even if through the mediation of different tribes, as the surface that government was to act upon.

Just as significant, however, indeed perhaps more so, was the substitution of the imagery of the Aborigine as a naked primitive for earlier photographic depictions of Aborigines as already well on their way to becoming self-civilising subjects. Jane Lydon's study of the photographs that were taken at Coranderrk Aboriginal Station over the period from its establishment in the 1860s through to the early 1900s is highly revealing here, showing how earlier conceptions of the Aborigine as possessing a human potential for improvement persisted into the early twentieth century. Located to the northeast of Melbourne, and within easy day-trip reach from the city, Coranderrk bore the imprint of a range of civilisational discourses – from Christian missionary ones to liberal ideals of self improvement – in its commitment to providing a site in which Aborigines, under white tutelage, might become self-civilising subjects. The Aborigines who lived there had their own complex reasons for complying with this civilisational regime while also negotiating and imbuing it with their own distinctive values. But these are less my concern here than the ways in which the inhabitants of Coranderrk were presented in over 40 years of being photographed – by professional Australian photographers, by visiting Europeans, and by the station's managers – and of the ways in which those inhabitants collaborated in the production of images of them as active participants in a civilising process in view of their realistic assessment of the role that their circulation played in organising the interfaces between white and black Australia.

I shall present Lydon's analysis of just three of the photographs she discusses. The first, *The Yarra Tribe Starting for the Acheron 1862*, is a mythical, biblical framing of the initial establishment of Coranderrk. It depicts a staged re-enactment of the departure of the Yarra people for Coranderrk, with a group of fully clothed Aborigines – men, women and children – walking across a clearing in front of a bush setting. It thus marks their departure from a condition of nomadism set against a scene of nature to a place of permanent settlement. It is also clear from the tools they carry that they are setting off for a life of agriculture (whose absence, under the influence of Lockeian ideas, had served as the primary justification for the dispossession of Aborigines under the doctrine of *terra nullius*). Both their tools and their Western clothes – making them indistinguishable from the station manager who accompanies them – separate the Aborigines from the scene of untamed nature that is the backdrop for their journey. The second picture, Charles Walter's portrait, *Timothy*, is of middle-aged Aboriginal man from Coranderrk. Timothy is show fully-clothed and Walter deploys the conventions of European portrait photography, including Timothy's holding an opened book in his right hand, as a sign of his acquisition of literacy as a key marker of a capacity for self-civilising. The only photograph Lydon presents of an unclothed Aborigine is the half-naked *Australian de Coranderrk* taken by the French photographer Désiré Charnay and eventually ending up, fittingly enough, at the Musée de L'Homme. Charnay's purpose had been to produce an anthropometric portrait after the fashion recommended by Thomas Huxley (see Spencer, 1992) – that is, naked and arranged against standard measuring devices – which, as we have seen, informed Spencer's photographic practice. The significance of this photograph in relation to Coranderrk, however, is its rarity: the inhabitants of Coranderrk usually refused to be photographed other than fully clothed as they were only too aware of the association of nakedness with notions of savagery. Yet it was an exception that confirmed the rule. Lydon tells us that Charnay paid a considerable amount for the privilege, recording that this particular subject who, quite apart from the fact that he had clearly kept his trousers on, charged 5 shillings.

If we compare Spencer's photographs with those from Coranderrk we can see how Spencer contributed to the development of a nature-culture in which Aborigines were, so to speak, jumped backwards in developmental time. For most of these images either post-dated or were contemporary with those from Coranderrk. As such, they both represented and were instrumental in effecting the transition from one nature-culture to another: from earlier liberal humanist and Christian conceptions in which Aborigines were viewed as a part of a collective humanity that was distinct from nature and therefore as capable of being civilised and, eventually, of civilising themselves, to one in which they were forever poised at the stage of an incomplete transition from nature into culture. The same was true of the arrangement of the Aboriginal collections at the National Museum of Victoria which depicted Aborigines as occupying the position of an 'evolutionary degree zero' representing the base level from which human evolution elsewhere had proceeded, but not in Australia. This nature-culture formed part of a revival of earlier innatist conceptions associated with polygenetic conceptions of race in which the apparent 'unimprovability' of the Aborigine had been accounted for in terms of an absolute racial difference. According to Kay Anderson and Colon Perrin, this was later translated into a matter of being 'too late' as, in the interpretations of Darwinians like Spencer, the problem was not that Aborigines absolutely lacked any capacity for improvement but rather that, having languished for so long on the cusp between nature and culture, there was not sufficient time for them to acquire the material, intellectual and cultural resources needed to compete effectively with a superior race before the inexorable laws of racial competition lead to their extinction (Anderson, 2006; Anderson and Perrin, 2007).

In the early years of the twentieth century, then, depictions of Aborigines were inscribed within two different nature-cultures which jostled for space with one another within Melbourne's public visual culture. At a time when the National Museum of Victoria had been moved from the University of Melbourne to a more popular location in the city centre, so Coranderrk also attracted thousands of day-trip visitors annually from Melbourne while Spencer's public lectures – involving lantern shows and film screenings depicting Aborigines as 'howling savages' – provided a popular evolutionary counterpoint to the Coranderrk experience. The disjunction between these two public versions of Aboriginality, it is important to add, cannot be accounted for in terms of a supposedly natural encounter with naked primitives when Spencer moved from Melbourne into the desert regions of Central Australia. As Wolfe notes, the readers of Spencer's and Gillen's texts would have had no sense that the Arunta had been brought under the influence of a Lutheran missionary ten years before Spencer and Gillen encountered them, or that they had earlier been photographed fully clothed alongside Strehlow and his family in texts which, since they were written in German, were little-known in either Australia or the English-speaking scientific community (Wolfe, 1999: 155). Spencer reflected revealingly on these issues in a letter to fellow anthropologist, the Reverend Lorimer Fison. Expressing his concern as to whether 'it was fit and proper to exhibit in public cinematograph pictures of natives who do not wear all the clothing that they ought to,' and noting that he could show slides 'to which not even the most strict Presbyterian elder could take exception,' he argues that this could only mean 'the elimination of the best of things … the real native' (Spencer, cit. Cantrill and Cantrill, 1982: 37).

Racial, individual and governmental times

I have drawn on Latour's account of the role of collecting institutions within the processes through which worlds are made and mobilised in view of the emphasis it places on assembling as a practice which, by rendering the things it brings together readable, combinable and presentable with one another in new ways, makes new realities thinkable and actionable. Tania Li, in commenting on the virtues of assemblage theory, similarly stresses how, in contrast to terms like apparatus and *dispositif* which focus on what are often presented as settled or even completed formations, assemblage 'flags agency, the hard work required to draw heterogeneous elements together, forge connections between them and sustain these connections in the face of tension' (Li, 2007: 264). A further advantage of the concept, she argues, is that of bringing together the 'material content of assemblages (bodies, actions, passions) and enunciations (statements, plans, laws)' (Li, 2007: 265) on the same plane, linking them not hierarchically in relations of causal dependence or in the order of the real and its representations but as elements that are reciprocally inserted within and presuppose one another. Insofar as they relate to bodies, however, assemblages, as Deleuze and Guattari put it, constitute 'a precise state of intermingling of bodies in a society, including all the attractions and repulsions sympathies and antipathies, alternations, amalgamations, penetrations, and expansions that affect bodies of all kinds in their relations to one another' (Deleuze and Guattari, 1988: 90).

The history of the relations between white and black Australia has witnessed a plethora of the coming together of statements, plans and laws with bodies, actions and passions to effect varied, strenuously resisted, orderings of the relations between black and white bodies – and the various shades in between – within Australian social space. This has, for the main part, involved compulsory rearrangements of the relations between racialised bodies brought about by the removal of Aborigines from their lands, camps, kinship and tribal structures, particularly via the abduction of Aboriginal children, and their relocation in sequestered environments to be subjected to varied forms of management (Commonwealth Government, 1997; Haebich, 2000; McGregor, 2002). Baldwin's address to the British Association for the Advancement of Science was delivered in the same year (1914) that a new way of arranging bodies in social space was introduced with the opening of the first institution in the Northern Territory designed expressly for 'half-caste' Aborigines.[15] This constituted a significant stage in the development of a new governmental rationality in which anthropological expertise was put into play in effecting new forms of somatic co-mingling and separation which plucked the half-caste away from the full-blood in accordance with a new civilising strategy whose underpinnings were those of the absolutely racialised Other that Spencer's texts and collections enunciated.

The category of the half-caste was not, of course, a new one; but it had not previously been accorded any significance in the management of Aboriginal populations. Bain Attwood notes that although the distinctions between full-bloods, half-castes, quadroons and so on had long been recognised, they had, in Victoria, been denied any legal or administrative significance as late as 1877 (Attwood, 2003: 21–27). When, a few years later, these categories were used as the basis for ejecting half-castes from Coranderrk, this was on the basis that they were not owed the same compensation or 'duty of care' as the full-blood Aborigines whose beckoning destiny was extinction. And in the missionary domain, at Hermannsberg, half-castes were regarded as inferior to full-bloods through into the 1920s, their skin colour functioning as a sign of spiritual dilution. Spencer, too, in the preliminary report he prepared during the year (1912) he served as Special Commissioner and Chief Protector of Aborigines of the Northern Territory invested no special positive value in the half-caste.[16] Indeed, he argued that they posed a threat of deterioration because the Aboriginal mother 'is of very low intellectual grade' (axiomatically) while the white fathers were (usually) from the 'coarser and more unrefined members of higher races', with the consequence that their offspring were unlikely to be of 'much greater intellectual calibre than the more intelligent natives' (Spencer, cit, McGregor, 1997: 80–81). Nor did Spencer at this time support separating half-castes in special institutions. He was adamant that no half-caste should be left in native camps recommending that if they lived near or worked in towns they should be placed in compounds, and that they should be placed in reserves if they lived in remote areas in a 'wild condition'. However, both compounds and reserves were places where all Aborigines, half-castes and full-bloods, were to be placed in order to receive education and training to lift them to a higher stage of civilisation.

In a later report he prepared for the Department of Home and Territories in 1922 Spencer followed through the logic of his 1914 address in investing a positive racial value in the half-caste. To ensure that they could realise their potential of achieving a higher level of development than the 'pure-blood blacks' (Spencer, cit. McGregor, 1997: 145) he recommended the establishment of a half-caste station equipped with dormitories, bathrooms, dining rooms, school, smithy, carpenter's shop and other facilities for industrial and technical training. It would, he now argued, 'be a fundamental mistake and most prejudicial to their welfare to place [half castes] on a station along with full-blooded aboriginal children', urging that '*the half castes must be encouraged to marry amongst themselves*' (Spencer, cit. McGregor, 1997: 146). Viewed in the context of the legal restrictions on inter-racial sexual relations that were introduced in 1922 to stem the increase in the number of half-castes, this constituted a programme that aimed to breed out the colour of the existing 'rump' (there were an estimated 624 half-castes in the Northern Territory in 1922) of past miscegenation.

The modes of interaction between white and black that were thus performed across these new institutional arrangements can only be understood in terms of the relations between racial time, individual time and the new forms of governmental time associated with the development of the Aboriginal domain. As we have seen, Spencer effects a new racialisation of Aboriginality in the role he accords race, rooted rigorously in bloodline and skin colour, to account for the shared substratum of Aboriginality that gives Aboriginal culture its underlying unity in spite of varying customs and practices among different tribes. At the same time, however, a dual temporality is attributed to Aboriginal culture as a result of the contradictory way in which Spencer inserts it into evolutionary time. On the one hand, it is a culture that lacks an inner temporality having been more-or-less static for millennia as a consequence of its grounding in a race which, lacking any competition, has failed to evolve. On the other hand, once faced with such competition as a result of European occupation, the Aborigine faces annihilation. Aborigines thus enters into evolutionary time for only a split second, at the very moment they are destined to leave it by being driven to extinction. Yet Spencer also provides for a different temporality at the level of the individual. While the laws of racial competition destine full-blood Aborigines to extinction, managed inter-marrying among half-castes provides a route through which they and their offspring might survive, but only on the condition that they cease to be Aboriginal in the sense that is, for Spencer, defining and constitutive, that is, racially.

It is, to go back to Wolfe, this racialised production of the Aborigine as an absolute and undifferentiated Other that formed the new 'transactional reality' underpinning the development of a new governmental time of assimilation in the context of the early twentieth-century development of the Aboriginal domain.

For it opened up a space in which half-castes could be separated from full-bloods and absorbed into white society through a programme that was simultaneously one of progressive whitening and progressive civilising that would eventually prepare them for citizenship. It was precisely this civilisational and epidermal advantage that early national governmental rationalities sought to promote. As Tom Clarke and Brian Gallagan (1995) show, these distinctions provided the crucial terms in which the relations between the Aboriginal domain and the distribution of citizenship rights and duties were managed in the context of the independent national polity that was developed in the first two decades following the 1901 Federation of Australia. And in a series of photographs that formed a part of this new assemblage, Spencer depicted the half-castes brought together in these stations much like Timothy at Coranderrk, fully clothed and accompanied by the trappings of European civilisation – except that these were now markers of their incipient whiteness.[17]

Notes

1 Spencer, a product of Mancunian liberalism, was originally trained as a natural historian and was an early supporter of Darwinism. His substantive position at Melbourne was as professor of biology but his interests progressively shifted to anthropology. Spencer met Gillen, a postmaster and Justice of the Peace at Alice Springs, during the Horn expedition. They subsequently developed a lifelong collaboration in which the distinction between the roles of field collector and university-based interpreter, while remaining intact, was also significantly blurred.

2 I shall follow Wolfe here in retaining the orthography of Spencer and Gillen, rather than using the corrected form of the Arrernte, since my concern is with the operation of this category in nineteenth-century Eurocentric discourses.

3 It is these issues, I think, that Howard Morphy (1996a, 1996b) loses sight of in castigating Wolfe as a post-modernist constructivist whose interpretation of the dream-times as entirely a property of white discourse fails to appreciate how they were 'an integral part of the conceptual structure of Aboriginal society, the recognition of which was part of a process of value creation that ran counter to the colonial process' (Morphy, 1996a: 164). In Wolfe's analysis, the later take-up of the language of the dream-times by different Aboriginal communities constituted a form of acquiescence to the terms in which Aboriginality had been encoded in anthropological discourse. Morphy's response to this is to suggest that Aboriginal take-up of the term was prompted by the fact that it 'fitted a lexical gap in Aboriginal languages' (Morphy, 1996a: 178). It allowed a semantic field which stressed the primacy of ancestral beliefs and values to the organisation of Aboriginal modes of sociality that was prominent in most Aboriginal languages to achieve a common currency across tribal groupings in ways that were of salience to Aboriginal people in the context of anti- and post-colonial political mobilisations. Although Morphy thus clearly wants to stake out a different political position from Wolfe by stressing the agency of Aborigines, this is still an agency exercised in the context of a new set of realities and relationships that have been historically constructed in the relations between coloniser and colonised. The key issues concerning the dream-times and their successors in this regard are not whether they are or are not realities that pre-exist(ed) their inscription in anthropological discourse but, as John Law (2004: 122–142) suggests, the functioning of the different ways in which they have operated within the different method assemblages – ways of producing and enacting truths – within which the relations between black and white Australia are complexly enacted.

4 Although they do not use the terminology I have proposed here, a similar understanding of Aboriginal culture informs a number of recent studies including Pat O'Malley's (1998) account of how indigenous practices of resistance have shaped practices of colonial rule as well as being shaped by them; Bain Attwood's (2003) account of the mobile constructions of 'Aboriginality' that have informed both state practices of indigenous governance and the development of Aboriginal rights and political movements; Chris Healy's (2008) account of the ways in which the strategic forgetting, and subsequent re-remembering, of Aboriginal culture has mediated the relations between 'mainstream' and indigenous Australians; Tim Rowse's (2009) account of how the statistical assembling of indigenous populations in official censuses constitute new transactional realities that are mobilised as parts of the process of collective subject formation on the part of Aboriginal political movements; and Fred Myers' (2002) account of the relations between Aboriginal and Western art practices and institutions.

5 Alfred Haddon's role in relation to the Cambridge 1898 Torres Strait expedition and the 1902 period of fieldwork among the Todas by W.H.R. Rivers (who had also been a member of the Torres Strait expedition) are the examples Morphy cites, although Franz Boas's participation, while at the American Museum of Natural History, in the 1897 Jesup North Pacific Expedition is also relevant. See Herle and Rouse (1998) for discussions of the Torres Strait expedition, and Rexer and Klein (1995) for the Jesup expedition.

6 The role of Spencer's work on the Arunta in shaping Durkheim's account of the elementary forms of religious life (Durkheim, 1915) has been subject to extensive commentary and is discussed by both Wolfe and Morphy.

7 The consequences flowing from the inclusion of Aboriginal 'art' in art exhibitions has been extensively studied in this regard. See Griffiths (1996) for a discussion of the ripple effects of the Melbourne 1929 Aboriginal Art Exhibition and Myers (2002) for the whole series of adjustments and counter-adjustments of government policy agencies, international art markets, Aboriginal artists, cultural intermediaries, etc. to one another flowing from – aptly enough – the *Dreamings: The Art of Aboriginal Australia* exhibition of acrylic dot painting at the 1988 Asia Society Galleries in New York.

8 The distribution of rations had often been used as a means of managing relationships across the colonial frontier on a private basis. What was new after 1880 was the supplementation of the philanthropy of police and pastoralists in this regard by government-run ration depots (Jones, 2007: 369).

9 I have discussed these elsewhere: see Bennett (2004).

10 The meeting was attended by Bronislaw Malinowski on his first visit to Australia (Stocking, 1991: 35).

11 He does not, though, regard the Aborigine as a pure race, seeing it as a probable blend of earlier black races.

12 The qualification is important. Spencer acknowledges that the introduction of Reckitt's Blue into Australia by the white man led to an acquired capacity to recognise it and its use in Aboriginal art. This is then re-presented as the proposition that the use of blue in any Aboriginal artefact is proof that it is a corrupted form: 'the presence of a blue pigment on any Australian ornament or implement that finds its way into one or other of our museums is regarded by all Curators as clear proof that the tribe from which it comes has lost its primitive outlook on art' (Spencer, 1921: 4).

13 The passage is from a paper that E.B. Tylor presented on Howitt's behalf to the Anthropological Institute in Britain in 1883.

14 See, for example, Gary Wilder's account of the account of the part played by the practices of 'colonial humanism' associated with the inter-war phase in the development of French anthropological fieldwork in ordering the relations between France and its African colonies (Wilder, 2005).

15 I use the terms of this racial vocabulary ('half-castes', 'full-blood', etc.) rather than the contemporary vocabulary of 'mixed descent' as the language that belonged to – indeed, constituted – the historical realities I am concerned with here.
16 It is important to note that Spencer was the first to serve in this capacity after, in 1911, responsibility for the administration of Aborigines in the Territory was transferred to the Commonwealth Government.
17 See McGregor (1997) for a detailed discussion of these.

References

Anderson, Kay (2006) *Race and the Crisis of Humanism*, London and New York: Routledge.

Anderson, Kay and Colin Perrin (2007) ' "The miserablest people in the world": Race, humanism, and the Australian Aborigine', *The Australian Journal of Anthropology*, 18 (1), 18–39.

Attwood, Bain (2003) *Rights for Aborigines*, Sydney: Allen and Unwin.

Batty, Philip, Lindy Allen and John Morton (eds) (2005) *The Photographs of Baldwin Spencer*, Melbourne: The Megunyah Press and Museum Victoria.

Blackburn, Kevin (2002) 'Mapping Aboriginal nations: the "nation" concept of late nineteenth century anthropologists in Australia', *Aboriginal History*, vol. 26, 131–158.

Cantrill, Arthur and Corinne Cantrill (1982) 'The 1901 cinematography of Baldwin Spencer', *Cantrills Filmnotes*, 37/38, 27–42.

Commonwealth Government, Human Rights and Equal Opportunity Commission (1997) *Bringing them Home: National Inquiry into the Separation of Aboriginal and Torres Strait Children from their Families*, Canberra: Australian Government Publishing Service.

Deleuze, Gilles and Felix Guattari (1988) *A Thousand Plateaus: Capitalism and Schizophrenia*, London: The Athlone Press.

Dias, Nélia (2004) *La mesure des sens. Les anthropologues et le corps humain au XIXe siècle*, Paris: Aubier.

Durkheim, Emile (1915) *The Elementary Forms of the Religious Life*, London: George Allen & Unwin Ltd.

Foucault, Michel (2008) *The Birth of Biopolitics: Lectures at the Collège de France*, London: Palgrave Macmillan.

Griffiths, Tom (1996) *Hunters and Collectors: The Antiquarian Imagination in Australia*, Cambridge University Press.

Haebich, Anna (2000) *Broken Circles: Fragmenting Indigenous Families, 1800–2000*, Fremantle Arts Centre Press.

Healy, Chris (2008) *Forgetting Aborigines*, Sydney: University of New South Wales Press.

Herle, Anita and Sandra Rouse (eds) (1998) *Cambridge and the Torres Strait: Centenary Essays on the 1898 Anthropological Expedition*, Cambridge University Press.

Hill, Barry (2002) *Broken Song: F.G.H. Strehlow and Aboriginal Possession*, Sydney and New York: Vintage.

Jones, Philip (1996) 'The Horne Expedition's place among nineteenth-century inland exhibitions' in S.R. Morton and D.J. Mulvaney (eds) *Exploring Central Australia: Society, Environment and the 1894 Expedition*, Chipping Nortin, NSW: Surrey Beatty.

—— (2007) *Ochre and Rust: Artefacts and Encounters on Australian Frontiers*, Kent Town, South Australia: Wakefield Press.

Latour, Bruno (1990) 'Drawing things together' in Michael Lynch and Steve Woolgar (eds) *Representation in Scientific Practice*, Cambridge, Mass.: MIT Press.

—— (1999) *Pandora's Hope: Essays on the Reality of Science Studies*, Cambridge, Mass.: Harvard University Press.

Law, John (2004) *After Method: Mess in Social Science Research*, London and New York: Routledge.

Li, Tania Murray (2007) 'Practices of assemblage and community forest management', *Economy and Society*, 36 (2), 263–293.

Lydon, Jane (2005) *Eye Contact: Photographing Indigenous Australians*, Durham, NC, and London: Duke University Press.

McGregor, Russell (1997) *Imagined Destinies: Aboriginal Australians and the Doomed Race Theory, 1880–1939*, Melbourne University Press.

—— (2002) '"Breed out the colour", or the importance of being white', *Australian Historical Studies*, 120, 286–302.

Morphy, Howard (1996a) 'Empiricism to metaphysics: in defence of the concept of the Dreamtime' in Tim Bonyhady and Tom Griffiths (eds) *Prehistory to Politics: John Mulvaney, the Humanities and the Public Intellectual*, Melbourne University Press.

—— (1996b) 'More than mere facts: repositioning Spencer and Gillen in the history of anthropology' in S.R. Morton and D.J. Mulvaney (eds) *Exploring Central Australia: Society, Environment and the 1894 Expedition*, Chipping Nortin, NSW: Surrey Beatty.

Mulvaney, D.J. and J.H. Calaby (1985) '*So Much That is New*': *Baldwin Spencer, 1860–1929: A Biography*, Melbourne University Press.

Myers, Fred (2002) *Painting Culture: The Making of an Aboriginal High Art*, Durham, NC: Duke University Press.

O'Malley, Pat (1998) 'Indigenous governance' in Mitchell Dean and Barry Hindess (eds) *Governing Australia: Studies in Contemporary Rationalities of Government*, Cambridge University Press, 156–172.

Patton, Paul (2000) *Deleuze and the Political*, London and New York: Routledge.

Rexer, Lyle and Rachel Klein (1995), *American Museum of Natural History, 125 Years of Expedition and Discovery*, New York: H.N. Abrams and the American Museum of Natural History.

Rowse, Tim (1992) *Remote Possibilities: The Aboriginal Domain and the Administrative Imagination*, Casuarina (Darwin): North Australian Research Unit, Australian National University.

—— (1996) 'Rationing the inexplicable' in S.R. Morton and D.J. Mulvaney (eds) *Exploring Central Australia: Society, Environment and the 1894 Expedition*, Chipping Nortin, NSW: Surrey Beatty.

—— (1998) *White Flour, White Power: From Rations to Citizenship in Central Australia*, Cambridge University Press.

—— (2009) 'The ontological politics of "closing the gaps"', *Journal of Cultural Economy*, 2 (1–2).

Spencer, Baldwin (1914) 'The Aboriginals of Australia' in G.H. Knibbs (ed.) *Federal Handbook prepared in connection with the eighty-fourth meeting of The British Association for the Advancement of Science held in Australia*, August 1914, Melbourne: Commonwealth of Australia.

—— (1921) 'Blood and shade divisions of Australian tribes', *Proceedings of the Royal Society of Victoria*, New Series, vol. 34, part 1, 2–6.

—— (1922) *Guide to the Ethnological Collection Exhibited in the National Gallery of Victoria*, 3rd edition, Melbourne: Government Printers.

Spencer, Baldwin and Frank Gillen (1899) *The Native Tribes of Central Australia*, London: Macmillan.

Spencer, Frank (1992) 'Some notes on the attempt to apply photography to anthropometry during the second half of the nineteenth century' in Elizabeth Edwards (ed.) *Anthropology and Photography 1860–1920*, New Haven and London: Yale University Press in association with the Royal Anthropological Institute.

Stocking, George W. Jr. (1991) 'Maclay, Kubary, Malinowski: archetypes from the dreamtime of anthropology' in Stocking (ed.) *Colonial Situations: Essays on the Contextualisation of Ethnographic Knowledge*, Madison: University of Wisconsin Press, 9–74.

Wilder, Gary (2005) *The French Imperial Nation-State: Negritude and Colonial Humanism between the two World Wars*, Chicago and London: University of Chicago Press.

Wolfe, Patrick (1991) 'On being woken up: the Dreamtime in anthropology and in Australian settler culture', *Comparative Studies in Society and History*, 33 (2), 197–224.

—— (1999) *Settler Colonialism and the Transformation of Anthropology: The Politics and Poetics of an Ethnographic Event*, London: Cassell.

Index

Page numbers for figures are given in **bold**